Sociological Ana

CW01079827

FOUNDING EDITOR FATOS TARIFA, *Eastern Michigan University / Albanian Institute of Sociology*

EDITORIAL BOARD ALEKSANDRA ÅLUND, *University of Linköping*
INES ANGJELI-MURZAKU, *Seton Hall University*
JUDITH BLAU, *University of North Carolina - Chapel Hill*
GEORGINA BORN, *University of Cambridge*
MICHAEL BURAWOY, *University of California - Berkeley*
CRAIG CALHOUN, *New York University / Social Science Research Council*
GIOVANNA CAMPANI, *University of Florence*
LIQUN CAO, *Eastern Michigan University*
DANIEL CHIROT, *University of Washington*
ANNE CRONIN, *Lancaster University*
ISMET ELEZI, *Albanian Institute of Sociology*
JON ELSTER, *Columbia University*
AMITAI ETZIONI, *George Washington University*
BAS DE GAAY FORTMAN, *University of Utrecht*
KRISTO FRASHËRI, *Albanian Academy of Sciences*
ILIR GËDESHI, *Center for Economic and Social Studies - Tirana*
KLARITA GËRXHANI, *University of Amsterdam*
ARJAN GJONÇA, *London School of Economics and Political Science*
BARBARA HEYNS, *New York University*
ARNE KALLEBERG, *University of North Carolina - Chapel Hill*
LISA KEISTER, *Duke University*
ZEF MIRDITA, *University of Zagreb*
KLEJDA MULAJ, *University of Exeter / Albanian Institute of Sociology*
VICTOR NEE, *Cornell University*
CLAUS OFFE, *Hertie School of Governance - Berlin*
SERVET PËLLUMBI, *Albanian Institute of Sociology*
JAN NEDERVEEN PIETERSE, *University of Illinois - Urbana Champaign*
RAYMOND ROSENFELD, *Eastern Michigan University*
SASKIA SASSEN, *Columbia University*
MICHAEL SAVAGE, *University of Manchester*
PAMELA SMOCK, *University of Michigan - Ann Arbor*
LEKË SOKOLI, *Albanian Institute of Sociology*
ENKELEIDA TAHIRAJ, *University College London*
JAY WEINSTEIN, *Eastern Michigan University*
ERIK OLIN WRIGHT, *University of Wisconsin - Madison*

Sociological Analysis

Sociological Analysis (ISSN 1097-7147) is an international journal affiliated with the Albanian Institute of Sociology, a nonprofit, independent professional organization of sociologists and other social scientists in Albania. *SA* is published annualy. The opinions expressed in articles, comments, and other contributions published in *Sociological Analysis* are those of the authors and do not necessarily reflect the views of the Albanian Institute of Sociology, those of the Editors or their supporters.

Sociological Analysis publishes papers, comments and other writings on topics of professional and disciplinary concern to sociologists and other social scientists. Empirical research and theoretical work reporting on how sociological knowledge relates to a variety of political, economic, social and cultural issues of broad public concern are especially encouraged. All areas of sociology are welcome. Emphasis is on exceptional quality, general interest.

MANUSCRIPT FORMAT AND SUBMISSION REQUIREMENT

All submissions are processed electronically. Articles, comments and book reviews intended for publication should be word-processed documents and submitted as e-mail attachment to ftarifa@emich.edu or via regular mail to Dr. Fatos Tarifa, Editor, *Sociological Analysis*, Eastern Michigan University, Department of Sociology, 712 Pray Harrold, Ypsilanti, MI, 48197, USA. An abstract of no more than 150 words and a brief bibliographical statement should be sent separately as e-mail attachment. Manuscripts should conform to *The Chicago Manual of Style*, 14th ed., and be typewritten in English. All text, including notes and block quotations, should be double-spaced. Notes, kept to a minimum, should be marked in the text at a point of punctuation. Tables and figures must be camera ready. Authors are responsible for the accuracy of all quotations. *Sociological Analysis* will not accept manuscripts submitted simultaneously to other journals.

SUBSCRIPTIONS

Subscriptions rates are $15 per year to individuals and $50 to institutions. Within the U.S. postage is included. Add the appropriate postage for Foreign Surface Mail or Airmail for subscriptions outside the United States. All correspondence regarding subscriptions and back issues should be addressed to ftarifa@emich.edu. Information on recent issues or back issue rates supplied on request. Remittance must be made by money order or check payable in U.S. dollars to *Sociological Analysis*. Subscribers must notify *SA* six weeks in advance of an address change. Claims for undelivered copies must be made no later than two months following the regular month of publication. When the reserve stock permits, the Editors will replace copies of *SA* that are lost because of an address change. Current rates and specifications may be obtained via e-mail by writing to ftarifa@emich.edu.

Copyright © by *Sociological Analysis*. All rights reserved. No portion of this work may be reproduced in any form without written permission from SA. Copyright is retained by author when noted.

Sociological Analysis acknowledges with appreciation the facilities and assistance provided by the Department of Sociology, Anthropology and Criminology at Eastern Michigan University.

Graphic Design: Roland Lelaj, Toronto, Canada (rlelaj@yahoo.ca)
Published by Globic Press (Chapel Hill, NC) on behalf of the Albanian Institute of Sociology
Printed in the United States

Sociological Analysis

Volume 1, Autumn 2007

SOCIOLOGICAL ANALYSIS (SA) is not a new title, but it is a new journal. In 1998, a group of Albanian scholars launched the first sociological journal in the history of Albania. We named it *Sociological Analysis* and I had the honor to serve as its Editor for those two years that we were able to publish it. *SA* was printed in Chapel Hill, North Carolina, but it was affiliated with the New Sociological Research Center in Tirana, Albania, and was published under the auspices of — and with tremendous help by — the Department of Sociology at the University of North Carolina at Chapel Hill as well as by the editorial office of *Social Forces*, housed in that department. I remain deeply beholden to Prof. Arne Kalleberg, then Department Chair and currently President of the American Sociological Association, as well as to a number of distinguished UNC sociologists who either contributed to *Sociological Analysis* with their work, or served in its International Advisory Board, such as (in alphabetical order), the late venerable Peter Blau, Judith Blau, Kenneth Bollen, Craig Calhoun, Glen H. Elder Jr., Lisa Keister, Sherryl Kleinman, Charles Kurzman, Anthony Oberschall, Michael Savage, and Angelika von Wahl.

After seven years from the publication of its last issue in 1999, in November 2006, an enthusiastic group of Albanian sociologists established the Albanian Institute of Sociology (AIS) in Tirana, the first of its kind in the country. In May of this year, the Institute launched the first issue of its official journal in Albanian, *Studime Sociale (Social Studies)*. Today, the AIS is introducing to the public — both inside and outside of Albania — the first volume of the renewed *Sociological Analysis*.

The launching of a new sociological journal in English requires some justification. Ours is manyfold, resulting by clearly defined goals.

First, *SA* is a response to many new developments that have occurred in Albania, in the Balkans, and in much of the world as the 21st century has began to unfold. First of all, *SA* is committed to serving as a positive force in the revival of Albania's academic life, particularly in the field of social sciences, and to playing an important role in the expansion of the public sphere in which civil society can further develop as a democratic institution. *SA* itself, like the AIS, is organized as an experimental social institution intended to stimulate new thinking, promote tolerance and understanding, act as a serious forum for social scientists — both in Albania and in other countries — bring together their concern with theoretical knowledge and practical recommendations and voice their opinions on numerous important issues facing Albanian society today, as well as those of its neighboring societies and the broader community of nations.

Second, we believe that there is a significant amount of valuable sociological research and knowledge produced by Albanian social scientists which cannot easily reach international journals. Our purpose thus is to provide an outlet for quality scholarly work written by Albanian social scientists. Publishing their work in English in *SA* Albanian scholars may have their efforts and achievements recognized internationally in a truly professional way. This will also enable social scientists from other countries who have a particular interest in Albanian politics, culture and society, or more generally in postcommunist Eastern Europe, to consult an important source of information on Albanian society and, more specifically, on the state of sociology in Albania.

Third, a further consideration in establishing *SA* is our belief that in a postcommunist society, such as Albania, social problems and other issues of a sociological nature have an urgency equal to other issues pertaining to political and economic transformation, yet the response to such issues has, so far, been disappointing. Social problems continue to be neglected and underesearched. We would like to cultivate this field and hope that *SA* will encourage empirical work among Albanian sociologists and serve a catalytic role in setting — and constantly raising — the standards of scholarship, contributing to the development of empirical — but theory guided — sociological research and to the discipline of sociology in Albania.

Fourth, it is particularly hoped that *SA* will be able to provide Albanian sociologists with valuable information on the state of — and the current trends in — the discipline of sociology internationally. The need to make such information available to Albanian social scientists is particularly important given the fact that very few sociological books and journals in the social sciences are available in Albanian libraries and book-stores today. *SA* will offer Albanian scholars and students in the social sciences, as well as a larger public that is interested in sociological issues, the opportunity to read quality work in sociology — and other related disciplines — produced by scholars from other countries, many of whom have already expressed their collegial and sincere interest to collaborate with *Sociological Analysis* and with the Albanian Institute of Sociology. By urging sociologists and other social scientists to contribute to this journal original work in English, we will attempt to fill a gap that has very negatively affected the development of sociology — and the social sciences in general — in the past.

Fifth, an integral part of *SA*'s overall purpose is to promote the exchange of ideas among Albanian and foreign sociologists through a publishing outlet accessible to both sides, as well as encourage scholarly collaboration among them. Ideas are the stock in trade of social scientists in the global market place of academic activity and cultural production. *SA* is intended to break down the long-time isolation of Albanian social scientists from the international community of scholars, help them integrate their scholarly work and achievements with theirs, and provide a serious forum for the discussion of sociological issues of common interest. Good social science is portable: it abstracts ideas of broad relevance from specific national contexts. As an international journal, *SA* feels a special obligation to make authors differentiate carefully between conclusions specific to one nation at one point of time, and conclusions that can still be relevant after crossing national borders.

These considerations together with the repeated assurances of our Albanian, American and European colleagues for a journal devoted to sociological analyses, prompted us to begin the publication of *Sociological Analysis* in the first place. In 1998 the birth of *SA* was probably *premature*; in 2007, it may be considered *delayed*. Yet, with the establishment of the Albanian Institute of Sociology this is an *appropriate* time for *Sociological Analysis* to reemerge. In Albania's current conditions, nothing could be more *natural* than the publication of a sociological journal like *SA*.

SA was established with the hope that it would play an important role in meeting all of the needs mentioned above. This prerogative is, indeed, the *raison d'être* of this new journal.

SA is committed to open thought, pluralist ideas, and examinations from a variety of sociological and social science perspectives. As Craig Calhoun once wrote for *Sociological Analysis*, "Openness to different ideas and research projects will help to further the basic goal of developing the highest quality of sociological understanding." The orientation of *SA* is potentially integrative of the social sciences. The focus on political, economic, cultural and social processes clearly transcends the conventional distinctions between sociology, political science, economics, and cultural studies. Therefore the subject matter of the journal will be drawn from interests that transcend not only the boundaries of the discipline of sociology, but also the boundaries of a single country. It will include theory — social, political, and economic — as well as problems of social and political organization that are global in their general character although national in specific characteristics.

These words of introduction would be incomplete without an acknowledgment of the jovial encouragement we have received from our colleagues in Albania, the United States, and several European countries, whose moral support, intellectual enthusiasm, and academic advice have contributed tremendously to help *Sociological Analysis* start its long and difficult journey. In particular, I acknowledge with gratitude the support given by the Department of Sociology at Eastern Michigan University. Even before the work for the preparation of the first issue of *SA* began, the announcement of our venture was received with extremely encouraging words by several eminent sociologists such as (in alphabetical order), Judith Blau, Georgina Born, Michael Burawoy, Craig Calhoun, Daniel Chirot, Jon Elster, Amitai Etzioni, Anthony Giddens, Arne Kalleberg, Victor Nee, Claus Offe, Saskia Sassen, Erik Olin Wright, etc., to whom I am particularly thankful.

I would be remiss if I did not express enormous gratitude to my old friends and distinguished colleagues, Bas de Gaay Fortman, Barbara Heyns, Lisa Keister, Jan Nederveen Pieterse, Michael Savage, Jay Weinstein and all those sociologists in and outside of Albania who remain supportive of our venture. I hope *SA* will properly justify the efforts of all those who have contributed to make this courageous endeavor come true. Most importantly, my Albanian colleagues and I hope that the format and scope of *SA* will meet both the needs of the Albanian social scientists and the expectations of all those supporting this journal or interested to publish their scholarly work in its pages.

I am aware that many shortcomings will crave the indulgence of the reader. I am confident, however, that the reader will extend to the enterprise not only his indulgence, but also his friendship and collaboration.

FATOS TARIFA

The foundational meeting of the Albanian Institute of Sociology
(Tirana International Hotel, Tirana, November 23, 2006).

The inaugural issue of *Studime Sociale* (*Social Studies*), the official journal
of the Albanian Institute of Sociology, launched on April 2007.

Anti-Social Science, Dehumanization, and Social Policy: The Legitimation of Social Injustice

By Jay Weinstein

Abstract

This paper seeks to establish a parallel between (a) the race science/race policy/ Holocaust linkage during the Nazi race war and (b) the linkage between a group of contemporary "anti-social" sciences we refer to as "SRM"/neo-conservative social policy/and class war raging today, especially—but not exclusively—in the US. "SRM" refers to sociobiology, rational choice theory, and medicalization of relational disorders. We argue that a set of social policies has been crafted from the main assumptions of SRM that support such tendencies as plutocracy, paternalistic rule, militarization of the public sector, elimination of public-sector support for vulnerable groups (privatization of social services, underwriting of "faith-based" programs), and marginalization of liberal and radical perspectives. In an application postscript, we ask if sociologists today can formulate an attack on SRM as did F. Boas and A. Montagu on race science. We certainly have the intellectual resources; but do we have the courage?

*A*NY AMERICAN sociologists today, especially those who identify as practitioners, believe that the political climate in the United States is essentially hostile to their interests. We are not referring to a perceived indifference, or lack of understanding, on the part of our potential publics. This is something against which sociologists and other social scientists have had to struggle since our fields were founded. And, thanks to Professor Michael Burawoy, the fact that it is a subject of concern was concisely expressed in the 2004-05 American Sociological Association's annual meeting theme of "Public Sociology." The perception of at least some of "our publics" that is currently at issue is far more serious and far more sinister than ignorance or indifference. Some people and organizations, it appears, are determined to invalidate the epistemological foundations of our field.

JAY WEINSTEIN is Professor of Sociology at Eastern Michigan University and an Honorary Member of the Albanian Institute of Sociology. He is the Editor of Journal of Applied Social Science *and author of many books, including his groundbreaking work* Sociology/Technology: Foundations of Postacademic Social Science *(1982),* The Grammar of Social Relations *(1984), and* Social and Cultural Change: Social Science for a Dynamic World *(2005).*

In a systematic—although not necessarily consciously planned—manner, certain essential elements of what Louis Schneider first referred to as "the sociological way of looking at the world" are under attack. The process does not constitute a direct assault, although this too is occurring in a limited way.[1]

More typical than an explicit attack, however, is the set of loosely-related counter approaches that have been developed and—with increasing support—have gained legitimacy in some intellectual and, of strategic importance, certain political circles. I refer to these here as *anti-social sciences*, in full recognition of the double entendre: (1) that the offending approaches are arrayed against society and (2) that they are arrayed against the fields that study society.[2]

The aim of this article is to describe these anti-social sciences, to consider the sources of their development and (selective) acceptance, to examine their role in what I believe to be the undermining of our traditional perspectives, and to speculate on the likely (dire) consequences of their continued growth. My explanation is, broadly, functionalist. That is, I see the anti-social sciences as involved in a reciprocal relationship with powerful groups whose ideology is justified by the sciences and which, in turn, materially and culturally support the fields and their practitioners—all of this to the detriment of applied sociology. As a model for this explanation, I draw on a well documented historical case in which little doubt remains that a certain kind of science and certain ideologically committed political and intellectual elites found themselves in a mutually supportive relationship, with disastrous consequences. This is the relationship between race science and the leaders of Nazi Germany that—along with other causes—eventuated in the Holocaust.

ON SCIENCE AND IDEOLOGY

AN IMPLICIT PREMISE of this discussion is that the SRM approaches are ideologies that are accepted, at least among some influential groups, as scientific accounts. Although the distinction between science and ideology is notoriously elusive, it is crucial in assessing the argument put forth here. Thus, in the following few paragraphs, I indicate what I believe to be the difference between the two.

To begin with, both scientific and ideological accounts are linguistic entities consisting of words and sentences, constructed via discourse among like-minded people. Both purport to describe an aspect of the world, in our case the world of human behavior. And both are based in part on observation and in part on deduction. Broadly speaking, they differ as to the purposes that their creators and/or users intend them to serve. That is, the goal of scientific accounts is to provide an accurate depiction of reality that can serve to advance knowledge via future research. In contrast, ideologies are meant to promote a

---

[1] For example, the Consortium of Social Science Associations has taken a special interest in what it refers to as "politically motivated attacks on peer review." In 2003 this organization informed the public that "The nation's basic science community was riled again this week by a new potentially serious development regarding National Institutes of Health (NIH) supported research involving sexual behavior and drug abuse issues critical to the nation's health" (COSSA 2003)

[2] I cannot claim credit for coining the term. David Rhind of London's City University used it in a review a few years ago (Rhind 2003), and I would guess that this was not the first time it appeared in print.

specific line of action and to avoid others. The problem with this contrast lies in the realm of applied science, whose aim, it can be argued, is also to promote action. We return to this issue below.

An ideology is a distorted account that serves the interests of some group for itself.[3] It distorts not by telling untruths but through its focus on only the facts that support its case. Karl Mannheim (1968), the first to develop a systematic theory of ideology, distinguished between *ruling ideologies* and *utopias*. This distinction emphasizes how some accounts justify the past or present, whereas others (the latter) are oriented toward a promised future. Both are kinds of ideologies, in that they have the same structure and function (Frankfurt Institute 1972: ch. VI). The former, however, are associated with groups that hold power, or ultraconservative groups that seek to recapture it; the latter characterize protest movements, especially left-wing political causes.

Ideologies (and utopias) have two parts, or phases, the *report* and the *command* phases (Gouldner 1975-76). The first part is *descriptive*, a report on the health or proper functioning of some established practice or institution. In ruling ideologies, evidence is selected to show that all is well and that the established ways are intact and effective. Movement utopias, in contrast, seek to prove that something is wrong and that the fault is with the system. The command phase is *prescriptive*; it is a therapy that tells people what to do to make things better. In ruling ideologies, this is a directive to behave in such a way that the status quo is maintained; in movements, it is a command to change things in a particular direction. Ideologies and utopias differ from ordinary myths and fictions in their degree of elaboration: they are relatively long, involved accounts that seem to explain everything. They are the products of conscious, collective, and partisan efforts often extending over generations. Some tell a convincing tale that, nevertheless, is crafted to benefit a movement, party, or regime.

Marx and, in his subsequent critical work, Mannheim were the first to draw a sharp contrast between ideology and science, although we now understand the difference between the two to be quite subtle, if not at least partly arbitrary. In a strict sense, all highly elaborated descriptive reports about reality — even scientific ones — must be distorted to some extent. For we are always bound to draw conclusions before the last possible piece of evidence is unearthed (Rudner 1953). Moreover, we act on our imperfect diagnoses in ways we more or less strongly feel, but never know for certain, are in our interests. So we make mistakes.

In this respect, scientific accounts differ from ideologies in the understanding that no particular party's interest is to be served by their depiction of reality and that no particular therapy is endorsed (a difficult ideal to achieve, as noted). This promotes science's stubborn quest for exceptions and disconfirming evidence, which is something ideologues seek to avoid. In this light, the difference between science and ideology is technically quite narrow, resting on a leap of faith — that the scientist will remain faithful to the principle of truth before "cause," no matter how just it may be. The ideologue, on the

---

[3] The word *ideology* has French roots and was originally used in the late eighteenth century by Destutt de Tracy (1817/1970; Head 1985) and Helvetius (1810/1969; Horowitz 1954), to refer to any system of ideas. With Marx and Engels's *The German Ideology* (1864), the concept was given its current connotation as an interest-serving distortion. See also Bendix (1971), Zeitlin (1968).

other hand, must promote the cause, even if literal truths must be bent. This, it seems to many sociologists of science, is a very important but rather fragile distinction.

THE RACE SCIENCE / RACE POLICY CONNECTION
IN NAZI GERMANY

THIS SECTION SUMMARIZES a thesis that Nico Stehr and I developed and first published in the journal *Social Epistemology* (Weinstein and Stehr 1999). In brief, we argue that the findings and theories of race science (*Rassenwissenschaft*) were employed to justify Nazi racial policy. Subsequently, this policy was used as the legal framework that legitimated the Holocaust. The parallel I am drawing here between race science and the currently burgeoning anti-social sciences was noted by Stephen Jay Gould in his *The Mismeasure of Man* (Gould 1981). Gould takes issue with the claims of sociobiology, in particular, which he sees as a sanitized version of the now-discredited racial determinist theories of an earlier era. Stephanie Herman (2003) observes that Gould rightly criticizes a similar type of prejudicial "science" of the 18th and 19th centuries that supported the belief that blacks were an inferior race. "The pervasive assent given by scientists to conventional rankings arose from shared social belief," Gould wrote, "not from objective data gathered to test an open question. Yet, in a curious case of reversed causality, these pronouncements were read as independent support for the political context"[4]

Race Science as Legitimate Science?

The question of whether or not race science was authentic, as opposed to "prejudicial" or pseudo-science, is a difficult one to answer. Certainly, with benefit of hindsight, it was largely bogus. But it is equally clear that at the time it was viewed as entirely legitimate. No less an authority than Carolus Linneaus viewed race as a meaningful biological category that encompassed physical features such as skin color along with aspects of temperament and intelligence. The following is Linneaus' 1735 classification scheme, verbatim.

Americanus: reddish, choleric, and erect; hair black, straight, thick; wide nostrils, scanty beard; obstinate, merry, free; paints himself with fine red lines; regulated by customs.

Asiaticus: sallow, melancholy, stiff; hair black; dark eyes; severe, haughty, avaricious; covered with loose garments; ruled by opinions.

Africanus: black, phlegmatic, relaxed; hair black, frizzled; skin silky; nose flat; lips tumid; women without shame, they lactate profusely; crafty, indolent, negligent; anoints himself with grease; governed by caprice.

---

[4] Quoted in Herman (2003), "Political Science" *American Partisan* (January), http://www.american-partisan.com/cols/herman/010300.htm

Europeaeus: white, sanguine, muscular; hair long, flowing; eyes blue; gentle, acute, inventive; covers himself with close vestments; governed by laws.[5]

By the late 1800s, the field—based largely on Linneaus' observations—enjoyed world-wide acclaim. Courses and research on the effects of racial differences were being pursued at the leading universities in England, France, Germany, the U.S. and other countries. In addition to their reliance on Linneaus, practitioners drew from the work of Darwin, Robert Knox, and Joseph Gobineau and from other fields such as agronomy, genetics, and anthropometry. In any case, as the impact of evolutionary ideas spread throughout the scientific community, so too did the influence of race science.

The Case of Ernst Fischer

An especially instructive case of the intersection of biography and the history of race science is that of Ernst Fischer. Fischer was born in Germany in the late nineteenth century. Trained as an agronomist but distinguished as a eugenicist, he, remarkably, survived World War II with his professional career intact.

Prior to the First World War, Germany had established itself belatedly as a European colonial power. Its principal colonial holding, German Southwest Africa (now Namibia), was the site of Fischer's major empirical work, published in 1913 as *The Rehoboth Bastards*. The book presents detailed evidence, including numerous photographs—a relatively new tool of science—"proving" that the offspring of marriages between Europeans and native Hottentots invariably had lower levels of intelligence and poorer physical characteristics than those of either parent. Throughout the book Fischer mounts a powerful argument against "race-mixing" (*Mischlenge*).

In 1921, with Fritz Lenz and Otto Bauer, two highly respected biologists, Fischer incorporated his findings in what was to become the leading text in German race science, *Human Heredity*. In June of 1933, less than six months after Hitler assumed power; Fischer was appointed Chancellor of Humboldt University of Berlin. Now a member of the SS and occupying the highest academic post in the *Reich*, he oversaw the incorporation of race science into his university and other institutions throughout the country.

These developments did not go unchallenged. Anthropologists such as Franz Boas and sociologists, including Max Weber, understood that racial explanations ignored or actively denied the importance of sociocultural factors. As the popularity of race science in scientific communities began to wane outside of Germany, the social sciences gained acceptance in academic circles. However, in Germany non-racial theories became increasingly suspect and social scientists who did not accept racial determinism were ostracized.

Under the Nazis, the German Anthropological Society was renamed the German Society for the Study of Race. And, in one of the most absurd manifestations of the race scientists' battle against sociocultural explanations, Boas' rejection of racial explanation was claimed by his fellow anthropologists to be the result of a Jewish racial trait. That

---

[5] Source: http://www-personal.umich.edu/~jonmorro/race.html

is, Jews have a hereditary disposition that renders them incapable of understanding how race shapes human behavior!

From Race Science to Race Policy: Nuremberg to Judenrein to Auschwitz

Hitler's first cabinet included a Minister of "Racial Hygiene." The post was occupied by Julius Streicher, a journalist and virulent anti-Semite whose newspaper carried the quote from Treitsche on its masthead: *Die Juden sind unser Ungluck* ("The Jews are our misfortune"). Streicher was unequivocal in his view that Jews were not only a race, but also a race of which Germany needed to be "cleansed." Thus, as race science became legitimate science, the religious anti-Semitism that had prevailed throughout the Christian world for nearly two millennia was transformed into "scientific" anti-Semitism.

By 1935, the findings of race science were being used to justify race policy. The first of the Nuremberg Laws, passed in that year, made explicit reference to heredity (the "one-grandparent" principle) and mixed marriage. At about the same time, the notorious Reich Office of Racial Hygiene (RHO) was established within Steicher's ministry. Its first director was Robert Ritter, an anti-Semite who also had a special "fascination" with Sinti and Roma people ("Gypsies"). These and related developments forged an important linkage between *Rassenwissenschaft* and the policy of *Judenrein* (cleansing of the Jews).

The rest is well-documented history. *Judenrein* was carried out in successive steps—from humiliation, to segregation, to deportation, to ghettoization, to annihilation. It bears repeating that every stage occurred within a (rapidly evolving) legal framework. The *Reich* law that legitimated the treatment of the Jews and other victims was an expression of official government policy. And the policy was justified by what was understood to be (not just in Germany but throughout the "civilized" world) authentic science.

In the remainder of this paper I will attempt to demonstrate that a parallel process is occurring today, especially in the U.S. In referring to it as "parallel" I mean to stress that race is no longer the issue—at least not explicitly. Rather than *race war*, we are now in the midst of *class war*. Further, I do not mean to suggest that we are experiencing or are about to experience mass slaughter of innocent civilians—although a nation at war is always in danger of such excesses. Rather, we are in danger of experiencing increasing impoverishment, political marginalization, and unemployment among all but the wealthiest of our citizens. Whereas science legitimated genocide during the Nazi era, today science appears to be legitimating the injustices of gross social inequality.

THE "SCIENTIFIC" ATTACK ON SOCIAL SCIENCE

I HAVE SELECTED three approaches to explaining social phenomena to illustrate my claim that sociology and related disciplines—especially applied sociology—are currently in danger of being displaced by anti-social sciences. Two of the three ought to be familiar to all sociologists, as they have been widely discussed, criticized, and defended in scholarly literature for the past two decades. The third, whose roots extend back decades as well, represents a more recent development. Thus, it requires the largest share of our attention in the discussion that follows.

The two more familiar approaches are sociobiology (denoted by an upper case "S") and rational choice theory ("R"). The third is the psychiatric theory that seeks to medicalize "relational disorders" ("M" — for medicalization). I will refer to them collectively as SRM. Although no doubt embattled, these "theories" have assumed a considerable degree of credibility among numerous scholars and, in their popularized versions, among members of sociology's publics as well.[6] Especially ardent followers of one or more of the SRM perspectives believe that a true breakthrough has been achieved in understanding human relationships. For these loyalists, not only does the perspective provide a valid explanation of social behavior, it provides the *only* explanation. That is, it is argued, the approach supersedes traditional explanations. If this claim is accepted widely enough (whether or not is can be substantiated), then SRM would truly displace its competitors.

The Programs and Power of SRM

In this section, I outline an argument to the effect that, if accepted, the premises of SRM would undercut key principles of traditional sociology. This, in turn, would (further) challenge the values of egalitarianism and social progress on which applied sociology is based.[7] And, ultimately, it would provide a justification for a "scientific" cleansing of social welfare and democratic reform.

Sociobiology

Of the three SRM theories, sociobiology is undoubted the best known, the most widely accepted, and the most frequently criticized.[8] It is also the one with the most direct links to classic race science on which Nazi race policy was based. The name of entomologist E.O. Wilson is closely associated with the foundations of the approach, and with good reason. For his *Sociobiology: A New Synthesis* (Wilson 1975) initiated a virtual storm of subsequent research and debate that continues to the present. Yet the principal thesis of the approach originated decades before the publication of Wilson's study.

Darwin himself and, more explicitly, Darwinian biologists have held that most consequential human social behavior is — like that of ants and other species — genetically determined and thus the result of evolutionary processes such as natural selection. Lawerence and Nohira (2002) provide a recent and unequivocal argument in support of this view, with generous acknowledgement of Darwin. Even the term, *Sociobiology*, itself has been

---

[6] Proponents often refer to the approaches as theories; and I shall follow this convention, using the term interchangeably with "approach" and "perspective." Nevertheless, in my view, this is another instance of careless (but conveniently so?) use of the term. See Weinstein (2000) for a more extended discussion.

[7] This argument, and the necessary qualifications to the effect that this pro-democracy strain is a tendency rather than an inherent feature of sociology, is explored at length in Weinstein (2004).

[8] Gregory and Silver (1975) edited an early collection that includes a statement by Wilson along with supportive and critical essays.

used in scientific literature since 1949 or earlier (see Alled et al. 1949).

One of the main points of contention associated with this claim is that, if true, then a core belief of applied sociology and related fields would be rendered invalid.[9] This is the belief that socioeconomic inequality among individuals, classes, nations, gender relations, and various forms of social injustice are the contingent outcomes of sociocultural processes. I say "contingent" to indicate that they are not necessary and—contrary to sociobiological principles—can thus be altered through political reform and planned social change.

Rational Choice Theory

Whereas sociobiology is clearly rooted in evolutionary biology, rational choice theory is a synthesis of neo-classical microeconomics and a variant of functionalist sociology. As is true of Wilson in relation to sociobiology, a single dominant scholar is virtually universally credited with founding (or at least popularizing) the approach. In this case it is James S. Coleman.

Coleman's *Foundations of Sociological Theory* (1990; also Coleman 1986) is premised on the assumption that social behavior is the outcome of rational deliberation in which the actor considers and compares the options that are available. The behavioral choice that results from this process is the one that the actor understands to have the greatest payoff in social rewards (material benefits, power, and prestige). Social interaction is thus seen as a process of negotiation in which participants attempt to maximize their gains and, to the extent that the encounter involves a zero-sum game, to minimize the gains of the other.

The theory is heavily laced with the terminology and major premises of economic price theory. The basic principle of rational choice theory states that the probability that an action will be carried out is a function of the gain in utility an actor expects from that action's outcome multiplied by the probability he or she attributes to the action's capacity to bring about the outcome. In a situation of choice, an actor carries out that action for which the value of its utility multiplied by the probability of such an outcome is the highest (Coleman 1990: 13-19; Münch 1993: 37).

If social relations did in fact follow these principles, then some fairly simple and fairly credible outcomes could be explained and/or predicted for a wide range of phenomena. But, of course, social relations are far more complex and varied than rational choice theory suggests. In fact, the theory is a nearly ideal example of *theoretical sociology* posing as *sociological theory* (see Weinstein 2000). As Richard Münch (1993: 70-71) has observed:

> The theory attains comprehensiveness only by reduction; that is, by reducing whatever exists outside the sphere of economics to the laws of economics....The strategy of achieving comprehensiveness by reduction is common to the whole movement of rational choice theory (1993: 70-71).

As is true of the economic perspective from which it is derived, rational choice theory is a deductive as opposed to an inductive formulation. As is true of other instances of

---

[9] See Gregory and Silvers (1978) for a review of this and other criticisms of the approach).

theoretical sociology, it is an explanatory system based on simplifying assumptions about mental processes and social relations. And this is the source of both its appeal and its flaws. Among the most serious flaws from the standpoint of applied sociology is that it assumes away altruism. For rational choice theorists, altruism is either irrational or illusory. Egoism, on the other hand, is understood to be an entirely natural and rational orientation.[10]

Relational Disorders

The Diagnostic and Statistical Manual of Mental Disorders (DSM) plays a role in the psychiatric profession that is unique among technical publications in other fields. For its entries literally define what is to be counted as an emotional or mental disorder (see Cloud 2003). When a type of behavior is included in the DSM, it is henceforth officially a disease whose diagnosis and treatment are the responsibility of accredited psychotherapists and other psychopathologists. Thus, inclusion is an extremely serious matter. "The DSM contains a cautionary statement saying it takes clinical training to tell the difference" between symptoms of disorder and perfectly normal behavior.

> But many nonspecialists use the book too: insurers open the DSM when disputes arise over the proper course of treatment for particular conditions, (If your treatment does not jibe with the DSM, you may not get reimbursed.) DSM diagnoses can be used by courts to lock you in a mental hospital or by schools to place your child in special-education classes. A DSM label can become a stigma (Cloud 2003).

The editors are now preparing the manual's newest and most comprehensive 5th edition, DSM-V, scheduled for publication in 2010. It was recently announced that a new entry is being considered for what has been termed "relational disorders." A relational disorder is defined as a serious problem in interactions between spouses, siblings, parent and child, and so forth. The individuals involved may be perfectly normal, except when they are relating to the relevant other(s). Thus, it is the relationship that is "diseased," not the individuals who comprise the relationship.

Dr. Michael First, associate professor of psychiatry at Columbia University and one of the principal figures behind the push, puts the case for the novel diagnosis this way: "There is evidence that relationships and how people interact in particular relationships can be disordered in a way that's very similar to mental disorders" (Kirn and Anh 2002).

The movement to include relational disorders has not gone unchallenged (see Blatner 2002). Some psychiatrists and lay observers have noted parallels between this proposal and the now highly controversial decision to include homosexuality in DSM-I and DSM-II. Several controversies were associated with the official designation of homosexuality as a disease. The most significant among these is that inclusion gave credence to the claims of religious and secular homophobes; and it continues to do so despite the fact that it was

---

[10] See Weinstein (2003). In this and other papers on altruism, I have posed the following dilemma. (The latter two scenarios entail rational choice theory's denial of altruism).

removed in 1973 from DSM-III and did not reappear in DSM-IV (see Kaplan and Sadock 1985). R.L. Spitzer provided the following summary in the *American Journal of Psychiatry*.

The issue of whether homosexuality is a disease has been one of the more controversial matters that has faced the framers of the various DSMs over the last few decades. The very first edition of the *Diagnostic and Statistical Manual of Mental Disorders* (DSM-I) classified homosexuality as a sexual deviation, as did DSM-II in 1968. However, in December of 1973, the DSM-II was modified by the Board of Trustees of the American Psychiatric Association (APA), who voted to eliminate the general category of homosexuality, and replace it with sexual orientation disturbance (Spitzer 1981).

The proposal to include relational disorders has also reinvigorated the longstanding debate about the arbitrary nature of diagnosis itself, to which Thomas Szasz famously contributed (Gergen et al. 1996; also Blatner 2002 on Szasz). But in addition to these issues, applied sociologists have an equally fundamental concern. If relational disorders are included in DSM-V, a range of what are traditionally viewed as social problems will *ipso facto* become medical problems. Considering the recent radical shift in the psychiatric profession from psychotherapy to psychopharmacology, it is virtually inevitable that interpersonal conflict and the like will be treated with prescription drugs (especially those over which major pharmaceutical companies hold a monopoly).

Sociologists are trained to seek the causes and the amelioration of such problems at structural and cultural levels. That is, a well-defined pattern—not an isolated incidence, of course, but a near-"epidemic"—of, say, spousal abuse is understood to be a symptom of crisis in the institutions of marriage, gender relations, and/or other larger structures. Thus, the diagnosis and treatment of relational disorders, such as spousal abuse, based on DSM guidelines represents a complete reversal of one of the very foundations of the sociological imagination. That is, public issues will be seen as private problems! The obvious corollary is that social reform will be rendered irrelevant, at least until we run out of psychotropic drugs.

A SUMMARY OF SRM IMPACTS

EACH OF THE SRM theories in itself presents a challenge to the traditional sociological perspective. Their potential impacts are magnified by the fact that they are also mutually supportive. That is, the theories either directly share some premises, or the basic assumptions of one complement those of another. Most broadly, with their roots in zoology, neoclassical economics, and behavioral psychology, they all tend to reject explanation at the superorganic level.[11] Instead, they attempt to reduce sociocultural objects and events to purely mental and/or genetic levels. From this it follows that:

Social structure is hard-wired; social reform is futile and ultimately impossible;

Social problems have a somatic origin and can be treated with chemicals;

---

[11] Herbert Spencer apparently introduced the term superorganic into social science. It was also used by A.L. Kroeber and P.A. Sorokin, among others. It refers to the phenomena that are the products of human interaction and that include an element of intentionality or purposefulness. These include material culture, non-

Late-sensate values are equated with human nature: Selfishness is more than a virtue; it is both natural and uniquely rational;

Altruism is a deviant or pathological form of behavior: What appears to be altruism can be understood as a manifestation of rational egoism and/or an instinctual response related to self-preservation.

The following section examines a key set of political implications of these elements of contemporary anti-social science.

SRM and Social Policy

The fact that several prominent theories contradict or invalidate key principles of sociology certainly has had an impact in academe where courses in the field are taught. However, their efficacy would be limited to this unless an ideologically motivated political party, group or faction were to embrace these theories and put them into practice via policy, as was the case with race science under the Nazi regime.

E.O. Wilson is one of the most explicit and most astute SRM proponents regarding the political implications of his work. "Already half the legislation coming before the United States Congress contains important scientific and technological components," he warns in *Consilience*. "Most of the issues that vex humanity daily—ethnic conflict, arms escalation, overpopulation, abortion, environment, endemic poverty...cannot be solved without integrating knowledge....Only fluency across the boundaries will provide a clear view of the world as it really is, not as seen through the lens of ideologies..." (cited in Herman 2003).

In 1976, a "discordant element" of evolutionary theory became potentially useful in our understanding of sociopolitical arrangements; Richard Dawkins published his theory naming the gene as the "basic unit of selfishness." According to Dawkins, natural selection favors the gene best able to replicate itself. How does a gene exhibit its superior ability? "A predominant quality to be expected in a successful gene," goes Dawkins' theory, "is ruthless selfishness" (Herman 2003).

In tracing the ideological linkages of SRM, two trends are immediately apparent. First, SRM and its premises have been widely and enthusiastically embraced by intellectuals associated with the Heritage Foundation, the Cato Institute, the Hoover Institution, the Mises Institute, and similar policy centers. These think tanks share a fundamental commitment to what they refer to as free-market capitalism and are well funded by the Coors family, Robert Welch, and other politically involved corporate actors. This connection, especially regarding sociobiology and rational choice theory, has been discussed and documented by Stephanie Herman (2003) and Roger Backhouse (2004), among others.

Included among this group of intellectuals who, typically, have connections with academic SRM and conservative think tanks is Don Lavoie. Lavoie, who died in 2001, taught at George Mason University and worked for the Cato Institute. He was consid-

---

material culture, and social structure. Thus, the family and other institutions, language, values, and norms are *superorganic* phenomena and, it is argued, can be explained only at the *superorganic* level. Durkheim's concept of *emergent*—the opposite of *reductionist*—is closely related.

ered an expert in the field of sociobiology.[12] Another is Terry Moe, William Bennett Monroe Professor of Political Science and Department Chair, Stanford University. Moe is a specialist in rational choice theory, a Cato Institute affiliate, and a Senior Fellow, Hoover institution.[13]

The second trend is that these intellectuals and the organizations they represent invariably discredit all critiques of SRM and its principles as left-wing rhetoric. Indeed, some of the most vicious attacks from the right I personally have read in years are those launched against "liberals" and "Marxists" in defense of SRM. The effect of this line of criticism is worth noting. That is, it conflates left-wing ideology with well-established and widely accepted tenets of sociology and related fields (not to suggest that sociology's critics have never before accused us of being left-wing apologists). This, in turn, politicizes a debate—in favor of the right—that has a perfectly scientific and thus legitimately falsifiable method of resolution. In this context, politicization denies a role to empirical investigation in resolving differences because one side is simply right and the other is wrong.

SRM's Ideological Champions

The "Tory" blog from the UK, *Conservative Commentary*, recently posted an extended defense of Richard Dawkins' (1989) sociobiology classic, *The Selfish Gene*. The reviewer, Peter Cuthbertson leaves little doubt about why some on the political right have embraced the theory.

> The first thing visiting aliens will ask about humans is whether we understand evolution; each individual gene exists to survive and replicate itself, even at the expense of its host; a huge amount of human behaviour can ultimately be traced back to our evolutionary inheritance. It's a solid scientific judgment, and one supported by much theory and evidence—and some beautiful exposition (Cuthbertson 2004).

Dawkins, Cuthbertson and others, in response to the charge that this position amounts to biological determinism, have allowed for the possibility that, despite the fact that behavior is the result of inheritance, the outcomes can be altered.

> Further to that: if, as evolutionary psychology and sociobiology suggest, our natural instinct is to be protective first of ourselves and our families, to be indifferent to the col-

---

[12] See http://psol.gmu.edu/dlavoie.nsf

[13] Closer to the Heartland, is Arthur Fleischer, Professor of economics at Metropolitan State College (Denver, Colorado). On a course syllabus posted online, he recommends "The Cato Institute: http://www.cato.org/ (Excellent site for discussion on social security reform)." His instructions to his students are indeed instructive: "We are going to show the relevance of economic methodology to these and other public or non-market choices. As you will find out soon enough, we emphasize that the "rules of the game" and institutions matter. If we see "bad" results in the real world, most people jump to the conclusion that the "rules of the game" must be bad. To change outcomes we must change the rules. When we do change the rules, good/bad things occur. Policy changes (isn't that what you do-gooders care about?) REQUIRE us to look at alternative rules. Bad results imply bad rules ONLY if you can show me alternative rule(s) that give us better results! Bad results can be optimal results—get over it! I believe that rational choice theorists have a comparative advantage in asking the key question—"compared to what?" (http://www.mscd.edu/~econ/47504b. syl.doc).

lective good save when leveled up against another group, to seek chaste, maternal, beautiful wives and hard-working, wealthy, dutiful husbands, then that too should not be regarded as a state of affairs we should passively accept...this position is perfectly consistent with Dawkins' science and his political convictions (Cuthbertson 2004).

We are not aware of a clear and direct formulation or program by sociobiologists that would allow us to actively alter such a "state of affairs." But I do get the impression that lurking just beneath the surface is the specter of eugenics. In any case, it is curious that one would find it admirable that a position is "perfectly consistent with" one's "science and his political convictions."

The flagship periodical of the intellectual right, *National Review* has created a list of the 100 best non-fiction books of the century. In first place is Winston S. Churchill, *The Second World War* Followed by Alexander Solzhenitsyn, *The Gulag Archipelago*. In an interesting juxtaposition, number 10 is Milton Friedman, *Capitalism and Freedom* whereas number 14 is Max Weber, *Economy and Society*. In this distinguished company, we find at number 17, E.O. Wilson, *Sociobiology: A New Synthesis*. The inscription reads "Darwin put humanity in its proper place in the animal kingdom. Wilson put human society there, too."

The Mises Institute is one of several conservative organizations that have championed the cause of rational choice theory (the Cato Institute and the Hoover Institution among them). The Institute's scholars generally view the theory as an extension of the strongly pro-market approach of Ludwig von Mises, the famed Austrian economist after whom it is named. Mises historian in residence, Joseph Stromberg, makes this case forcefully in his review of a book by James Aune (2001). Aune's analysis of rational choice theory is similar to that of Münch, summarized above. Stromberg, in turn, defends the theory in asserting that "Aune uses dubious empirical studies to defend minimum wage laws and farm subsidies, he proceeds with the only part of the book where the actual existence of anything outside of language plays much of a role" (Stromberg and Tucker 2001).

Attack on "the Left"

In what appears to be a well-coordinated strategy, ideological defenders of SRM have strengthened their position, at least in the public consciousness, by categorizing all criticism of the theories as left wing and/or Marxist rhetoric. No doubt, much criticism of the theories has been politically motivated. But equally as much has been formulated by social scientists whose training and research seriously incline them to take exception to major claims of the theorists. In contending that anyone who disagrees with E.O. Wilson, James Coleman, Michael First, or their associates is a "leftist" their defenders are able to dismiss serious scientific skepticism about a set of approaches that invite skeptical scrutiny.

The review by the Mises Institute's Peter Stromberg, cited in the previous section, concludes with the following, classic *ad hominum* attack: "Like many leftists, [Aune] sides with competitive losers like Betamax, seeking thereby to demonstrate constant market failure. Since Austrians have produced solid critiques of the market-failure school, we need not linger over Aune's thin rebuttals."

In a more vigorous, but no less characteristic manner, Peter Cuthbertson (2004) argues that challenges to sociobiology encapsulate the left's horror at the implications of the science for their own projects of permanent revolution, social radicalism and sexual egalitarianism. For while they can still hold to those goals, sociobiology certainly undermines a thousand claims that it is simple prejudice, custom and social convention that prevents them being realized. This liberal horror should be matched on the right by quiet satisfaction from all those who have no interest in the remodeling of human nature nor faith in the power of the state to make us all perfect little citizens, devoid of all the self-interest, distrust and unkind judgment that makes the liberal dream so unachievable. It is only a small exaggeration to say that nature is on our side.

One wonders how exactly an experiment can be devised to determine whose side nature is on! In any case, Cuthbertson's tone makes it seem as if at issue is something that goes far beyond differences of opinion over the value of one or another scientific theory. Rather, it appears more like a war is being waged; and indeed a war is being waged, as I will discuss presently.

Some sense of just how much enmity exists among SRM proponents against those who would disagree with them can be discerned from this final passage of Cuthbertson's critique. I quote it at length because it provides a very clear statement of the linkage between the anti-social sciences and the anti-social policies that they appear to justify.

> For anyone who sees the best government and worldview as one that goes with the grain of human nature and everyday instinct, sociobiology opens up a whole new perspective on the same social and political questions. As the *National Review's* Steve Sailer puts it: "The left has long denounced sociobiological research for validating what conservatives have assumed all along: that human nature—with its sex differences and its stress on individual, family, and ethnic self-interest—is an innate heritage, not a blank slate that can be wiped clean by speech codes, sensitivity workshops, and re-education camps." This is a point of profound importance, and which has implications for all of politics. It has regularly astounded me when discussing cultural and social issues not that people often disagree with the conservative perspective, but that they tend to do so in such a way as to suggest they think it has all simply been pulled out of the air as an arbitrary edict. Do they really think a father is superfluous in the raising of children?, I ask myself. Do they honestly think marriage is merely a piece of paper, that the link between sex and procreation is a thing of the past? Can they possibly believe that a marriage of multiple men and women would work just as well if social conventions only changed a little? From the Marxist, postmodernist and liberal left to the libertarian right, such blank slate attitudes are commonplace. But then I realize that without a basic grounding in sociobiology, I would likely think the very same (Cuthbertson 2004).

THE CONTRIBUTIONS OF SRM TO CLASS WAR

IT PROBABLY GOES without saying that the think tanks whence the defense of SRM — along with the attacks on its critics — emanates have inordinate influence on the policies that are formulated and promoted by the current administration. Of course, this is equally true of liberal think tanks during Democratic administrations. However, a kind of ideological orthodoxy (and polarization) that may well be unprecedented characterizes the political culture in the US today. Thus, the organizations that support intellectual activity in and around Washington, DC now play a unique role.

As Figure 1 indicates, the principles of SRM, which originate in academic science, are adopted and elaborated on by the intellectuals in the think tanks. Those who adopt their work, in turn, have the power to create and implement social policy based on these principles. It is not at all unusual for the same individual to participate in two or all three spheres, sometimes simultaneously and sometimes at different stages of a career. The system is self-sustaining through reciprocity by virtue of the fact that policy makers can and routinely do allocate resources to private organizations and universities.

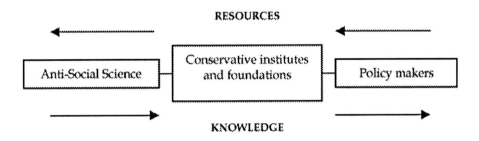

Figure 1: Science to Science Policy

This is obviously a highly simplified model of science-justified state policy. In particular there are in reality many more actors involved in the process, which makes for a far more elaborate system of communication, feedback, and the like. Moreover, when academic organizations—universities, laboratories, and research institutes—are involved, peer review plays a crucial role in legitimating the knowledge at issue. Nevertheless, in its basics, it covers not only contemporary SRM approaches but Nazi science as well (see Burleigh and Wimpermann 1991, esp. Chs. 2-5). To the extent that one accepts the treatment of peer review developed by proponents of the Strong Program in the philosophy of science, the distance between science and ideology in this context is narrowed even further, and the parallels with Nazi policy become even closer.[14]

During the Nazi era, race science and race policy based on that science were employed to wage race war. Today, evidence exists to suggest that SRM and policy based on it are increasingly being employed to wage class war.[15] Separately or in combination, the principles of SRM, especially as interpreted by the Heritage and Cato intellectuals, are being used to support policies that promote the following:

> A confluence of private wealth and state power. Plutocracy is becoming the dominant form of rule;
>
> "Security" takes precedence over civil liberty. This is a key feature of paternalistic rule;
>
> Militarization of the public sector. Government resources are increasingly direc-

---

[14] On this point see Chubin and Weinstein (1987).

[15] It is impossible to provide in this brief paper an effective argument that would substantiate this claim. But, along these lines, Florida (2004), Kinsley (2003), and Ivins and Dubose (2003) each makes a convincing case.

ted away from social programs and toward the military industrial complex;

Elimination of public-sector support for vulnerable groups (e.g., privatization of social services, underwriting of "faith-based" programs);

Marginalization of liberal and radical perspectives that might mitigate these trends.

POSTSCRIPT

IMPLICIT IN THE foregoing analysis is a call to action. Sociologists, especially applied sociologists, are currently seriously embattled. Our core principles of sociocultural determinism, the reality of both egoism *and* altruism (a paired concept coined by Auguste Comte), and the commitment to social justice are, in some highly influential circles, being dismissed as unscientific. Considerable energy and money are being expended to promote the cause of SRM. Indeed, we are faced with a formidable foe.

Many of the proponents of SRM are extremely politically astute. In a campaign of academic McCarthyism, they have been quite successful in characterizing their critics as left wing ideologues. But the criticism of sociobiology, rational choice theory, and the relational disorder movement from the standpoint of traditional sociology is far removed from ideology. These are not merely theories that offend our political sensibilities; they offend our understanding of humanity. So, I ask, can we today formulate an attack on SRM as did Franz Boas, Max Weber, and Ashley Montagu on race science? We certainly have the intellectual resources; and I hope we have courage.

NOTE

I extend my thanks to Robert Arnold, school psychologist, for his assistance on the relational disorders issue. Earlier versions of this paper were presented at the Annual Meeting of the North Central Sociological Association (Pittsburg, Pennsylvania), on April 8, 2005, and at the 37th World Congress of the International Institute of Sociology (Beijing, China), on July 6, 2005.

REFERENCES

Alled, W.C., A. E. Emerson, O. T. Park, and K.P. Schmidt. 1949. *Principles of Animal Ecology.* Philadelphia: W. B. Saunders.

Aune, James Arnt. 2001. *Selling the Free Market: The Rhetoric of Economic Correctness.* New York: The Guilford Press.

Backhouse, Roger. 2004. "A Suggestion for Clarifying the Study of Dissent in Economics." *Journal of the History of Economic Thought* 26, 2: 261-71.

Bendix, Reinhard. 1971. "Sociology and Ideology." In E. A. Tiryakian, ed., *The Phenomenon of Sociology.* New York: Appleton-Century-Crofts.

Blatner, Adam. 2002. "Re-Story-ing the Soul." www.Blatner.com/adam/level2/ restrs/htm.

Burleigh, Michael, and Wolfgang Wippermann. 1991. *The Racial State: Germany, 1933-1945.* New York: Cambridge University Press.

Chubin, Daryl E., and Jay Weinstein. 1987. "War Painters and Western Science." *Sociological Inquiry* 57, 2: 120-43.

Cloud, John. 2003. "How We Get Labeled." *Time*, January 20: http://www.time. com/time/magazine/article/0,9171,1004091,00.html

Coleman James S. 1986. *Individual Interests and Collective Action: Selected Essays.* Cambridge, UK: Cambridge University Press.

_____. 1990 *Foundations of Social Theory.* Cambridge, MA: Harvard University Press.

Coss A. 2003. "Politically Motivated Attack on NIH Peer-Reviewed Research Continues." *Timely NEWS of Interest to Researchers* at http://www.cossa.org/consortium of social science associations

Cuthbertson, Peter. 2004. "Darwin's a Tory at Heart." *Conservative Commentary* (http://concom. blogspot.com/2004_01_11_concom_archi-ve.html)

Dawkins, Richard. 1989. *The Selfish Gene.* Oxford: Oxford University Press.

Destutt de Tracy, Antoine Louis Claude. 1817/1970. *A Treatise on Political Economy.* New York: A.M. Kelley.

Florida, Richard. 2004. "Creative Class War: How the GOP's Anti-Elitism Could Ruin America's Economy." *Washington Monthly* (January/ February).

Frankfurt Institute for Social Research. 1972. *Aspects of Sociology.* Boston: Beacon Press.

Gergen, Kenneth J., Lynn Hoffman, and Harlene Andersen. 1996. "Is Diagnosis a Disaster: A Constructionist Dialogue." In F. Kaslow, ed. *Relational Disorders.* Hoboken, NJ: John F. Wiley and Sons.

Gould, Stephen Jay. 1981. *The Mismeasure of Man.* New Your: Norton.

Gouldner, Alvin W. 1975-76. "Prologue to a Theory of Revolutionary Intellectuals," *Telos* 26, 1: 2-36.

Gregory, Michael S., and Anita Silvers. 1978. *Sociobiology and Human Nature: An Interdisciplinary Critique and Defense.* San Francisco: Jossey-Bass.

Head, Brian. 1985. *Destutt de Tracy and French Liberalism.* Boston: Kluwer Academic Publishers.

Helvétius, Claude. 1810/1969. *A Treatise on Man; His Intellectual Faculties and His Education.* New York: B. Franklin.

Herman, Stephanie. 2003. "Political Science" *American Partisan* (January) http://www.american-partisan.com/cols/herman/010300.htm

Horowitz, Irving Louis. 1954. *Claude Helvetius: Philosopher of Democracy and Enlightenment.* New York: Paine-Whitman.

Ivins, Molly, and Lou Dubose. 2003. *Bushwhacked: Life in George W. Bush's America.* New York: Random House.

Kaplan, H.I., and B.J. Sadock. (eds.). 1985. *Modern Synopsis of Comprehensive Textbook of Psychiatry,* 4th ed. Baltimore: Williams and Wilkins.

Kim, N.S., and Ahn, W-K. 2002. "Clinical Psychologists' Theory-based Representations of Mental Disorders Predict their Diagnostic Reasoning and Memory," *Journal of. Experimental Psychology* 131: 451-75. http://citeseer.ist. psu.edu/kim02clinical.html

Kinsey, Michael. 2003. "The Return of Class War: Bush and the New Tyranny of the Rich." *Slate Online* (June 5). http://slate.msn.com/id/2084002/

Lawrence, Paul R., and Nitin Nohira. 2002. *Driven: How Human Nature Shapes our Choices.* San Francisco: Jossey-Bass.

Mannheim, Karl. 1968. *Ideology and Utopia.* New York: Harcourt, Brace & World.

Münch, Richard. 1993. *Sociological Theory: Development since the 1960s.* Chicago: Nelson-Hall Publishers.

Rhind, David. 2003. "Antisocial Science." A Review of *Great Expectations: The Social Sciences in Britain.* http://www.soc.surrey.ac.uk/~scs1ng/C.UnivGt. Expecta-tions.pdf

Rudner, Richard S. 1953. "The Scientist Qua Scientist Makes Value Judgments." *Philosophy of Science* 20: 1-6.

Spitzer, R. 1981. "The Diagnostic Status of Homosexuality in DSM-III: A Reformulation of the

Issues." *American Journal of Psychiatry* 138: 210–15.

Stromberg, Joseph, and Jeffrey Tucker. 2001. "Mises vs. Marx: The Battle Continues". Mises Institute, February 16. http://www.mises.org/fullstory.aspx

Weinstein, Jay. 2000. "The Place of Theory in Applied Sociology: A Reflection." *Theory and Science* 1, 1.

_____. 2003. "Why Altruism is Considered Deviant Behavior." In Arthur B. Shostak, ed., *Viable Utopian Ideas: Shaping a Better World*. Armonk, NY: M.E. Sharpe.

_____. 2004. "Civics as Applied Sociology." *Social Justice* (Spring).

Weinstein, Jay, and Nico Stehr. 1999. "The Power of Knowledge: Race Science, Race Policy, and the Holocaust." *Social Epistemology* 13, 1.

Wilson, E.O. 1975. *Sociobiology: The New Synthesis*. Cambridge, MA: Harvard University Press.

Zeitlin, Irving M. 1968. *Ideology and The Development of Sociological Theory*. Englewood Cliffs, New Jersey: Prentice-Hall.

❧ ❧ ❧ ❧ ❧ ❧ ❧ ❧

ANTI-SOCIAL SCIENCE:
THE USE AND ABUSE OF SOCIOLOGY

David J. Hartmann
Western Michigan University

*T*HE TRUTH OF Max Weber's words becomes more clear as time goes on: "The materialist conception of history is not to be compared to a cab that one can enter or alight from at will, for once they enter it, even the revolutionaries themselves are not free to leave it." The analysis of thought and ideas in terms of ideologies is much too wide in its application and much too important a weapon to become the permanent monopoly of any one party. Nothing was to prevent the opponents of Marxism from availing themselves of the weapon (of the concept of ideologies) and applying it to Marxism itself (Mannheim 1936: 75).

With Mannheim looking on, I'd better try to be clear about where I am as I start this response. Where I am is squarely in agreement with Jay Weinstein's conclusions and advice. Professor Weinstein's is unequivocally right—I am however, not sure that his argument is correct. The distinction is precisely what I hope to elaborate in these few pages and is at its core one of method in the Deweyian sense: that of legitimate forms of inquiry. Anti-science (the parent problem to anti-social science) is definable at two levels. The first is lack of fidelity to the accepted principles of logic and method that make up a discipline (Toulmin 1972). The key point is that these are not absolute principles, no rationality with a capital "R". They are productively thought of as evolving attempts to sustain a dialogue among peers in pursuit of common (and themselves changing) problems.

These are the standard debates of method that literally define legitimate science but we would do well to remember that honest people can and should disagree even about such fundamental issues. Particularly when the presuppositions or assumptions of method are in conflict, it is difficult to see—and consequently difficult to have—the open conversation that is required of science. The absence of that conversation is the second level of anti-science referred to above. Science is definable as the open, critical, inherently doubting pursuit of ideas in application to commonly defined problems. If the problems are not—at least substantially—commonly defined and if dogma rather than doubt is allowed too much a role, something other than science is taking place. This second level of standard is, unlike the first, constant across differences in first level methods and assumptions.

Commentary

In a nutshell, science can go wrong at both levels and become something other than science, or even anti-science. The situation is further complicated by the recognition that scientific thought is only worth while to the extent that it is useful—useful to solve intellectual problems and to improve the chances for successful adaptation to physical, social, and ethical environments. So science, including our social science, must be used. As Marshall Sahlins (1976) captured in the title of his book on sociobiology, when the stakes are high, the potential for problems is present. "The Use and Abuse of Biology" is a fine phrase—it captures what we must do with science and what we must guard against as we do so. What I hope is clear by this point is that values—including those that infuse the political realm of our lives—are inevitably a part of science since they are part and parcel of the problems we address and the methods (level one) we use to address them. Values are inherent at level two as well though they are treated as more enduring there. This account is by the way, quite close I think, to Weinstein's discussion of ideology and science. I particularly like his line about "science's stubborn quest for exceptions and disconfirming evidence, which is something ideologues seek to avoid."

All this said, is "SRM" and its links to policy anti-science? If so, can we mount a challenge? The answers are *sometimes* and *yes*. At the risk of distracting the reader from my fundamental agreement with Weinstein's argument, I will point out a few modest disagreements (not to the level of weaknesses in the inquiry) and posit a few cautionary counter-examples. The key point is that while I am almost positive that Jay is right, I cannot really—or comfortably—be positive about anything in this science business and so, Hamlet-like, I will dispute. Whether we, as a set of disciplines, can long maintain such distinctions and still serve the stated purposes of science (improvement, satisfaction, understanding…) is a constant struggle perhaps to be taken up in a future discussion.

For this discussion, I take it as given that scientists are responsive to personal, disciplinary, and larger demands. These demands are intellectual, moral, ethical and so on. Weinstein points out that many of us are faced with a part of that environment which "appears" to be actively hostile to logical (Weinstein says "epistemological") assumptions and practices "of our field." I do not like that phrase, "of our field," or even the one in the following paragraph—"the sociological way of looking at the world." They are dogma in the sense of the second level mentioned above, but I understand his point. We, as professional people, as disciplinarians, have certain ways of thinking and parts of our publics are at odds with us on these scores.

Rightly (and correctly) Weinstein focuses on counter approaches that compete for our legitimacy as advisors and as a source of enlightenment for policy debates in the larger society. The anti-social sciences are against our values ("against society") and against our disciplinary pursuit of those values. He argues that one may understand this phenomenon in functionalist terms and, again, I think he is right. But, as Weinstein knows quite well, functionalist arguments at this level of abstraction tend strongly to the teleological. Much like functionalist descriptions of natural selection in biology (which he rightly criticizes in sociobiology), the accounts can be compelling even if they are not technically useful. Note that this criticism does not apply to the case that Weinstein elaborates, that of race theory in Nazi Germany, precisely because the details are presented and stand on their own. Particularly important to the credibility of this argument, as always, is elaboration of the mechanisms through which selective affinity of ideas and environment (institutional power in this case) are nurtured. This is also the case for useful versions of natural selection where the approach was rescued from tautology by the development of the science of genetics and of rational choice where an a priori assumption of the rationality of action was replaced by modeling of the limits of rationality.

Weinstein elaborates the case for the anti-science of SRM in the remainder of his article. The basic claim is that science, or anti-science, is "legitimating the injustices of gross social inequality." To that, I can without hesitation say, "amen". I can also say and have often said that quality social science works against such conservative beliefs and policies. In sum, I am sure we (Weinstein and I) are right in our stance and efforts. But I must stop short of saying that I am sure that our science is correct. Science is never correct; it is not in its power to be so. It is inherently tentative in the sense of knowing it can do better.

Does one therefore refrain from policy discussions or magically shift from scientist to citizen when discussing policy? I have heard such advice but I think it misses a central point. Recall that the purpose of science and of thought generally is to act and to do so toward the betterment of the current condition. Minimum levels of credibility are required before acting and we are not always in the best position to know if those levels are met. But action must eventually be forthcoming and must be credibly related to our scientific thought. It follows, by the way, that since science is action oriented it is knee-deep in values — we aspire not to value freedom so much as to open-mindedness.

Let us quickly examine the three strands of SRM. Sociobiology has, indeed, had proponents that have made outrageous claims, some of which might invalidate much of the social sciences. On the other hand, much of the science of sociobiology is far more limited in its scope and claims basically arguing that natural selection at the genetic level might set a broad range of potentiality within which cultural evolution and agency have worked. Even in the first years after Wilson's 1975 book, the range of statements (c.f., Wilson 1978; Sahlins 1976; and Dawkins 1976), is quite broad. Ruse (1979) and Caplan (1978) and now many others have surveyed this territory with care. The key point for sociologists is, I think, that sociobiology focuses attention on the limits of genetics and on the interdependence of agency, culture, and extra-sociological constraints. Those constraints need be nothing more than vague limits, distant in evolutionary and pragmatic terms.

But what if a fanatic took the obvious but limited import of a genetic foundation and ignored all else? Well, then we have trouble of the same kind as seen in many sloppy or narrowly trained thinkers. Perhaps because the possible implications of sociobiology seemed all too familiar to those familiar with the eugenics debates of the early part of the century, the arguments quickly became ideological in precisely Weinstein's sense. This happened on both sides however and the first salvo may well have come from the right (our) side, the left politically, with the Science for the People Sociobiology Study Group letter to the *New York Review of Books*. My own take as a non-expert is clearly reflected by the age of my citations. I thought this was interesting twenty-five years ago but the discussion has subsequently been either too technical or too ideological to hold my interest, in particular given the overheated rhetoric one is sometimes forced to sift through. The lesson for anti-science studies is that ideology is always nearby in issues that matter and can easily jump to the point that it swamps what might have been passable inquiry but clearly is no longer. This invasive and distracting ideology, by the way, reminds me of Horowitz' (1994) critique of several radical positions in "our field" when he talks of the politicization of American sociology. In any case, I do not think it is inherent in sociobiology that it be inimical to a sociologically informed understanding of inequality or of other elements of our societies.

Similarly, rational choice theory can be naively substituted for sociological analysis but it need not be. Indeed, the assumption of rationality is a starting point for many other theories including theories of bounded and other rationalities but also of phenomenology, Marxism (recall that the real, that is, rational interests of the bourgeoisie and of labor for that matter are the starting point for understanding history and required change) and, as mentioned earlier functionalism of various hues. Rational choice theory models the limits of rationality and often gets those limits wrong. The attempts may nevertheless be instructive even to those primarily interested in other factors.

Biology may be like rationality — they are part of us but not the only parts and, to sociologists, it is at their limits that our interest is peaked. Medicalization may be different in kind from these — it is after all a sociologically defined process (genes for example have no discernable role in this tendency in recent history though rational considerations of clinical utility might) but as an explanation it points to individual cases not to trends or patterns. It may or may not be appropriate for understanding individual cases but it is not a meaningful competitor for sociological explanations. If "social disorders" are increasing, for example, the explanation is not seriously medical, it is social. We may, of course, use medical metaphors (such as contagion or unhealthy environments) as we have since Durkheim. For an individual spouse abuser, however, individual treatment may be ameliorative. Even if causes are social, cures can include individual interventions. Substance use issues and gambling are classic examples of what are in most interesting ways social problems that nevertheless admit of individual (clinical) interventions. I, and most of whom I would call colleagues, would predict that individual medicalized interventions will be relatively ineffective because they treat manifestations or symptoms rather than the whole array of social causes. But such treatments are only dangerous when they are allowed to rule out the importance of fuller and multilevel understandings and policies. To borrow another medical metaphor, it would be a myopic policy person indeed, who would see drugs and psychotherapy as obviating polices on the socio-structural and cultural bases of crime, poverty, abuse (drugs, gambling, relational) and so on. Such people exist and we have a professional obligation to diagnose and prescribe cures for their myopia.

Furthermore, each strand of SRM can be supportive of social justice. Biology's fascination with altruism is deep and long (at least since Darwin) and sociobiology's most important insight may well be that we are genetically predisposed to care about each other and that stubborn resistance to that insight is ideological. Its next most important insight may be that human evolution has long since passed to the cultural stage so that biology is at best a part of the "deep heart's core" that is mastered through the million variations that make up comparative history. Gould was instructive in quoting Stevenson on biological evolution: "The world is so full of a number of things, I'm sure we should all be as happy as kings." Human culture and ideas have produced a similar abundance. The problem, of course, is that some of it is not so wonderful and we would like to continue to try to improve it. Sociobiology offers nothing against this program and reminds us that this has long been our business. Rational choice theory can be linked to the right side as well. Willie and Alves, for example, built their "controlled choice" plans for equitable public education on market processes of the kind championed for other ends by Terry Moe. Medicalization too, can and must serve humanity—not blame or further subjugate it – though again, it will not be terribly sociological in doing so.

As to the champions of SRM who bend it to their own ideological needs, it should not surprise those of us who were drawn to social science by its potential to free ourselves and our societies from an unrelenting determinism or flux. We must not lose sight of Weinstein's fundamental insight, that elements of SRM (I would argue of all functionalist accounts) lend themselves to conservative thought. It is a form of reification. But real science, including the pursuit by real scientists of SRM, rejects reification and dogma on its face. That is, after all, the final safeguard against complacency and despair. Our response to the misuse of science must always be to champion the dual nature of science—doubt and hope—and through them social justice. Liberal politicians (including social scientists in their public role) may perform roles in which nuance and doubt are left aside. Scientists *qua* scientists can not give in to that temptation.

Summary

In thought and in policy, there is no question that reductionist attachment to biology or rationality or their individual level combination in clinical medicine is incomplete, wrong-headed, and even dangerous. That is "misuse" of science and those who think otherwise are indeed engaged in anti-social science. Jay Weinstein is right. The question remains, however, whether these ideas or approaches are bad in themselves. I do not think they are. I think that they may have use in precisely the way all scientific ideas may—as tools to approach problems and search for a better future. Whether we call them scientific depends on their adherence to the two levels of methodological standards described at the beginning of this paper. But even if an idea does not rise to the current standard of science—standards are, after all, intersubjectively negotiated and constantly in flux—it may still be useful. In fact, James' standard of consistency and Dewey's of future use will do for how seriously we entertain most ideas. Among other important lessons, Weinstein's paper reminds us that the designation as "science" is, among other things, a historical artifact the prestige of which is, like all such distinctions, fleeting. To build policy on science is essential. To dismissively build policy on science as settled is a misunderstanding.

David J. Hartmann

References

Caplan, Arthur L. 1978. *The Sociobiology Debate*. Harper and Row: New York.
Dawkins, Richard. 1976. *The Selfish Gene*. New York: Oxford University Press.
Horowitz, Irving Louis. 1994. *The Decomposition of Sociology*. New York: Oxford University Press.
Mannheim, Karl. 1936. *Ideology and Utopia*. New York: Harcourt Brace Jovanovich.
Ruse, Michael. 1979. *Sociobiology: Sense or Nonsense?* Holland: Reidel.
Sahlins, Marshall. 1976. *The Use and Abuse of Biology*. Ann Arbor, MI: University of Michigan Press.
Toulmin, Stephen. 1972. *Human Understanding*. Princeton, NJ: Princeton University Press
Wilson, Edward O. 1978. *On Human Nature*. Cambridge, MA: Harvard University Press.

David J. Hartman is Professor and Chair of the Department of Sociology at Western Michigan University. His most recent publications appeared in Discourses on Applied Sociology: Theoretical Perspectives, *edited by S. Dasgupta, and in the* Journal of Applied Social Science.

❦ ❦ ❦ ❦ ❦ ❦ ❦ ❦

Jay Weinstein's "Anti-Social Science, Dehumanization, and Social Policy"

William DuBois
Southwest Minnesota State University

*I*N AN EXCELLENT ARTICLE, Jay Weinstein explores the current War on Social Science and its implications for social policy. There is a movement afoot to replace Social Science with primitive explanations of human behavior that were popular before sociology, psychology and anthropology painted a more complicated picture. Weinstein details three of these pretenders against which conscientious social scientists particularly need to stand up. He calls them SRM—sociobiology (S), rational choice theory (R), and the medicalization of relationship disorders (M).

Sociobiology represents the ultimate dehumanization. It eliminates any suggestion that the human is special in the realm of nature. Mind is reduced to matter. Social Science is territorialized and replaced by physical science and biology. This is all accomplished by simply decreeing it so with virtually no understanding of the philosophical underpinnings of what science is. Sociobiologists take it as doctrine of ultimate faith that all can be reduced to the physical.

We have long ago demolished the foundations of rational choice theory. Albion Small who chaired the first sociology department in the United States said his whole life's work was to overcome the "individualistic superstition." But the superstitions are making a comeback. Much of it is but an extended rationalization to justify the ideology of the rich and the powerful. Weinstein writes, "Rather than a *race war*, we are now in the midst of a *class war*." Rational choice theory demands individuals make better choices and ignore the social conditions in which they struggle. If you're not making it, it's your own fault. Pull yourself up by your own bootstraps is the pet advice of an irresponsible elite which feels winners have no obligation to put part of their winnings back into the game so the rest of us have a chance—or to acknowledge the social resources that enabled their success. It is insensitivity to others particularly the vulnerable. And we certainly are not supposed to look at those who are profiting off the ways things are.

Rather than being prejudiced against race, we are prejudiced against the poor—and prejudiced against all underachievers—when we decree that their problems are entirely of their own making, and

Commentary

they would be successful if they only tried harder and made better choices.

Social science originated as part of the Enlightenment tradition that knowledge about human behavior can be used to instruct government how to improve social conditions to reduce social problems. The rich elite who promote SRM would deny that there are things that can be solved by collective social action. In their mind, it is folly to try and intervene in human affairs to make them better. Above all, they want to avoid any suggestion that we need to raise taxes to address social problems.

Everything is reduced to the "rational" choice of a primitive economic cost-benefit analysis. Greed and "more, more, more" become the only hallmarks of a successful economy. We are supposed to ignore the ease with which the lives of the middle class and powerless become collateral damage under the wheels of the corporate machine.

The sociological imagination properly understood means personal problems are tied to larger social issues and that *we can apply that insight*. By *understanding the situations* in which people struggle, we can *invent social resources* that would be helpful to people in similar situations. However, the SRM crowd doesn't want to invest in the Good Society. Weinstein rightly sees SRM as a reversal of the sociological imagination—an emerging tendency to reduce public issues to private ones and pretend social reform is unnecessary. Rather than solving social problems, it's popular to blame individuals. Sociobiologists follow right behind claiming this is human nature and there is no way that improving social conditions will make things better. Any social problems and relationship problems would be medicated.

SRM proponents would strike love from the equation. Weinstein writes, "Among the most serious flaws [of rational choice theory] is that it assumes away altruism [as] either irrational or illusionary." Selfishness is assumed to be the supreme value. But there is a crucial difference between selfishness and enlightened self interest. Social psychology shows the nature of the social bond is that *self* and *others* are intimately interwoven. Realistic self fulfillment takes place in the context of community. In the long run, selfishness that takes a nonchalant view of others is simply not practical. It is also often immoral. Let us not forget that imprisoned former Enron CEO Jeff Skillings's favorite book was Dawkin's *The Selfish Gene*. The leaders at Enron claimed they were the "smartest guys in the room." But as Theodore Roosevelt once said: "To educate a person in mind and not in morals is to educate a menace to society."

David Hume says that all of morality stems from two things—"enlightened self interest" and the fact, that as he puts it, "the suffering of others makes us feel uncomfortable." Altruism is intrinsic. From an evolutionary standpoint, we are all in this together. The idea of the "Selfish Gene" is an unevolved view—a genetic throwback.

Sociobiologists say human nature is not a blank slate as they claim social scientists say it is. But sociobiologists are setting up a straw man they can tear down. We have human needs. The early social scientists set out to discover "the social forces" which they considered to be human needs and purposes. Some things are not changeable. But some are. The sociobiologist's claim that everything is exactly as it must be and cannot change is nothing more than dogma. It is the ultimate conservative bias. Social scientists have learned a great deal about how to solve social problems and create societies and organizations in which people thrive. SMR would delete all this knowledge.

My only caveat about the article is that I wish it would have expanded medicalization of relational disorders section to focus on all medicalization of deviance. Weinstein is certainly right that the new medicalization of relational disorders represents the newest absurd threat. However, the psycho-pharmaceutical assault on sanity needs to be rolled back at every corner. Take juvenile delinquency for example. Large proportions of school children are being placed on medications for "conduct disorders" while their actual problems are largely ignored.

For those who think that Jay Weinstein's reference to Nazi race science is over the top, please note that what is at stake in today's arena is the size of the human soul. Getting it wrong about race led to terrible atrocities as policy makers acted on those theories. Getting it wrong about human beings will have even worse results. We can try to force people to fit into theories with no room for the human spirit and into the kind of society that results. But Social Science has eloquently detailed the side effects of such an approach—crime, wars, mental breakdowns, social problems, terrorism and all the other consequences of human alienation.

The SRM approach is ignorant of everything social scientists have learned about human behavior. It is simply a disguise to justify untaxing the rich, abolishing social programs and treating with indifference anyone except the super rich at the top of society. Ultimately, it represents a war on humanity and who we are as human beings.

Notes

[1] *Enron: The Smartest Guys in the Room.* Director: Alex Gibney. Screenplay by Alex Gibney from the book by Bethany McLean and Peter Elkind. HDNet Films.2005.
[2] David Hume. *An Enquiry Concerning the Principles of Morals.* 1751.

William DuBois *is Assistant Professor of Justice Administration at Southwest Minnesota State University.*

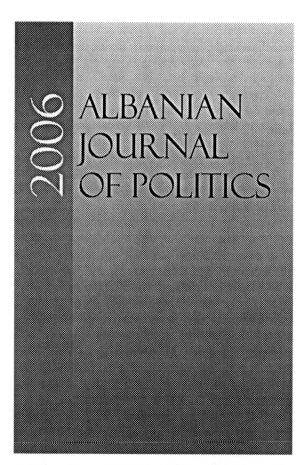

Albanian Journal of Politics is the official journal
of the Albanian Political Science Association

Substantive Democracy: Some Considerations

By JUDITH BLAU AND ALBERTO MONCADA

Abstract

Among many western political philosophers, direct, participatory democracy has been the ideal, the standard against which all other forms of democracy have been compared. Abraham Lincoln implicitly referred to such a democratic form in his Gettysburg Address, but he did not elaborate. The U.S. and other western countries embrace indirect democracy and with it, competing political parties that have their origins in the class divisions that accompanied industrialization. Yet there are lessons that westerners can learn from non-western societies in which more popular forms of democracy are practiced. Recognizing the extraordinary relevance of new technologies, we present a sketch of how substantive, participatory democracy might function, using the United States as the example.

*T*HE *RAISON D'ÊTRE* of the state, according to the classic conception, is to make the welfare of the people its aim which it does through government. But since the state *is* the people we could say that the people ought themselves be both the objects and the subjects of government. To understand that this is not an entirely new conception in the United States, we can turn to Abraham Lincoln. Consecrating the cemetery at Gettysburg, on November 19, 1863, he stated that the "great task remaining" after the end of the long civil war was to create a nation with "a new birth of freedom." Newly conceived, this nation would have a government "of the people, by the people, and for the people."[1]

Lincoln was clear that the objective is self-governance, so we can set this aside for a moment to consider how feasible it is. In the nineteenth century, his vision may have

---

[1] Abraham Lincoln, Gettysburg Address," November 19, 1863, Transcript of the "Nicolay Draft:" http://www.loc.gov/exhibits/gadd/gatr1.html

JUDITH BLAU is Professor of Sociology at the University of North Carolina at Chapel Hill and an Honorary Member of the Albanian Institute of Sociology. She has authored, co-authored and edited more than fifteen books. ALBERTO MONCADA is President of "Sociologists without Borders." He has taught at the University of Madrid, Stanford University, the University of Lima, Florida International University, and Alcalá University. Both authors are co-editors of the journal Societies without Borders. *This paper is a revised version of a chapter from their volume* Freedoms and Solidarities: In Pursuit of Human Rights *(2007).*

seemed to his contemporaries as impossibly utopian. It probably was. Self-governance requires dense communications networks that allow for deliberative processes in real time, consultation, and voting on given substantive issues. Citizens need to feel they are themselves accountable and self-governance must meet efficiency standards, just as is the concern with representative democracy (Kjaer 2004: 15). In Lincoln's time only large cities were connected by telegraph, and the invention of the radio, the telephone, television, the Internet, the worldwide web, and cell phones all lay in the future.

However, at the beginning of the twenty-first century, new technologies make self-governance more feasible. People use the web interactively for making purchases, banking, taking a college course, learning a language, managing retirement accounts, participating in online chat rooms, and signing petitions. Exploiting these new technologies UNESCO has had amazing success with its e-governance projects.[2] Each phase of the World Summit on Information Society (WSIS) has advanced an understanding of how the Internet can be used to achieve nonhierarchical and decentralized participation in governance. WSIS is also a global forum for ongoing discussions about the principles and the technical requisites for inclusive, grassroots democracy (Maclean 2004; Badshah et al. 2005; Avgerou 2002). These efforts are motivated by the same principles that Abraham Lincoln advocated at Gettysburg.

Democratic self governance is an important goal, we believe, because it is only through participatory democracy that the rights and freedoms of all people are inclusively advanced, and, besides, participatory democracy can ensure the public availability of collective goods. In his *Where do We Go From Here: Chaos or Community?* Martin Luther King wrote: The good life for any of us depends upon satisfying the democratic mutuality conditions for all of us" (quoted in Green 1999: 157). Such mutuality can only be realized, King suggests, is through participatory, democratic communities and societies.

WHAT IS DEMOCRACY?

IN THE WESTERN, liberal tradition, government by representatives has been naturalized although as Carole Pateman points out, there have been western political theorists, including John Stuart Mills and Jean Jacques Rousseau, who developed and defended direct and participatory principles of governance. Pateman's book, *Participation and Democratic Theory*, published in 1970, became a classic, inspiring interest in the conceptual and empirical underpinnings of self-governance, particularly in communities and the workplace.[3] However, implementing self-governance has been elusive on any large scale, and many have contended that participatory democracy is only practical on a small scale, much like the Athenian Forum, but hardly in large metropolises or on the scale of a nation-state. Yet scholars continued writing on participatory democracy and self-governance, distinguishing representative democracy from direct democracy, and highlighting

---

[2] See UNESCO World Summit on Information (WSIS) "Action Directory": http://www. unesco.org/webworld/wsisdirectory/pages/_ICT_Applications/Egovernment/index.htm; UNESCO, "Internet in the Service of Democracy,": http://www. unesco.org/bpi/eng/ unescopress/2002/02-72e.shtml.

[3] Others built on Pateman's arguments in the 1970s; for example see Abrahamsson (1977).

that political processes were not the ends of democracy, but rather the means to further collective and individual social and economic welfare (Baiocchi 2005; Bachrach 1992).

The principle behind representative government is that individual voters will express their preferences for this or that candidate, in this or that election, and the candidate who wins will solemnly exercise the will of the people (see Schumpeter 1943). It is hard to say who benefits from this charade since it trivializes the issues, insults the intelligence of voters, and generates high levels of apathy. This system is extremely expensive. Campaign costs in a major election year top 2 billion dollars, more than a tenth of total annual federal spending on education.[4]

The rationale for representative democracy, never very powerful, is fading. Representative democracy is not democratic, even by its own internal standards, because voter turnout is low; corporations play powerful roles through campaign contributions and lobbying, and in recent U.S. national elections there has been egregious election fraud. With media and public outcry for reforms, political leaders call for reforms but they hardly address root problems. But isn't reform beside the point? For people to be sovereign and self-determining, they need more than the right to elect proxies who in turn make substantive decisions. Such a procedure is not efficient; true preferences are veiled and obscure unless they have a context.

What has transformed peoples' thinking most about democracy, is what José Nun describes as a "transcendent event" — the approval, in 1948, of the University Declaration of Human Rights (UDHR). The UDHR puts political rights into a larger context that includes economic, social and cultural rights. Since all people share fundamental positive rights to their welfare and agency, they also share political and civil rights to participate in democratic processes that advance these rights. The title of Brian Clark's 1979 play "Whose Life Is It Anyway?" simply evokes the principle. Because people all share entitlements to healthcare, housing, to protections against the effects of illness and unemployment, to nondiscrimination, and so forth, they ought be entitled to participate in decisions that ensure these entitlements. Political rights, therefore, are not simply ends in and of themselves (though they are that), but also the means to achieve these other rights. For that reason, we refer to direct or participatory democracy as *substantive democracy*. It has nothing to do with partisanship and everything to do with advancing individual and collective interests and welfare.

This conception shares with "deliberative democracy," advanced especially by Joshua Cohen (1989), that democracy should be an inclusive and rational process, and draws from Jürgen Habermas' the idea that democratic processes ought to be transparent and public (also see: Nino 1996; Habermas 1984; Gutmann and Thompson 1996). However, our conception of substantive democracy, which draws from the work of José Nun (2003), Judith Green (1999), and Carol C. Gould (2004), differs from Cohen's and Habermas's in that participation is thoroughly grassroots, and what is not decided at the grassroots level is decided by people who are accountable to the grassroots. Thus, substantive democracy involves decision-making where people directly participate in all decisions that immediately affect them, and where oversight is radically decentralized,

---

[4] For cost estimates, see: Public Citizen: http://www.citizen.org; Institute for Public Accuracy: http://www.accuracy.org

possible through local-state-federal linkages. Our conception of substantive democracy starts from our assumption that freedoms are the means and ends of human development, and that through the exercise of their freedoms people advance the common good.

SUBSTANTIVE DEMOCRACY

POLLSTERS MOSTLY ASK questions about polarizing issues that divide Americans, but when they ask Americans what it is they want Americans are in amazing agreement. They not only mention things like full employment, better wages, fair government, a healthy environment, better schools, and universal healthcare coverage. They also attach importance to fairness and equity.[5] For example, in a U.S. poll that asked questions about what government should be doing, substantial majorities reported that government should help working families (76 percent), increase the minimum wage (84 percent), provide health insurance to laid off workers (87 percent), and extend unemployment benefits (82 percent).[6] Such answers as these are hardly consistent with politicians' and pollsters' views that the members of the electorate think in categorical bipolar, Blue-Red terms. Furthermore, Americans' confidence in national political institutions has declined. The Pew Research Center finds that American confidence in the federal government, the executive branch, and congress has declined sharply in the last decade, suggesting to us a widespread disillusionment with representative democracy.[7]

Along with declining trust in the state and political leaders there has been a dramatic growth in citizen action and civil society. Citizen action is hard to measure in the aggregate, although one indicator is the number of NGOs (nonprofits).[8] For the United States, the Independent Sector, a coordinating agency for nonprofit organizations, estimated that in 2004 there were 1.3 million NGOs in the United States.[9] The nonprofit sector is also growing considerably faster than the for-profit sector, in the U.S. there has been a doubling in the number of employees between 1977-2001, while the number of employees in the private sector for the same time period increased only by about a third.[10]

Thus, while civil society is an abstraction its most evident concrete manifestation are NGOs. In fact, NGOs in most countries, the U.S. included, have become something like a

---

[5] Linda Gordon, "Budget Priorities," Institute for Public Accuracy," http://www.common-dreams.org/pressreleases/july99/072999g.htm

[6] Poll carried out by the Ms. Foundation, summarized by Robert Kuttner, "What Voters Really Want," The Boston Globe February 20, 2002: http://www.comondreams.org/views 02/0220-04.htm

[7] Pew Research Center for the People & the Press, "Public Sours on Government and Business," October 25, 2005: http://people-prss.org/reports/print.php3?Page ID=1010; "Confidence in government is remarkably constant and surprisingly low, about 40%," April 12, 2000: http://people-press.org/reports/display.php3?ReportID=41. In repeated multi-year Newsweek surveys, starting in 2003, which ask Americans how satisfied or dissatisfied they are "with the way that things are going in the U.S." the majority in virtually every survey are dissatisfied: http://www.pollingreport.com/right.htm

[8] The number of NGOs is the indicator commonly used at the international level (see Edwards and Gaventa 2001).

[9] Independent Sector. Panel on the Nonprofit Sector, Final Report, June 2005: http://www. nonprofitpanel.org/final/

[10] Independent Sector, "Nonprofit Almanac," http://www.independentsector.org/PDFs/npemployment. pdf

shadow government as they center their activities around social change as well as promoting peoples' substantive rights—housing, education, food security, and the special needs of vulnerable populations, such as immigrants, minorities, women, children, the disabled and retarded. They also promote the democratic imagination by providing egalitarian, inclusive, and empowering opportunities for citizens (Perrin 2006). New Orleaneans in the aftermath of Katrina made it crystal clear that through NGO partnerships, people could fight for their rights as citizens and advance the common good, often in opposition to local, state, and federal government agencies. The rights for which they fought included housing, decent jobs, education, healthcare, municipal services, and pluralism (ending racism, sexism).[11] Therefore, civil society can be advocates for peoples' rights, advance peoples' rights, and engage, as Frances Fox Piven (2006) describes, "disruptive politics" to promote social change. NGOs can, in other words, be advocates for citizens and vehicles for social transformation. However, they are not especially democratic, at least in the traditional sense.

EMERGING PUBLICS

WITHIN THE BROAD NGO framework around the globe is a surge in local mobilization, which cannot be understood within the framework of liberal democracy. These mobilizations do not reflect the partisan divisions of representative democracy, nor can they be mapped onto electoral politics. Instead, the issues are substantive, such as protection of land from development, preservation of natural wilderness areas, expansion of parks and recreational areas, public transportation, clean water, safe energy sources, sustainable local farming and agriculture, bilingual programs in local schools, recycling, food banks, and so on (Low and Smith 2006). Civil society duality is such that citizens can participate in "cool" deliberative processes—for example, compiling land use maps—or they can engage in "hot" politics—for example, cutting wire fences that officials erected around housing projects in New Orleans. A nation-wide example of this are the Living Wage campaigns, which have mushroomed around the country in just a few short years.[12] These campaigns involve citizens in the methodical tasks of collecting data on wages and jobs for cities, counties, and states, and also entail protests and labor strikes. Yet, these are not systematically democratic. They only await a structure for them to become democratic. Nevertheless, they are broad based, with coalitions of union leaders, academics, workers, and concerned citizens.

Many campaigns are mobilized nationally, with one or several NGOs at the campaign's hub, linked in turn to the grassroots in different ways.[13] These various campaigns

---

[11] To give an example, see Common Ground: http://www.commongroundrelief.org/; Editors, "One Year After," The Nation, September 18, 2006: http://www.thenation.com/ issue/20060918

[12] Living Wage campaigns are organized at the city and county levels Since 1994, 120 counties or city units have adopted a living wage ordinance. See, Political Economy Research Institute, University of Massachusetts, "Living Wage and Labor Markets:" http://www. peri.umass.edu/Labor-Market-L.197.0.html

[13] On children's rights (Children's Defense Fund, Child Rights Information Network, Children's Rights Council); racial justice (NAACP, Rainbow Coalition/PUSH, Congress of Racial Equality, Southern Poverty Law Center); rights of Hispanics (La Raza, United Farmworkers, Immigrant Justice Action Network); women's rights (Feminist Majority, NOW); affordable housing (Habitat, ACORN); the rights of persons with autism

universalize the principles of inclusiveness and equality, and although each campaign usually has a particular substantive focus, they sometimes forge coalitions, especially when working on issues at the local level (such as immigrant rights or the anti-war movement).

At the local level there are environmental groups, campaign finance reform organizations, peace groups, anti-poverty organizations, campaigns against gun violence, groups that advocate gay and lesbian justice, racial justice organizations, just to mention some goals of NGOs. This phenomenon—secular civil society—is relatively new in the United States, emerging roughly around the time that American cities were beginning to experience dislocations from deindustrialization (Powell and DiMaggio 1987) and accelerating with the collapse of welfare programs, and as globalization exacerbated social and economic problems in America (Derber 2002). Yet these nonprofits and campaigns and the civil society that they compose provide interesting examples of how American communities are beginning to help shape citizens' engagement.

NGOs embed the principles of substantive democracy, and to a great extent that substance is defined in terms of human rights—children's rights, reparations, housing rights, and so forth. NGOs are democratic in the sense of being egalitarian, but they fail the litmus test of being democratic because they are neither participatory nor representative. As we will see, by doing away with liberal political structures, participatory democracy can draw from the substantive and advocacy principles of NGOs. Note too that NGOs are not rigidly organized as government hierarchies are, but instead tend to be consultative and egalitarian. Their very informality tends to promote collaboration around their substantive goals, such as reducing homelessness, providing services for abused women, organizing programs for the disabled.

Such goals as these require networked coordination involving varieties of NGOs and agencies, and sometimes service providers and even businesses become collaborative partners. For example, one New York City NGO, We-Can, is largely run by homeless citizens as a recycling program whereby they pick up bottles and cans from community businesses to sell them to recycling companies. We-Can has what it calls its partners, such as schools, churches, and businesses, from which it regularly collects recyclables. We-Can is densely interconnected with other organizations, and its networks extend to for-profit businesses, clinics, colleges and universities, and churches that are a source of volunteers. Run by the homeless and formerly homeless, We-Can, along with its coalition partners, is not shy about confronting government agencies and elected officials in advocating the rights of the homeless.

PRELIMINARY CONSIDERATIONS

DEMOCRACY, THE LATE Argentinean legal scholar Carlos Nino (1996) contended, is not an end in itself, but a vehicle for a more just society. According to this conception, a just society can only be pursued through ongoing participatory or direct democratic

---

(Aspies for Freedom); environmental justice (Greenpeace, Greenaction, Sierra Club, Indigenous Environmental Network, Nature Conservancy); and fair wages (Students Against Sweatshops, Living Wage Campaign, Universal Living Wage, Faireconomy).

processes. In our view NGOs would be the precursory social forms at the core of these processes. Three concepts are useful when considering forms and processes of self-governance: cosmopolitan citizenship, normative indeterminacy, and mutualism. NGOs are themselves not participatory — although they can be — but they are organized around substantive ends, are often deeply entrenched in communities, and are passionate advocates of those they represent.

There are three main conceptual underpinnings for participatory democracy. First, *cosmopolitan citizenship* is the capacity to embrace social and cultural pluralism as an expression of moral equality whether in local communities, economic units, the nation, or the world. This definition is consistent with Carol C. Gould's (2004: 166), and with the one that David Held (1995) uses to describe overlapping and connected participation in ad hoc social arrangements. There is much about participatory democracy that is improvisational and messy, but it allows for redundant processes that ensure inclusivity. Cosmopolitan citizens and cosmopolitan practices promote multiculturalism and pluralism, which are often repressed in liberal democracy.

Second, participatory democracy is a process, according to Benjamin Gregg (2003), whereby values, worldviews, and ideas evolve in a space in which there is *normative indeterminacy*. Such normative openness, accompanied by cosmopolitanism, is requisite for negotiation, consensus building, give-and-take, and prevents the ossification of rigid decision-making and consolidation of power. The recognition of normative indeterminacy, or what Benjamin Gregg calls, "enlightened localism," allows for flexible decision-making within communities as well as flexible decision-making across communities and up and down jurisdictions.

Gould refers to the importance of *mutualism* in democratic communities, or what she terms, "the caring society" (2004: 165), and she highlights the importance of reciprocity, the universal recognition of rights and duties, regard of the other, and the welfare of community members. Certainly, any form of self-government must embody this principle of mutualism, as well as principles of empathy, caring, compassion, individual responsibilities and joint obligations. The community not only depends on members' mutualism for democratic processes, but the goals of such a democratic community encompass mutualism as a means whereby universal rights are advanced and achieved.

Now we can link these concepts to see their relevance for self-governance. Participatory democracy requires mutualism and interconnectedness, acceptance of normative indeterminacy, and structures that promote and sustain cosmopolitan citizenship. Such a democracy not only protects and promotes the political — or participatory — rights of all citizens, but empowers them to advance human rights and the collective good. Whether at the local, national or global level, cosmopolitan citizenship and cosmopolitan democracy promote solidarities among autonomous and self-determining and connected actors, whether they are individuals, groups, or collectives.

It should be clear that cosmopolitan, democratic communities are reinforced by and in turn reinforce democratic workplaces. It is useful to quote Seymour Melman to indicate that the democratization of economic entities is well underway in the U.S. Quietly — without fanfare, manifestos or plans — workers around the world have been inventing an economy that succeeds capitalism and communism as we have known them. In many different countries, workers are developing new rules for deciding about production —

their own work—and for allocating the product, basing their decisions on standards that are quite different from those of capitalism and communism" (Melman 2001: 19).

There is no single model for these new forms of workplace democracy. Their varied forms include employee management, employee ownership, consumer cooperatives, stock ownership, and mixed forms. Regardless of the form, democratic workplaces depend on and enhance the personal autonomy of workers, while ensuring accountability in structures of codetermination. As in the case of self-governing communities, workplace democracy is grounded in normative principles of equity and equality. Along side the flourishing of NGOs, which is dramatic and very recent, such new developments in workplace democracy bode well for the advance of democratic communities.

We have also proposed, along the lines that Immanuel Wallerstein (1998) has argued, that firms become nonprofit (see Blau and Moncada 2007). This would effectively refocus workers' and worker-owners' attention on customers and clients, and products and services. It would eliminate enormous waste and contribute to economic efficiencies. At a single stroke, this "decommissioning" of firms from capitalism would free up equity for redistribution and would eliminate the inefficiencies induced by inequalities in wealth.

JURISDICTIONS

THERE IS A DILEMMA: Is the locus of fundamental human rights and justice norms on the ground, deeply rooted in social processes? Or is this locus universalized and embodied in laws and doctrine at the highest jurisdiction? Consistent with Gould's and Green's positions, human rights are advanced relationally and interactively. Alternatively, fundamental human rights are lodged at the highest level possible so that they have unequivocal universal backing. This universalistic—or constitutionalist—perspective is defended by David Beetham, who writes,

> Entitlements ascribed to human beings everywhere; and the institutions involved in their implementation, both formal and informal or civic, proceed from the international to the national and local levels, rather than vice versa as is the case with democracy (1999: 137).

Similarly, political theorist José Nun (2003) emphasizes that the state's responsibilities to its citizens must be constitutionally guaranteed, formally lodged at the highest jurisdictional levels.

We take the position that both are necessary, and there is ongoing interaction between fluid, social practices in daily life and formally constituted standards promulgated and enforced by centralized bodies. For example, recent state laws in the U.S. ensuring gays and lesbians equal rights to marriage protections raises all citizens' consciousnesses about gays' and lesbians' sexual, social, economic, and legal rights, which in turn shapes attitudes and practices. Likewise, these attitudes and practices shape laws. Political and civil rights deal with the relationships between citizens and the state and therefore must be codified at the highest jurisdictional level even if they are normatively legitimized informally through attitudes and practices. Constitutions provide a meaningful touchstone for laws, values, standards, and peoples' expectations.

To elaborate, using an example that may be obvious, only a body with worldwide jurisdiction, such as the United Nations and its courts, have authority to craft and implement international standards, such as inter-state treaties regarding, for example, use of the oceans, and to promulgate international human rights, or to protect people that countries do not, such as refugees and stateless persons (Moore and Pubantz 2006: 85-86). Yet citizens and the media play important roles. The citizens' campaign against U.S. rendition practices increases the likelihood that the U.S. will be censored in an international arena. Peasant groups have sometimes turned to the Food and Agricultural Organization (FAO) of the UN for support for their cropping rights and food security, while FAO's policies on cropping and food security evolve through interaction with peasant groups.

Our examples suggest that questions about jurisdiction really boil down not to *which* jurisdiction, but *how* can multiple jurisdictions interact. The same sort of approach is useful when trying to sort out the role of experts and the role of citizens. Some decisions can only be made by experts—for example, designing a traffic grid—but citizens must have the right to make democratic decisions about policies. Informed citizens can express their priorities as to the development of rail, automobiles and roads, buses, and whether or not to encourage bicycle, moped and motorcycle use. Once priorities are established, experts implement them, while citizens can be kept in the decision loop. Similarly, citizens would vote on programmatic priorities, while specialized agencies—say ones devoted to mental health, education, parks, cultural activities—would do the planning required to implement democratic decisions about priorities. UNESCO's pilot programs in Milan and São Paulo demonstrate that networked residents can make very complex decisions about municipal budgets and programs.[14]

It is useful to mention differences between the Third World and First World countries because the former, for historical reasons, often tend to favor more decentralized democratic practices. The European countries, Australia, New Zealand, and North America have more centralized governance structures because they evolved on a historical path through various centralized configurations—empires, feudal monarchies, and kingdoms. We do not want to overstate the case because many Third World countries have dictators or are under military rule, but there are robust local democracies in Africa and Latin America especially, where communities are self governing.[15]

Some communities in Africa that have been self-governing for centuries have complex systems for subsistence, trade, and in drought-prone areas, systems for water preservation and distribution (see Legesse 1973; 2000; Kiflemariam 2000). In much of Africa, where indirect rule was enforced by colonial rulers, traditions of local democracy sometimes survived intact (Mamdani 1996). Self-governance in Latin America has been reenergized by peasant movements, such as Via Campesina, the Zapatistas (EZLN), and the Brazilian Landless Movement. All these provide examples of decentralized democratic orders.

Owing to the robustness of local communities and of the networks that link villages in much of Africa, it was possible in 2003 and 2004 to launch a full-scale pan-African

---

[14] See UNESCO websites for e-governance; accessible through: http://unesco.org/

[15] For interesting discussions of these comparative possibilities, see: Pecora (2001), and Mamdani (1996).

movement that enlisted volunteers to obtain signatures on an African Treaty to enhance the rights of women, specifically, the Protocol on the Rights of Women to the African Charter. This Protocol is quite remarkable for its provisions that accelerate the implementation of women's economic, social and legal rights in African countries, and provide for gender parity in governments.[16] African women used their far-flung networks to mobilize broad-based grassroots support for the Protocol. Supporters fanned out throughout the Continent to inform women in the most remote communities of the significance of the treaty and to ask their support. They obtained thousands and thousands of signatures "by pen, email, online and by text messaging (SMS)"[17] Their efforts were successful. The Draft Protocol was approved by the African Union in 2004 and it went into force in October 2005.[18] Such campaigns as these build on pre-existing propensities for democratic action. Here, they also help to illustrate that democracy is far more than simply voting; it is collective decision-making, mobilization, and grassroots campaigns.

Just as African women used the Internet, the web, and text messaging in their democratic campaign, electronic technologies can be expected to transform democracy, allowing for universal participation in community and national decision-making. UNESCO has carried out pilot projects in cities and communities utilizing electronic media for voting and deliberative decision-making, and has set up pilot projects for e-governance in local communities and cities throughout the world. UNESCO has also advanced the principle that democratic participation is particularly well suited to development in poor countries.[19] This vision is shared by the International Green Party, whose "four pillars" platform includes participatory grassroots democracy (see Melman 2001). A few countries have launched their own projects to implement participatory democracy.

A Peoples' Democracy

WE DEVELOP AN EXERCISE in this section that is grounded in the sorts of considerations that society would probably have to take into account if they would adopt practices that would promote participatory democracy. Citizens in such a democracy would be making substantive decisions and be deciding the procedures they would use. Citizens would be voting on their representatives to serve at higher levels, but these representatives would be selected on the basis of their proven performance at the local level in a particular area. The general principle is that embedded structures form chains of participation from communities to counties to state to nation. What joins one link of the

[16] African Union, "Solemn Declaration on Gender Equality in Africa." Addis Ababa, 6-8 July 2004: http://www.fasngo.org/en/whatnew/doc/Declarations%20Heads%20of%20States. pdf

[17] Equality Now, "Nairobi, Kenya—Solidarity for African Women's Rights SOAWR": http://www.equalitynow.org/english/pressroom/press_releases/africaprotocol_20051027_en.html

[18] Amnesty International, "Entry into force of Protocol on the Rights of Women in Africa positive step towards ending discrimination:" http://www.amnestyusa.org/news/document.do?id=ENGAFR010042005

[19] Boutros Boutros-Ghali, The Interaction between Democracy and Development, (Paris: UNESCO, 2002): 13; http://unesdoc.unesco.org/images/0012/001282/128283.pdf

chain to the next link, going up the chain, is the implementation of community decisions at broader and broader jurisdictions, and what joins one link of the chain to the next link, going down the chain, is the application of general principles to smaller jurisdictions. The nation-state and all of its subunits have as their central goals the welfare of citizens, as articulated in human rights provisions, and the protection and promotion of the collective good.

Preliminary Thoughts

American philosopher Ronald Dworkin (1999) defines political equality as "the state of affairs in which the people rule their officials...." He goes on to say that "...liberty and equality are, in general, aspects of the same ideal, not as is often supposed rivals." Dworkin makes an especially important point that has interesting implications for the ways we might consider publics and participatory democracy. First, people, who have their liberties (freedoms) as political equals, have the power to rule their officials. Second, engagement in public life — and we add economic life as well — does not presuppose competitive individualists but rather collaboration among sovereign equals. This is the idea that people bring their personalities, expertise, views, and opinions to the fully egalitarian public sphere.

Few have described such a public sphere as well as Miguel de Unamuno. For him, the public sphere was an arena where everyone discusses and debates the issues of the day, and participates in the creation of a true "opinión pública" (Unamuno 1996: 40). His views of public life — as participatory, democratic, and equalitarian — relate to his own distinctive understanding of a methodology for achieving a public sphere where all voices would be heard on matters of collective concern. For Unamuno, the public was "...a method, a way to solve, analyze, criticize the issues. It is, mainly, a method of free thinking. This society has to raise its head and say: Not everybody is ready to be treated as children (*ibid.*: 39).

Drawing from this conception, public life is open, fluid, contingent, responding to issues as they develop, with substantive topics crisscrossing and intersecting. Main priorities for the communities and neighborhoods would be bound up with national priorities, but in specific ways — the local schools, the practices of multiculturalism, community parks and recreational areas, community clinics and hospitals, retirement homes, green spaces, museums, cinemas, and so forth. Such realms for collective decision-making transform politics into substantive civil discourse that is itself nested into national discourses centered on enhancing the lives of all residents and on the health and vitality of the collectivity. Self-interest is enlightened because every individual relates through co-determination to the collective interests that are at stake.

Whether called "participatory democracy,"[20] or "deep democracy" (Green 1999), the principle is that decentralized decision-making is substantive, and it involves mutual recognition of equality, and democratic processes that are contingent and indeterminate (Gould 2004; Greg 2003). In Abraham Lincoln's trenchant phrase the goal is democra-

---

[20] For a general discussion, see: Shutt (2001) and Florini (2003).

cy that is "of the people, by the people, for the people."

An Exercise

When considering the rudimentary structures and processes required to advance Lincoln's idea of "a new birth of freedom," it is important to undertake exercises, however implausible they might initially appear. To encourage readers to try their hand at this, we sketch out some ideas. Readers may accept some of these ideas as workable and others not. Figure 1 provides an outline of the major points we will discuss. In this exercise we will focus most on the local, community level, while suggesting that active governance processes cascade up and down all levels.

Principles

Democracy is "for the people," which is to say the end of democracy and government is to promote peoples' freedoms, wellbeing, and security—that is, to promote peoples' fundamental human rights and the common good. Democracy is "by the people," in the sense that people are self-governing. Democracy is "of the people" in the sense that the large collectivity of all citizens is sovereign, not the state per se. Laws are transparent and clear, enforced with exacting consistency.

Firms-Markets-Polity

Strictly speaking there is no political economy if by that is meant the relation between the state and capitalism. As earlier posed, firms would be nonprofit and they would have no surplus to distribute to shareholders. Participating in markets, firms would nevertheless generate revenues that would be taxed, as would personal earnings, for government expenditures. Political parties, were they to exist, would not reflect the historical class divisions but reflect constellations of various substantive concerns, such as a Green Party, an Education Party, Housing Party, and so forth.

NESTED STRUCTURES

SUBSTANTIVE DEMOCRACY at the community level and above is entirely feasible with the technical capabilities of electronic communications. If we shop on line, we can certainly participate in decision-making on line! As earlier indicated, it is increasingly the case that peoples' rights are being advanced by NGOs, and, building on their successes, it would be desirable to make NGOs themselves or their *modus vivendi* a key part of local democratic processes. As Figure 1 indicates, all citizens would vote on major decisions, with recommendations and alternatives posed by committees. All citizens would also vote on representatives to serve them, at the community and higher levels.

Figure 1: Elements of Participatory Democracy

Principles

1. Constitutional provisions for human rights and preservation of public goods

2. Democracy is "for the people," and the goal of governance is to promote peoples' human rights and the public goods they share.

3. Democracy is "by the people," and people are self-governing.

4. Democracy is "of the people," making the people the sovereign collectivity, not the State.

5. Laws are clear and transparent, guided by principles of justice and enforced with exacting consistency.

Firms, Markets and Polity

6. Economic units are not-for-profit entities.

7. Taxes collected from individuals and economic units are revenues for governance units for distribution according to the democratic will

8. Political parties do not reflect class politics, but substantive foci

9. All elected offices filled by popular vote.

Nested Structures and Processes

10. Online voting is a responsibility of citizenship, and vacancies at each level (community, county, state, national) are filled by election. Referenda are also decided by ballot.

11. Community-wide town-hall forums used to debate controversial issues; committees meet to carry out deliberations.

12. All residents serve on, at the very least, one Community Working Committee, and may be elected to serve on a Working Committee or Coordinating Committee at a higher level.

13. Working Committees are unit-specific—e.g., the community, the county, and so forth; Coordinating Committees pool units—e.g., across communities, across counties, and so forth.

14. Communities, counties, states and federal levels are nested within one another.

15. Working Committees coordinate decision-making from bottom to top, and top to bottom; Coordinating Committees coordinate decision-making laterally.

The distinction between a Working Committee and Coordinating Committee in Figure 2 is made on the basis of what is being aggregated and the units being represented. Any Working Committee is devoted to a specific area, such as education, within a community, an entire county, an entire state, and at the federal level. A Coordinating Committee is devoted to the task of coordinating a particular area across communities, across counties, and across states. To simply illustrate (and it will be further clarified in Figure 2) the Housing Working Committee for the town of Xenia may have developed plans to rehabilitate old buildings in the town's center and puts its proposals before the residents of Xenia for a vote. It is evident, however, that there needs to be harmonization at the county level of all the towns' housing projects. The person elected to the county-level Housing Coordinating Committee will participate in county-wide deliberations about housing. Thus, we propose a dual structure—one that pools information within a given unit (town, county, state, and the nation as a whole), and another that pools information across units (for example, across towns and within a county; across counties and within a state). Needless to say, citizen input, recommendations, and votes would be sought throughout these various processes, and it is a matter of fine-tuning practices to set decision rules on what requires a vote or general referendum.

Figure 2: Nested Participatory Democracy

Communities
Working Committees ↑
Budget Committee allocates funds to all communities ↔
Conflict resolution courts
Community services and programs ↔
Elect representatives to higher level structures ↑
Carry out community-referenda ↔
Implement county and state programs ↓

Counties
Working Committees ↑
Coordinating Committees ↔
Budget Committee allocates funds to counties ↔
County courts
County services and programs ↔
Elect representatives to higher level structures ↑
Carry out county-wide referenda ↔
Implement state and federal programs ↓

States
Working Committees ↑
Coordination Committees ↔
Budget Committees allocate funds to states ↔
State courts
State services and programs ↔
Elect represents to federal level ↑
Carry out state-wide referenda ↔
Implement federal programs ↓

Federal
Working Committees generic to federal level ↓
Coordinating Committees for all states: ↔
Cabinet-level Committee: Representatives of Working Committees and Coordinating Committees. ↓
Federal Budget Committee
Federal courts
Federal services and programs ↔
Carry out national-level referenda ↔ and implement ↓

Note: A Working Committee is unit-specific (e.g., county-wide or state-wide); a Coordinating Committee includes representatives from all the units at a given level (e.g., all the communities in a county or all the counties in a state). Arrows indicate the flow of communications.

Figure 2 illustrates how democratic processes flow within the system and how each level relates to others. At each level there are both Working Committees and Coordinating Committees. Again, these two types of committees overlap substantively, except that Working Committees focus broadly on program areas for a single jurisdiction, such as a town, a county, or a state, and Coordinating Committees pool representatives from all sub-units within a given jurisdiction—that is, across all local units at the county level, across all counties at the state level, and across all states at the federal level.

At the state level, Coordinating Committees pool representatives from all the counties, whereas the members of Working Committee are county representatives. Likewise, at the federal level, Coordinating Committees pool representatives from all the states, whereas the members of Working Committees are representatives from individual states. We also indicate that Working Committees are responsible for communicating and implementing information and decisions at each level down to the next lower level, whereas Coordinating Committees diffuse information and decisions laterally, across each of the subunits. Because we highlight the importance of democratic decision-making in substantive areas we leave open such questions as the nature of a congressional body and cabinet, but suggest that representatives from Working and Coordinating Committees would play important roles at the federal level.

The scheme we propose helps to highlight that the objectives of governance reflect the objectives of all citizens and that government is indistinguishable from its citizens. Figure 3 provides a laundry list of topics that, with some consolidation, might be a basis for the individual Working and Coordinating Committees. Thus, for example, there would be a Working Committee and a Coordinating Committee to ensure universal adequate housing, each at the county, state and federal levels. Not every area of decision-making is relevant at all levels. For example, advocacy for aesthetically attractive communities may be only — or primarily — a community activity.

Figure 3: Local Democracy – Substantive Areas

Adequate universal housing
Adolescent programs
Adult learning centers
Aesthetically attractive communities
Bicycle paths
Bilingual education
Biodiversity provisions
Childcare facilities
Children's health and welfare
Clean air
Clean drinking water
Communications – universal access to ICT and telephones
Community holidays and fairs
Conflict resolution courts
Democratic workplaces
Dissemination of scientific and other knowledge
Domestic dispute counseling programs
Entertainment: theaters, cinemas, concert halls, and craft fairs
Energy: solar and wind technologies
Environmental sustainability
Farmers' markets
Free press
Health and healthcare: preventative care, neonatal and other clinics, hospitals
Industry compliance with labor and environmental laws
Integrated residential neighborhoods
Labor protections: wages, hours worked, holidays
Language proficiency programs

Living wage guarantees
Low levels of earnings inequality
Migrants' rights
Multicultural programs
Needs of the disabled
Needs of the elderly
Nondiscriminatory educational, housing, and employment provisions
Occupational safety
Playgrounds
Preservation of literary and oral traditions
Preservation of wildlife, fish stocks, wetlands, forests, streams, inland waterways and coasts
Primary through secondary schools
Programs to promote cultural, racial, ethnic, and language diversity
Protection of political and civil rights
Public health programs
Public libraries
Public parks
Public radio and television
Public safety
Public spaces: urban squares and green zones
Recreation and sports facilities
Recycling and zero-waste
Renewable energy
Restaurants and cafes
Retirement provisions
Spatial planning that is eco-friendly and reduces sprawl
Sports arenas
Support of pure and applied science
Sustainable, eco-friendly agriculture
Technical schools, colleges, and universities
Transparent governance and laws
Zero unemployment

We have mapped out the hypothetical substantive areas in Figure 3, and suggested that these areas would help to clarify democratic decision-making at various levels of governance. The elements listed in Figure 3 are substantive areas for decision making but they also are material expressions of human rights, and many embody the principles of collective goods. For example, preservation of literary and oral traditions is a human right because it affirms personal dignity, while it also affirms groups' identities, and also is a collective good that benefits everyone, because such preservation helps to ensure the continuity of traditions, a source of social solidarity. A robust public health program is a collective good that benefits all, but each and every person benefits.

The democratic state we have described would promote a high degree of public mindedness, encourage cosmopolitan citizenship, and promote the sort of empathy that is at the core of recognizing the rights of others. We have also shown how collective goods, human rights, and democratic values are indivisible in a democracy that is "of the people, by the people, and for the people." With nonprofit businesses, many problems that plague American communities would be nonexistent. There would be no economic incentives to exploit workers, disregard the environment, overcharge customers, overdevelop land or buy up property and land for speculation. That is, decisions would be made rationally on the basis of equality, need, and individuals' interests and capabilities. Wealth inequalities would gradually disappear.

As we have suggested, political liberalism assumes distrust—by the higher levels of the lower levels and by lower levels of higher levels. We also indicated that recent work in political theory suggests that democracy has the capacity to transform the preferences of people's self-interest into more altruistic and moral ones (Blau and Moncada 2006: 158). Alberto Calsamiglia (1999) defines democracy as a framework of cooperation and consensus building in which human rights are contextualized in the deliberative process—as the rights of moral human beings—and pursued through deliberative processes.

LOCAL DEMOCRACY – GLOBAL DEMOCRACY

ON JUNE 25, 1993, the Vienna Declaration and its Program of Action was adopted unanimously by 171 States. It provokes a clear understanding of the principles that underlie our proposals. Article 8 states:

> Democracy, development and respect for human rights and fundamental freedoms are interdependent and mutually reinforcing. Democracy is based on the freely expressed will of the people to determine their own political, economic, social and cultural systems and their full participation in all aspects of their lives.[21]

Various countries are already engaged in processes that would implement local democracy, in which all residents would participate in substantive decision-making. These include: Georgia, Armenia, Azerbaijan, Japan,[22] Switzerland,[23] Greece,[24] and Brazil.[25] These innovations are a response to the growing recognition that the nation-state is pluralistic, not homogenous as liberal democracy presupposes, that only citizens are experts on what they need in their own communities, and that liberal democracy is an exceedingly inefficient form for the advance of peoples' rights and security.

It is also useful to consider the analogies between the citizen of a state and a world citizen. Michael Byers summarizes what is meant by the relatively new term, "the global citizen." For him, global citizenship accompanies a sense of collective responsibility, an awareness of the importance of exchanges and interdependencies, an awareness of the realities of a shared environment and the effects of climate change, political engagement, and attentiveness to the peoples living under dire conditions in impoverished countries.

Thus, the global citizen, according to his conception, possesses a worldly, cosmopolitan conscience, and that requires a profound understanding of what it means to be inter-

---

[21] Vienna Declaration and Programme of Action, 12 July 1993 http://www.unhchr.ch/huridocda/huridoca. nsf/(Symbol)/A.CONF.157.23.En?OpenDocument

[22] E-democracy in the South Caucasus is documented in a paper prepared for the International Institute for Democracy and Electoral Assistance (IDEA): "Democracy at the Local Level: A Guide for the South Caucasus: http://unpan1.un.org/intradoc/groups/ public/documents/UNTC/UNPAN014977.pdf

[23] See Obinger (2000).

[24] See Latouche (2003).

[25] See Lowy (2000).

connected. Such qualities that describe the global citizen likewise describe the local citizen, as implied in our analysis of local democracy: when empowered, the local citizen has the capacity to act on collective responsibility, participate in exchanges and interdependencies, promote shared public goods, directly engage in decision making, and work to remedy the dire conditions that confront others. Local activism predisposes people to be global citizens, and global citizenship enhances the capacities of people to be local activists. In very general terms, through participation in self-governance, all people are empowered to exercise their positive freedoms in pursuit of common goals and their own needs and desires, and they do so through the pluralistic networks and institutions that they themselves collectively create. It can be said that government of, by, and for the people is a virtuous circle.

REFERENCES

Abrahamsson, Bengt. 1977. *Bureaucracy and Participation*. Beverly Hills: Sage.

Avgerou, Chrisanthi. 2002. *Information Systems and Global Diversity*. Oxford: Oxford University Press.

Bachrach, Peter. 1992. *Power and Empowerment: A Radical Theory of Participatory Democracy*. Philadelphia: Temple University Press.

Badshah, Akhtar, Sarbuland Khan, and Maria Garrido. 2005. *Connected for Development*. New York: United Nations Information and Communications Task Force.

Baiocchi, Gianpaolo. 2005. *Militants and Citizens: The Politics of Participatory Democracy in Porto Alegre*. Stanford, CA: Stanford University Press.

Beetham, David. 1999. *Democracy and Human Rights*. Cambridge, UK: Polity Press.

Blau, Judith, and Alberto Moncada. 2006. *Justice in the United States: Human Rights and the U.S. Constitution*. Lanham, MD: Rowman & Littlefield.

_____. 2007. *Freedoms and Solidarities: In Pursuit of Human Rights*. Lanham, MD: Rowman & Littlefield.

Calsamiglia, Alberto. 1999. "Constitutionalism and Democracy." Pp. 136-154, in Harold Hongju Koh and Ronald C. Slye (eds.), *Deliberative Democracy and Human Rights*. New Haven: Yale University Press.

Cohen, Joshua. 1989. "Deliberative Democracy and Democratic Legitimacy." Pp. 17-34, in Alan Hamlin and Phillip Pettit (eds.), *The Good Polity*. Oxford: Blackwell.

Derber, Charles. 2002. *The Wilding of America: Money, Mayhem, and the New American Dream*. New York: Worth.

Dworkin, Ronald. 1999. "The Moral Reading and the Majoritarian Premise." Pp. 81-115, in Harold Hongju Koh and Ronald C. Slye (eds.), *Deliberative Democracy and Human Rights*. New Haven: Yale University Press.

Edwards, Michael, and John Gaventa (eds.). 2001. *Global Citizen Action*. Boulder, CO: Lynne Rienner.

Florini, Ann. 2003. *The Coming Democracy: New Rules for Running a New World*. Washington, D.C.: Island Press

Gould, Carol C. 2004. *Globalizing Democracy and Human Rights*. Cambridge, MA: Harvard University Press.

Green, Judith M. 1999. *Deep Democracy: Community, Diversity and Transformation*. Lanham, MD: Rowman & Littlefield.

Gregg, Benjamin. 2003. *Coping in Politics with Indeterminant Norms: A Theory of Enlightened Democracy*. Albany, NY: State University of New York Press.

Gutmann, Amy, and Dennis Thompson. 1996. *Democracy and Disagreement*. Cambridge, MA: Belknap Press.

Habermas, Jürgen. 1984. *The Theory of Communicative Action: Volume 1, Reason and the Rationalization of Society*. Boston: Beacon Press.

Held, David. 1995. *Democracy and the Global Order*. Stanford, CA: Stanford University Press.

Kiflemariam, Abraham. 2000. *Governance without Government*. Amstelveen, the Netherlands: Boom Juridische Utigevers.

Kjaer, Anne Mette. 2004. *Governance*. Cambridge, UK: Polity Press.

Latouche, Serge. 2003. "Can Democracy Solve All Problems? *Democracy & Nature* 9: 373-377.

Legesse, Asmarom. 1973. *Gada*. New York: Free Press.

_____. 2000. *Oromo Democracy: An Indigenous African Political System*. Lawrenceville, NJ: Red Sea Press.

Low, Setha, and Neil Smith (ed.). 2006. *The Politics of Public Space*. New York: Routledge.

Lowy, Michael. 2000. "A 'Red' Government in the South Brasil," *Monthly Review* 52: 16-20.

MacLean, Don (ed.). 2004. *Internet Governance: A Grand Collaboration*. New York: United Nations Information and Communication Technologies Task Force.

Mamdani, Mahmood. 1996. *Citizen and Subject*. Princeton, NJ: Princeton University Press.

Mayo, Marjorie. 2005. *Global Citizens: Social Movements and the Challenge of Globalization*. London: Zed.

Melman, Seymour. 2001. *After Capitalism: From Managerialism to Workplace Democracy*. Alfred A. Knopf.

Moore, John Allphin, Jr. and Jerry Pubantz. 2006. *The New United Nations: International Organization in the Twenty-First Century*. Upper Saddle River, NJ: Pearson/Prentice Hall.

Nino, Carlos Santiago. 1996. *The Constitution of Deliberative Democracy*. New Haven: Yale University Press.

Nun, José. 2003. *Democracy: Government of the People or Government of the Politicians?* Lanham, MD: Rowman & Littlefield.

Obinger, Herbert. 2000. "The Swiss Welfare State in the 90s: Social Policy under the Instutitional Setting of Direct Democracy, *Zeitschrift fur Politikwissenschaft* 10: 43-63.

Pateman, Carole. 1970. *Participation and Democratic Theory*. Cambridge: Cambridge University Press.

Pecora, Vincent P. (ed.). 2001. *Nations and Identities*. Malden, MA: Blackwell.

Perrin, Andrew J. 2006. *Citizen Speak: The Democratic Imagination in American Life*. Chicago: University of Chicago Press.

Piven, Frances Fox. 2006. *Challenging Authority: How Ordinary People Change America*. Lanham, MD: Rowman & Littlefield.

Powell, Walter W., and Paul DiMaggio. 1987. *The Nonprofit Sector*. New Haven: Yale University Press.

Schumpeter, Joseph. 1943. *Capitalism, Socialism, and Democracy*. London: Allen & Unwin.

Shutt, Harry. 2003. *A New Democracy*. London: Zed Books.

Unamuno, Miguel de. 1996. "Un Discurso en la Sociedad 'El Sitio' de Bilbao," *El Liberal* (Bilbao), 6 January 1924). Pp. 28-41, in Stephen G. H. Roberts, *Miguel de Unamuno: Political Speeches and Journalism (1923-1929)*. Exeter: University of Exeter Press.

Wallerstein, Immanuel. 1998. Utopistics: Or, Historical Choices of the Twenty-First Century. New York: The New Press.

Bryan S. Turner

❧ ❧ ❧ ❧ ❧ ❧ ❧ ❧

SUBSTANTIVE DEMOCRACY AS CIVIL SPHERE:
FURTHER CONSIDERATIONS ON BLAU AND MONCADA

Bryan S. Turner
National University of Singapore

*I*N RECENT YEARS Judith Blau and Alberto Moncada have built up a substantial body of work on human rights and democracy. They have been effective critics of liberalism in search of a broader basis of human rights (Blau and Moncada 2005). We owe them our gratitude for bringing such important issues firmly within the scientific discourse of mainstream sociology. My critical comments are therefore based upon this prior sense of indebtedness, both theoretical and political. Let me start therefore on a note of agreement.

We live in an audit society in which individuals and public institutions are constantly measured against government audits (Power 1997). These regulatory procedures have imposed a considerable burden on society in the name of efficiency and cost effectiveness. These procedures have been particularly onerous, for example in British universities, where staff are constantly monitored to measure research and teaching activity. I am struck by the fact that, by contrast, governments and their presidents are rarely brought to account by a public audit apart from congressional communities or parliamentary committees, but these are not fully public instruments. Blau and Moncada suggest that with modern technology we could experiment with regular electronic referenda and other instruments to bring about more effective "substantive democracy." The Internet could be used in domestic politics at both national and local levels to impose a "democratic audit" on parties and politicians to measure how and whether they delivered their electoral promises.

At the moment, the most effective—and in many cases the only democratic audit available— is a periodic national election in which governments that have failed are in theory thrown out of office. This is the basic principle of participatory democracy that the electorate can eventually punish an incompetent or corrupt government. In practice, we know that this often fails. As Blau and Moncada point out, formal democracy in the United States is profoundly flawed. The electorate has a very low turn out rate; there is little to choose between political parties; politicians are too closely associated with Big Business; there is low consumption of newspapers and serious journalism; the party bureaucracies are too powerful; and there is low trust of politics and politicians. In addition, there are specific problems such as the erasure of a significant number of voters from the Florida electoral list during the election of the Bush administration. In the U.S. there is no viable oppositional politics offering a genuine alternative, partly because it is unclear what the Democratic Party actually stands for in policy terms (Bendavid 2007).

But we should not take the failures of American democracy to be an indictment of formal democratic values and institutions as such. Not all formal democracy is phony democracy. The recent elections in Northern Ireland to implement the resolutions of the peace process and to restore power to local Northern Ireland institutions represent a remarkably successful exercise of democracy. In this case, politicians overcame the prejudices of deeply divided communities. The elections in May 2007 in East Timor were peaceful and successful in a country that has been the victim of decades of violence. The Left may not welcome the outcome of the French presidential elections, but it was a remarkable display of viable democratic politics with over 80 percent of the French electorate turning out. Elections in post New Order Indonesia display a vibrant democratic culture after years of authoritarian, centralized rule. In short, we should not read the failures of American democracy as representing the failure of participatory democracy as such.

Blau and Moncada offer us what I will call a "civil-sphere theory of democracy" that in some respects follows the recent arguments of Jeffery Alexander in *The Civil Sphere* (2006). To understand a functioning democracy as sociologists we should look not to formal structures—opposition parties, elections, election campaigns, presidential offices and so forth—but to the substantial structures of NGOs, local neighborhood groups, social movements, citizenship action, the not-for-profit sector and so forth. This arena of political activity empowers ordinary citizens while futile elections only reinforce their distrust.

This perspective is powerful and persuasive, but it has one classic problem. It has to assume that in some mysterious way the civil sphere is a self-regulating and self-monitoring arena in which the activity of many social groups finds some form of equilibrium. What happens when civil society contains anti-social or criminal groups? How do we make that judgment? Can we regard the actions of mafia as making a contribution to the civil sphere? Mafia groups can be regarded as associations working for the interests of marginalized ethnic groups. In southern Italy, mafia works for the welfare benefit of its clients where state institutions are absent or have failed. In Australia, Sri Lankan diasporic communities, it is claimed, collect money through charitable foundations to further the military conflict in their homeland. In previous research, I tried to study the contribution of "voluntary associations" or "not-for-profit" organizations to the civil sphere and came to some negative conclusions: *voluntary associations are not democratic and transparent*; they tend to employ women at wage levels well below the market rate; they depress wages in the unskilled sector; and they do not—and do not attempt to—provide a universalistic service (Brown et al. 2000). Civil society solidarity can only work on the basis of pre-existing effective empowerment from citizenship and regulation from the rule of law. Americans have lots of *individual rights* but a weak framework of citizenship and welfare in terms of well embedded *social rights*.

Blau and Moncada say we should learn from developing societies in order to get a picture of how substantive democracy can work. Unsurprisingly they can look towards Latin America for good examples. However, the biggest problem for democracy in the developing world is *political corruption*, and perhaps the Philippines is a particularly good example of how celebrities have taken over electoral politics turning elections into symbolic carnivals in which real power stays with a small number of political families (Anderson 1998). This example poses an interesting sociological question as to whether ex-American colonies have a higher rate of political failure than ex-British or ex-French colonies.

My conclusion is that *substantive democracy can complement participatory democracy rather than replace it*, and perhaps the necessary linking institution is *citizenship* itself.

References

Alexander, Jeffrey C. 2006. *The Civil Sphere*. Oxford: Oxford University Press.
Anderson, Benedict. 1998. *The Spectre of Comparisons: Nationalism, Southeast Asia and the World*. London: Verso.
Bendavid, Naftali. 2007. *The 'Thumpin': How Rahm Emanuel and the Democrats Learned to be Ruthless and Ended the Republican Revolution*. New York: Doubleday.
Blau, Judith, and Moncada, Alberto. 2005. *Human Rights beyond the Liberal Vision*. Lanham, MD: Rowman & Littlefield.
Brown, Kevin M., Kenny, Susan, and Turner, Bryan S. 2000. *Rhetorics of Welfare: Uncertainty, Choice and Voluntary Associations*. Houndmills: Macmillan Press.
Power, Michael. 1997. *The Audit Society. Rituals of Verification*, Oxford: Oxford University Press.

Bryan S. Turner is the author of Vulnerability and Human Rights *(Penn State University Press, 2006).*

Sparring with Old Friends:
Further Considerations on Blau and Moncada

Nikita Okembe-RA Imani
James Madison University

*O*NE MIGHT DESCRIBE my piece as a "sparring with old friends." The engagement is friendly, but serious. From the very outset, the Blau-Moncada essay seeks to engage an ancient inquiry. How does one construct a political entity that represents the will of the people and serves as a facility for the wielding of their collective power in the common interest? To this problem was posited the notion of the Greco-Roman civil state, but it proved a failure for the task at hand, inevitably devolving to the oligarchic rule of the few or, even worse, the tyranny of the majority over the few, revealing itself to me not much more advanced than the feudal and monarchical constructions that were its contemporaries and progenitors. Alas, finally the European nation-state with its colonial appendages were born and it was refined until we had the birth of the American experiment that came to be known as "democracy." In its name, this construction borrowed from the classical Greek lexicon but the term was not being invoked in the classical Greek manner where the rule of the masses was to be the rule of the mob. The term was now applied positively and positivistically to this new configuration of state power which introduced elite rule in the form of electoral politics and "representative" or surrogate legislature, allegedly configured in a balance and separation of powers between administrative branches. The model argued that this balance of power would not preclude authoritarianism, but that it would constrain it in an equilibrium between the manifestations of this new "holy trinity."

This new contrivance, presented as the best that humanity could congeal out of its storehouse of knowledge, was limited from birth by force of its intellectual parentage. It was spawn of Platonic epistemology, specifically from Plato's conception of the universe as a material rather than spiritual artifice and of its proposed inherent dichotomization into subjects and objects. The latter perpetually controls the former and the relationship between them sets the state for the supposedly inevitable dichotomy of oppressor and oppressed that was to characterize the derivative colonial and postcolonial systems that these new nation-state "democracies" were to supervise.

This brings us back to Blau and Moncada's article, which begins with that very problematic Western dichotomization as would-be citizens are presented as being both subject and objects in relation to the state. To be subject to the state however, in the Platonic sense, is to forfeit ones power to control its actions. To be in the object relation with respect to the state is to control it and presumably relative to the aforementioned objects. There is not a recipe here for liberation however well-intentioned and noble the effort. Yet for most Western discourse, the equation of this form of "democracy" with the very concept of rule of the masses as the only possible rendering of the question is like a theoretical involuntary reflex that spurs perennial Pyrrhic political efforts that seek human political liberation and end up in jingoistic advocacies of more Westernization, read modernization, read Eurocentrism.

This difficulty is then compounded by the vehicle chosen for this entry into participatory democracy, which is essentially a Western technology and, of course, this technology is rendered diffuse by the other arm of Western expansionism, global capitalism. The motivation for the penetration of media and communicative forms throughout the continent of Africa for example, is not the participation of the masses, but greater capacity to penetrate and exploit the labor and consumer markets to the detriment in most cases of the political, economic, and social well-being

Commentary

of the native populations. This reminds me of the glorification of the mass media forms in general that characterized the work of Richard Thompson. In his work, he argued that the new mass communicative forms and vehicles were exposing people to the capacity to create media and thereby resist vested systems of power. Yet, such an argument must ignore the lack of diffusion of the technology, the absolute imbalance in social capital that facilitates the use of technology, the metropoles that control the symbolic cultural products that are marketed and disseminated through that technology, and so on.

Blau and Moncada posit a new substantive democracy, but it too is based on another Western philosophical proposition that is extremely destructive when applied outside of the Western context—the notion of the individual as the subject and locus of rational choice. Thus the focus of this new political model is like most forms of Eurocentrism—liberalism upon the empowerment of the individual collectivity. Critical theory shows us the problematic nature of the concept of the individual which is often merely the mirror reflection of the mass commodity culture imprinting on single personages whose personal opinions are mere echoes of false consciousness. I am reminded of El Hajj Malik el-Shabazz and his critique of a would-be liberatory democracy among slaves. He chided those who would advance that agenda, admonishing us that we should not ask a slave what he wants. "He doesn't know what he wants and because he doesn't know what he wants," in effect, he or she will attempt to integrate themselves more thoroughly into the system of oppression as a function of their choice.

Against this notion of the community as the collection of individuals, I posit the community as the collective itself and the individual as something apart, as representing that moment of the uniqueness, abstracted from the whole and that is largely responsible for the collapse of those narratives we codify under the rubric "human rights" themselves. Thus a true participatory democracy, although I must admit detesting the latter term, would involve representing collective interests and not individual interests. The very reason the West honors political and civil rights is because they are bought at the cost of social and economic rights which are necessarily collective, yet failure to provide for such rights precludes any real notion of or possibility for freedom.

It's ironic that the authors draw on Habermas, who perhaps more than any other descendant of the Frankfurt school discourse, occupied himself with the legitimation and rationalization of established order and the reassertion of conformity as a means of measuring social ethics. He is often criticized as being the most "non-critical" of those scholars considered "critical" for precisely this social conservatism in his theory. His is largely a throwback to Durkheimian functionalism, in which rationality also played a vital role in the conception of how "modern" societies are formed.

A question raised by this article is whether one can even have democracy in a non-democratic society. That is, to what extent is democracy a structural problem to be architecturally designed for, or a measurement of the socio-ethical stage of development of a particular society? Collectivity works when I see myself as part of a collectivity. In societies where this is the social mythology, communal structures emerge as a naturalized phenomenon and are viewed as inherently just and rational. Conversely, in a society that venerates individualism, capitalism, religious denominationalism, and so on, one would expect whatever organic political structures emerge to steadily devolve into competitive, partisan forms that the authors want to resist. It seems that we call for a political paradigm shift without calling for the necessary epistemological shift away from Eurocentrism.

The concept of cosmopolitan citizenship sounds a lot like traditional liberal rhetoric involving multiculturalism, cultural pluralism, et al and to the extent that it will remain grounded in the conception of the diversity of this concept of "individual," it is likely to be much more parochial, than truly global.

From an African traditional perspective, the idea of "normative indeterminacy" is extremely troublesome. The rationale for communitarian political forms in that context is out of and towards the provision of moral and ethical clarity for the society and mutual understanding of common interests and the legitimacy of those interests. "Indeterminacy" as it is conceived here, seems a kind of postmodernist vacuum into which will likely encroach partisanship, special interest, and then we may return to the default condition. I fail to see how that likelihood is to be avoided. Why would the "enlightened" not merely be the "elect" and ultimately the "elite," replicating the Protestantesque, Calvinist political forms characteristic in the West at present and currently oversold?

It is the concept of mutualism that I find most useful and progressive, yet for reasons previously discussed I fail to see how the cultural context for the spirit of mutuality is to be attained. And this mutualism is directly contradicted by the Western ideology of universalism which is affixed to human right. The primordial, non-colonialist "human right" would be the collective right to define human rights themselves. The positing of a pre-existing universality has the practical effect of a cloture of the democratic, discursive processes laid out in the model. Thus we are confronted with what Stephen Lukes (2005) describes in his *Power: A Radical View* as the "third face" of power, the power to determine the agenda for subsequent participatory discussion. This is much like Western universalism in science generally where you start by saying "taking so and so for granted, or controlling for such and such variable." Inevitably the divergent variables which are controlled for and the meta-assumptions agreed to are themselves the substance of the issue.

All in all, Blau and Moncada have made an excellent contribution to the standard discourse about human rights and democratization broadly conceived. This is a piece of the puzzle. Now we must open up the debate to even more theorists and writers outside of this discourse about democracy and the U.S. as a test case to those who begin from collectivity rather than individualism and from spiritual cosmogonies rather than Platonic epistemology. I hope my brief comments are contributory to this evolving discussion and I am grateful for an opportunity to read this excellent and thought-provoking piece. We remain friends.

Reference

Lukes, Stephen. 2005. *Power. A Radical View*, second edition. Basingstoke: Palgrave Macmillan.

Nikita Okembe-RA Imani is Associate Professor of Sociology and African Studies at James Madison University, and an associate graduate faculty member at Central Michigan University. He has authored and coauthored several books, most recently Head Games, *forthcoming in fall 2007 by the University Press of America.*

❧ ❧ ❧ ❧ ❧ ❧ ❧ ❧

SUBSTANTIVE DEMOCRACY, HUMAN RIGHTS, AND THE VOCATION OF SOCIOLOGY

Mark Frezzo
Florida Atlantic University

C ONCEIVED AS A RESPONSE to widespread calls for a blueprint for a new global architecture, Blau and Moncada's proposal for substantive democracy can be interpreted as an exercise in "grounded utopia" (Mittelman 2005). To the end of grounding their proposal, the authors take two steps. Their first step is to offer a "counter-memory" of the Enlightenment project

Commentary

of human emancipation by tracing the lineage of substantive democracy from such luminaries as Jean-Jacques Rousseau and Abraham Lincoln to such contemporary theorists as José Nun, Judith Green, and Carol C. Gould. In the process, they excavate the repressed memory of attempts to push democratic theory beyond parliamentary politics—the realm of routinized relations among parties, lobbyists, special interest groups, and think tanks—in the direction of self-governance. The authors' second step is to translate the practical undertakings of justice-oriented movements—whether in Latin America, the United States, or elsewhere—into theoretical terms. This involves elucidating the common denominator that underlies movements of indigenous peoples, peasants, workers, women, environmentalists, immigrants, and anti-corporate activists—namely, the meta-language of human rights. I intend to focus on the second step.

I begin by elucidating the scholarly context of the authors' intervention. Why is substantive democracy an issue for sociology (as opposed to political science, legal studies, and philosophy)? A number of events—including the collapse of the Soviet Union (and the ensuing re-organization of the inter-state system), a wave of financial crises sweeping across the global economy, and a proliferation of social movements challenging neoliberal policies—have inspired a flurry of research on transnational norms (Khagram et al. 2002), cosmopolitanism (Archibugi 2003), and global governance (Patomaki and Teivainen 2004). In the same period, the rapid growth of transnational coalitions—beginning with the Zapatista solidarity network in 1994 and continuing with the World Social Forum (WSF) in 2001—has prompted sociologists to analyze the role of NGOs in facilitating and constraining the activities of grassroots movements (Bandy and Smith 2005). While NGOs attempt to funnel their resources into promising movements (in exchange for influence on decisions about objectives, strategies, and tactics), movements attempt to make themselves attractive to NGO sponsors by embracing transnational norms (Bob 2005).

Notwithstanding their reservations about the phenomenon of "NGO-ization," Blau and Moncada find inspiration in the current trend among social movements in the global South—particularly in Latin America. Under the sway of secular and religious NGOs, popular mobilizations are embracing substantive democracy and human rights as objectives, while committing themselves to non-violent tactics of resistance. In this fashion, diverse movements in the global South have managed not only to thicken their ties to one another, but also to garner material support and sympathy from allies in the global North. As the authors note, these transnational coalitions have been facilitated by such cyber-activist techniques as e-mail campaigns, electronic petitions, blogging, and independent media (to complement more conventional protest repertoires). But the value of these communicative techniques consists in the propagation of common frame for a diverse array of mobilizations.

Where does this leave us? Though presented as an intervention in contemporary social and political theory, Blau and Moncada's article represents a significant contribution to the sociology of human rights—a field that has solidified in recent years. It is worthwhile to demarcate two tendencies in the sociology of human rights. Linked to the initiative for "public sociology" in the American Sociological Association, the first tendency involves building an advocacy of human rights into scholarly analyses of inequality, exclusion, poverty, environmental degradation, and other social problems. From this perspective, the sociologist's vocation is to push for such policies as living wage laws and national healthcare. Linked to recent studies of transnational norms, the second tendency involves analyzing how human rights circulate among different social actors—including social movements, NGOs, national governments, and inter-governmental organizations. From this perspective, the sociologist's vocation is to explain how various social actors contest, claim, and transform the doctrine of human rights. More to the point, the goal is to explain how movements—particularly in the global South—attempt to extricate the doctrine of human rights from the legacy of Eurocentrism and push "rights talk" into the economic, social, cultural, and environmental spheres. Both tendencies merit further elaboration.

References

Archibugi, D (ed.). 2003. *Debating Cosmopolitics*. London: Verso.

Bandy, J., and J. Smith (eds.). 2005. *Coalitions Across Borders: Transnational Protest and the Neoliberal Order*. Lanham, MD: Rowman & Littlefield.

Bob, Clifford. 2005. *The Marketing of Rebellion: Insurgents, Media, and Inter-national Activism*. Cambridge: Cambridge University Press.

Khagram, S., J.V. Riker, and K. Sikkink. 2002. *Restructuring World Politics: Transnational Social Movements, Networks, and Norms*. Minneapolis, MN: University of Minnesota Press.

Mittelman, J. H. 2005. "What Is a Critical Globalization Studies?" Pp. 19-29, in R. Applebaum and W. Robinson (eds.), *Critical Globalization Studies*. London: Routledge.

Patomaki, H., and T. Teivainen. 2004. *A Possible World: Democratic Transformation of Global Institutions*. London: Zed Books.

Mark Frezzo is Assistant Professor of Sociology at Florida Atlantic University and member of the Peace Studies Committee at that institution. He publishes and teaches in the areas of social movements, political economy and development sociology.

❦ ❦ ❦ ❦ ❧ ❧ ❧ ❧

ANOTHER DEMOCRACY IS POSSIBLE: REFLECTIONS ON BLAU AND MONCADA'S "SUBSTANTIVE DEMOCRACY"

A. Kathryn Stout & Ricardo A. Dello Buono

*B*LAU AND MONCADA RAISE many important issues in their essay "Substantive Democracy." The thrust of their work is to reaffirm the limitations of "indirect democracies" as practiced in Western countries while suggesting that important lessons can be drawn from more popular and participatory forms of grassroots democracy found in non-Western countries. The authors suggest ways to transform non-democratic societies through community based, democratic processes built around local issues which can hopefully expand to more regional, national and global levels.

Among their arguments is the notion that dense communication networks are necessary to help make the achievement of substantive democracy possible and this is favored by new technological developments such as electronic networking and internet based mechanisms of collective governance. Residents participate in "working committees" that focus primarily on single substantive issues (e.g., housing or education) at all levels of governance and interact with "coordinating committees." All residents (the authors use the term "citizens") have equal access to participation at all levels and every elected person is subject to the rules of transparency and accountability. Perhaps most critical to this model is the proposal to eliminate a profit based economy, replacing it with nonprofit firms. These ideas are presented in a model for democratizing and humanizing society, both in our everyday actions and in the larger macro structures in which we live.

We agree with the authors that there is a dynamic and transformative interaction between human agency, social structure and social change. While cultural practices can indeed result in social transformations, we feel that the overall structural constraints of capitalist social relations were minimized in this article. If understood as an ideal vision of what we would like society to become, their model makes a valuable contribution to those seeking progressive social change. But in terms of concrete plans for implementing such change based on existing examples of democratic processes and organizations, there are many reasons to remain pessimistic.

Blau and Moncada's analysis provides examples of effective NGOs in Africa and Latin America while they express hope in the potential of community based groups emerging out of crises in the United States. For example, homelessness and Post-Hurricane Katrina recovery efforts across the Gulf Coast region provide an important context for their discussion. They remain somewhat limited by restricting their attention to "progressive" groups, focusing on those whose principles include protecting human rights, equality, diversity, compassion, and so on. Absent is any mention of the effects of undemocratic organizations which have developed in direct response to progressive U.S. forces, for example the powerful forces of the "Christian Right" or persistent influence of the Ku Klux Klan.

We certainly agree with the authors that NGOs can serve as positive forces for social transformation while not being especially democratic in their structure. As noted in the article, remote control by donors is one of the obvious constraints on NGO contributions to democratization. While NGOs can facilitate social monitoring, as the authors point out, and this is one of their most common practices in Latin America and other regions of the global "South," they can also help to mobilize collective actions around a broad range of substantive issues in conjunction with social movement organizations (SMOs).

From our point of view, NGOs are better thought of as organizational expressions of the relations of domination in "actually existing" democracies rather than any form of more advanced democratic praxis. This can be readily observed, for example, in the police state environment of New Orleans during the immediate, post-Katrina period. The authors seem to focus too exclusively on the positive aspects of NGOs, stressing their political focus on specific substantive issues and their close proximity to the popular base instead of a more comprehensive analysis that weighs in on their structural limitations. We also do not agree that indicators such as the number of NGOs are universally valid for measuring citizen action in civil society participation or in the practice of "disruptive politics." Our experience with a variety of NGOs in Latin America further suggests that they are far from egalitarian. Their dynamics of consultation tend to be thwarted by donor interventionism or financially imposed exigencies, while traditional forms of internal authoritarianism abound, often including quasi-charismatic, patriarchic or "guru" forms of leadership.

Some initial dynamics in the Post-Hurricane Katrina period in New Orleans and the larger Gulf Coast region suggested, as do Blau and Moncada, a hopeful view of the power and possibilities of a grassroots democracy. As the dust began to settle, however, the prevailing social commitments to profit, structural inequalities and nondemocratic decision-making at virtually all levels proved to be the most powerful forces in shaping reconstruction. While it may appear from the outside that the growing number of grassroots groups, benevolent associations, and nonprofit organizations offer significant opportunities for social transformations, the most disenfranchised populations have remained displaced and "voiceless" nearly two years after the fact, many with little hope of ever returning to their communities.[1]

In the Katrina aftermath, the media bombarded the world with a steady parade of images showing politicians working tirelessly on behalf of the people, with open town hall meetings seemingly giving "voice" to residents across the region. This created a rather bloated illusion of "democracy in action." In reality, highly structured political processes and pre-defined economic exigencies have effectively dominated every aspect of the recovery process. One illustrative example is found in the gambling industry that had previously been prohibited from building their typically self-enclosed complexes of hotels and restaurants adjacent to the casinos. These regulations designed to protect the local New Orleans economy from "McDonaldization" soon became lifted under Post-Katrina economic conditions.[2]

The already developing process of privatizing education, crime control, and other formerly public institutions actually accelerated in New Orleans during the initial recovery period. This meant that pre-existing social conflicts between groups, especially across race and class, became notably exacerbated by the crisis. Elite and pro-establishment figures along with much of the media essentially celebrated the imposition of a police-state siege on New Orleans while poor and predominantly African American communities suffered the terrifying consequences.

We agree that there are numerous positive examples of popular democratic groups working around redevelopment issues. Some are new and even exciting, and it is true that some pre-existing groups have grown in membership. It remains to be seen if, as in the words of Blau and Moncada, "democracy has the capacity to transform people's self-interest into more altruistic and moral ones."[3] We suspect, however, that most of the groups who have survived this early period are already in the process of being co-opted or assimilated.

In a similar vein, we feel that Blau and Moncada's discussion of workplace democracy does not adequately recognize the nature of such alternatives as being structurally shaped by immediacies derived from severe capitalist crises and subsequently integrated into "recovery" schemes of cooptation. These characteristics contribute to their typically unstable organizational basis and tendency towards collapse in the most radical cases, while more stable cases become consolidated by reproducing market dynamics within and throughout "self-managed" structures. Clearly, there needs to be additional discussion about the ways and means of transforming capitalist enterprises into authentically nonprofit firms.

There is a growing sense, particularly in Latin America, that another world is possible; a more democratic one where ties of solidarity can be reconstructed in accordance with the interests of the popular sectors. Imperialism, the essence of un-democracy, makes this other democracy urgent and necessary in Latin America and the rest of the global South. Likewise, the response of NGOs to the Gulf Coast experience serves as an important empirical illustration for the need of more democratic political and economic processes within the "underdeveloped" regions of the global North. We agree with the authors that this process of democratization is one of struggle, not of contemplation. We believe that direct, more participatory democracy becomes possible not merely by reason, but by collective resistance and the creation of new organizational forms that can effectively challenge the status quo. In this context, new technologies unquestionably open new possibilities for challenging hegemony and forcing "indirect democracies" wider open.

But here, we return to our sober point of departure. Existing social class relations enable these same technologies to be wielded in new, more highly repressive forms as well. The capacity of reactionary states and aligned forces to monitor and conduct surveillance over electronic networks and communications is a documented and growing reality. There are obvious issues regarding equal access to new technologies and it is possible, as some have suggested, that electronic voting may be even more susceptible to electoral fraud than traditional balloting.

Repressive technologies also represent serious threats on the ideological level. This was substantially anticipated by Frankfurt School theorists whose critical while often pessimistic work was visionary in anticipating the depth of new forms of ideological control under advanced capitalism. In hindsight, these 20th Century thinkers may have underestimated the extent to which subtle and technologically driven forms of "democratic unfreedom"[4] could be intensified via reversion to more traditional forms of manipulation based in media-induced paranoia and the fabrication of imminent "threats" as seen in the post-9/11 period. Such trends convince us that the important contributions now being made by outstanding critical theorists like Blau and Moncada must be continually scrutinized against empirical cases in assessing positive movement towards more genuine forms of democracy.

Notes

[1] For more information on this point, see www.advancementproject.org/katrina.html.

[2] The term "McDonaldization was first popularized by George Ritzer, *The McDonaldization of Society.* Thousand Oaks, CA: Pine Forge Press, 1993.

[3] Cited in their present essay from another work: Blau, Judith, and Alberto Moncada. 2006. *Justice in the United States: Human Rights and the U.S. Constitution.* Lanham, MD: Rowman & Littlefield.

[4] A term popularized in Herbert Marcuse, *One Dimensional Man: Studies in the Ideology of Advanced Industrial Society.* Boston: Beacon Press, 1964.

A. Kathryn Stout was Associate Professor of Sociology and Criminology before returning to her hometown of New Orleans in 2005. She is currently an independent scholar-activist whose family was directly affected by Hurricane Katrina and still struggles within the recovery efforts. **Ricardo A. Dello Buono** *was previously Associate Professor of Sociology and International Studies at Dominican University before resigning his tenure in 2005 to take up residence abroad. He is the Global Division Chair of the Society for the Study of Social Problems (SSSP) and Editorial Board Member of the journal* Critical Sociology.

HUMAN

BEYOND THE LIBERAL VISION

RIGHTS

Judith Blau and Alberto Moncada

There is growing recognition around the globe that people's
fundamental human rights are being imperiled in a world
economy that is being driven by multinationals, investors,
and banks. The "race to the bottom" and insatiable greed has
intensified poverty and economic inequalities, fueled migration, and rapidly accelerated environmental degradation.
The fates of all nations are interdependent and even though
the U.S. is the prime driver of the new economy, Americans
have likewise experienced declines over the past decades.
Blau and Moncada outline the fundamental human rights
that all people are entitled to and the important role that
nations have in upholding these rights.

Human Rights is both a welcome contribution in its own
right and an intellectually engaging stimulus to further
work on its urgent themes. Human rights and global justice
are among the fundamental issues of our day and a sociological perspective such as this one is sorely needed.

Craig Calhoun, *New York University*
President, Social Science Research Council

New Trends in Globalization

By Jan Nederveen Pieterse

Abstract

The twenty-first century momentum of globalization is markedly different from twentieth century globalization and involves a new geography of trade, weaker hegemony and growing multipolarity. This presents major questions. Is the rise of East Asia, China and India just another episode in the rise and decline of nations, another reshuffling of capitalism, a relocation of accumulation centers without affecting the logics of accumulation? Does it advance, sustain or halt neoliberalism? The rise of Asia is codependent with neoliberal globalization and yet unfolds outside the neoliberal mold. What is the relationship between zones of accumulation and modes of regulation? What are the ramifications for global inequality? The first part of this paper discusses trends in trade, finance, international institutions, hegemony and inequality and social struggle. The second part discusses what the new trends mean for the emerging twenty-first century international division of labor.

*W*ITH 5 PERCENT of the world population the United States absorbs 25 percent of world energy supplies, 40 percent of world consumption and spends 50 percent of world military spending and 50 percent of world health care spending (at $1.3 trillion a year). U.S. borrowing of $700 billion per year or $2.6 billion per day absorbs 80 percent of net world savings. Meanwhile the U.S. share of world manufacturing output has steadily declined and the share of manufacturing in U.S. GDP at 12.7 percent is now smaller than that of the health care sector at 14 percent and financial services at 20 percent. This shrinking of the physical economy makes it unlikely that its massive external debt can ever be repaid (Prestowitz 2005).

According to IMF estimates, China and India are expected to overtake the GDP of the world's leading economies in the coming decades. China is expected to pass the GDP of Japan in 2016 and of the U.S. by 2025. In 2005 China surpassed the U.S. as Japan's biggest trading partner, surpassed Canada as the biggest trading partner of the U.S. and surpassed the U.S. as the world's top choice of foreign direct investment. If

JAN NEDERVEEN PIETERSE is Professor of Sociology at the University of Illinois at Urbana Champaign and an Honorary Member of the Albanian Institute of Sociology. His recent books include Ethnicities and Global Multiculture: Pants for an Octopus *(Rowman & Littlefield, 2007),* Globalization or Empire? *(Routledge, 2004),* Globalization and Culture: Global Mélange *(Rowman & Littlefield, 2003) and* Development Theory: Deconstructions/Reconstructions *(Sage, 2001).*

current trends continue, China will become the biggest trading partner of practically every nation. By 2025 the combined GDP of the BRIC—Brazil, Russia, India and China—would grow to one-half the combined GDP of the G-6 countries (the U.S., Japan, Germany, France, Italy and Britain). By 2050, according to a Goldman Sachs report, the combined BRIC economies will surpass that group. According to this forecast, "China, India, Brazil and Russia will be the first-, third-, fifth- and sixth-biggest economies by 2050, with the United States and Japan in second and fourth place, respectively." BRIC spending growth as measured in dollars could surpass the G-6 countries' levels as early 2009 (Whelan 2004).

Both these data sets are uncontroversial, almost commonplace, yet combining them raises major questions. How do we get from here to there and what does this mean for the course and shape of globalization?

The United States, Europe and Japan rode the previous wave of globalization, notably during 1980-2000, but in recent years their lead in economics, trade, finance and geopolitics is gradually slipping. The United States set the rules, in economics, through the Washington consensus, in trade, through the WTO, in finance, through the dollar standard and the IMF, and in security, through its hegemony and formidable military. Each of these dimensions is now out of whack. The old winners are still winning, but the terms on which they are winning cedes more and more to emerging forces. In production and services, education and demography, the advantages are no longer squarely with the old winners. In several respects in relation to globalization, the old winners have become conservative forces.

The twenty-first century momentum of globalization is markedly different from twentieth-century globalization. Slowly, like a giant oil tanker, the axis of globalization is turning from North-South to East-South relations. This presents major questions. Is the rise of Asia and the newly industrialized economies (NIEs) just another episode in the rise and decline of nations, another reshuffling of capitalism, a relocation of accumulation centers without affecting the logics of accumulation? Does it advance, sustain or halt neoliberalism? Is it just another shift in national economic fortunes, or an alternative political economy with different institutions, class relations, energy use and transnational politics? What is the relationship between zones of accumulation and modes of regulation? And what are the ramifications for global inequality?

Examining this poses methodological problems. Extrapolating trends is risky. The units of analysis are not what they used to be or seem to be. The story is not merely one of change but also continuity, and in some respects, seeming continuity.

Euro parliamentarian Glyn Ford notes, "The EU has more votes in the International Monetary Fund than the U.S., but has not yet used them to challenge the current neoliberal orthodoxy.... With support from Latin America, in the World Trade Organization, at UN conferences in Tokyo as well as from the Santiago-plus-five and Durban-plus-five groupings, an alternative world could emerge" (Ford 2005).

It could, but, so far, it doesn't. There is a certain stickiness and stodginess to social change. Power plays continue as long as they can. Policies continue old style until a policy paradigm change is inevitable—not unlike Thomas Kuhn's revolutions in science. There is a sleepwalking choreography to social existence, never quite in sync with actual trends; or rather trends are only trends when they enter discourse. (In a similar way what we teach in universities is often years behind what we know or what we're thinking about because there is no convenient structure or heading yet under which to place and communicate it.) Changes manifest after certain time lags—an institutional lag, discursive lag, policy lag; yet changes are underway even if the language to signal them isn't quite there yet. Some changes we can name, some we can surmise and some escape detection and will catch up with us. So at times it feels much like business as usual. We should identify structural trends and discursive changes as well as tipping points that would tilt the pattern and the paradigm.

According to Kemal Dervis, director of the UN Development Program, globalization in the past was a profoundly "unequalising process." Yet,

> Today, the process is rapidly turning on its head. The south is growing faster than the north. Southern companies are more competitive than their northern counterparts....Leading the charge is a new generation of southern multinationals, from China, Korea, India, Latin America and even the odd one from Africa, aggressively seeking investments in both the northern and southern hemispheres, competing head-to-head with their northern counterparts to win market share and buy undervalued assets" (quoted in Peel 2005).

This optimistic assessment counts economic changes—which this paper also highlights—but it doesn't address social questions.

About cutting-edge globalization, there are two big stories to tell. One is the rise of Asia and the accompanying growth of East-South trade, financial, energy and political relations. Part of this story is being covered in general media (Marber 1998; Agtmael 2007). In the words of Paul Kennedy, "we can no more stop the rise of Asia than we can stop the winter snows and the summer heat" (2001: 78). The other story, which receives mention only in distant, patchy ways, is one of major social crises in agriculture and urban poverty in the emerging countries.

The first section of this paper discusses the main trends in twenty-first century globalization by comparing trends during 1980-2000 and 2000-present in trade, finance, international institutions, hegemony and inequality and social struggle. I preface each trend report with a brief proposition. I don't discuss cultural changes in this treatment because they generally follow slower time lines than trends in political economy. In the second part I seek to understand what the new trends mean for the emerging twenty-first century international division of labor.

TRADE

GROWING EAST-SOUTH trade leads to a "new geography of trade" and new trade pacts.

Through the postwar period North-South trade relations were dominant. In recent years, East-South trade has been growing, driven by the rise of Asian economies and the accompanying commodities boom (particularly since 2003) and high petrol prices (since 2004). According to the UN Conference on Trade and Development, a "new geography of trade" is taking shape: "The new axis stretches from the manufacturing might and emerging middle classes of China, and from the software powerhouse of India in the south, to the mineral riches of South Africa, a beachhead to the rest of the African continent, and across the Indian and Pacific oceans to South America which is oil-rich and mineral- and agriculture-laden" (Whelan 2004).

Brazil opened new trade links with the Middle East and Asia. Chile and Peru are negotiating trade agreements with China (Weitzman 2005). "The Middle East has started looking to Asia for trade and expertise;" trade has expanded threefold in the past years and the fastest growing markets for oil are in China and India (Vatikiotis 2005). Growing Sino-Indian trade combines countries with 1.3 and 1.2 billion people each (Dawar 2005).

During 1980-2000, American led trade pacts such as NAFTA, APEC and the WTO played a dominant role. In the 2000s, these trade pacts are passé or in impasse. Dissatisfaction with NAFTA is commonplace. In Latin America, Mercosur, enlarged by Venezuela and with Cuba as associate member, undercuts the Free Trade Association of the Americas (FTAA). The association of Southeast Asian nations, ASEAN, in combination with Japan, South Korea and China (ASEAN+3) sidelines APEC, which is increasingly on the backburner, and reduces Asian dependence on the American market. As Michael Lind (2005) notes, "This group has the potential to be the world's largest trade bloc, dwarfing the European Union and North American Free Trade Association."

During 1980-2000, the overall trend was toward regional and global trade pacts. The G22 walkout in Cancún in November 2003 upped the ante in subsequent negotiations. Advanced countries that previously pushed trade liberalization now resist liberalizing trade and retreat to "economic patriotism." The United States has been zigzagging in relation to the WTO (with steel tariffs and agriculture and cotton subsidies). Given WTO gridlock in the Doha development round and blocked regional trade talks (the Cancún walkout was followed by the failure of the FTAA talks in Miami) the U.S. increasingly opts for FTAs, which further erode the WTO (Nederveen Pieterse 2004b).

Thus in North-South trade there has been a marked shift toward bilateral free trade agreements (FTAs). American terms in free trade agreements typically include cooperation in the war on terror, exempting American forces from the International Criminal Court, accepting genetically modified food, and preferential terms for American multinationals and financial institutions. FTAs include Chile, Colombia, Central America, Jordan, Morocco, Oman and Singapore and are under negotiation with South Korea, Thailand and Australia.

In South-South and East-South trade, however, the trend is toward regional and interregional combinations such as Mercosur and ASEAN. China has established a free trade zone with ASEAN. India may join ASEAN+3 in the future. Since 2003 there are talks to establish a free trade zone of Brazil, South Africa and India (IBSA).

The old "core-periphery" relations no longer hold. The South no longer looks North but sideways. South-South cooperation, heralded as an alternative to dependence on the West ever since the Bandung meeting of the Nonaligned Movement in 1955, is now taking shape. "Already 43 percent of the South's global trade is accounted for by intra-South trade" (Gosh 2006: 7).

The downside is that much of this is sparked by a commodities boom that will not last. Note for instance the rollercoaster experience of the Zambian copper belt (Ferguson 1999), which now experiences another upturn, spurred by Chinese investments, which will be as precarious as the previous one. Only countries that convert commodity surpluses into productive investments and "intellectual capital" will outlast the current commodities cycle.

FINANCE

THE CURRENT IMBALANCES in the world economy (American overconsumption and deficits and Asian surpluses) are unsustainable and are producing a gradual reorganization of global finance and trade.

During 1980-2000 finance capital played a central role in restructuring global capitalism. The return to hegemony of finance capital ranks as one of the defining features of neoliberal globalization (Duménil and Lévy 2001).

The role of speculative capital led to the diagnoses such as casino capitalism and Las Vegas capitalism. International finance capital has been crisis prone and financial crises hit Mexico, Asia, Russia, Argentina and Latin America. Attempts to reform the architecture of international finance have come to little more than one-sided pleas for transparency. The trend since 2000 is that NIEs hold vast foreign reserves to safeguard against financial turbulence: "the South holds more than $2 trillion as foreign exchange reserves" (Gosh 2006: 7). Emerging economies view financial markets as the next arena of strategic competition—beyond trade, resources, manufacturing and services.

During 1980-2000, the IMF was the hard taskmaster of developing economies; now year after year the IMF warns that U.S. deficits threaten global economic stability (Becker and Andrews 2004).

Through the postwar period the U.S. dollar led as the world reserve currency, but since 2001 there has been a gradual shift from the dollar to other currencies. In 2001-05 the dollar declined by 28 percent against euro and a further 12 percent in 2006. In 2002 the leading central banks held on average 73 percent world reserves in dollars, by 2005 this was 66 percent (Johnson 2005) and the trend for 2006 is towards 60 percent. China and Japan with 70 to 80 percent of their foreign reserves in U.S. dollars, reflecting their close ties to the American market, deviate markedly from the world average. Of China's $1.3 trillion in foreign reserves up to $1 trillion is in dollars. The current trend is for China to diversify its foreign reserves gradually towards 65 percent in dollars (McGregor 2006).

In the wake of the 1997 Asian crisis the IMF vetoed Japan's initiative for an Asian monetary fund. Since then Thailand's Chiang Mai Initiative established an Asian Bond Fund. Japan, China and South Korea—*if* they would be able to settle their differences— may develop a yen-yuan-won Asian reserve, or an "Asian dollar." Venezuela, backed by petrol funds, has withdrawn from the IMF and World Bank and proposes a Bank of the South.

Western financial markets have long been dominant, arguably since the seventeenth century. In the 2000s financial sources outside the West play an increasingly important role, reflecting the rise of Asia, the global commodities boom and high petrol prices. The accumulation of petro money during 2005-2007 is three times the annual Asian surpluses from exports (Magnus 2006). A new "east-east" financial network is emerging. China's initial public offerings are increasingly no longer routed via New York and London, but via Saudi Arabia (Timmons 2006). East Asian countries are active investors

Jan Nederveen Pieterse

in Latin America and Africa. Thirty seven percent of FDI in developing countries now comes from other developing countries. China emerges as a new lender to developing countries, at lower rates and without the conditions of the Washington institutions (Parker and Beattie 2006). China's foreign aid competes with Western donors. Venezuela plays this role in Latin America.

Financial instability also affects institutions in the West, such as the collapse of LTCM in 1998, the Enron episode along with WorldCom, HealthSouth and other corporations in 2001, Parmalat in 2003, the Amaranth fund in 2006 and mortgage lenders in 2007. New financial instruments such as derivatives and options are increasingly opaque and out-of-control. Hedge funds have become more active international players than investment banks. In 2006 there are 10,000 hedge funds with $1.5 trillion in assets, the daily global turnover in derivatives is $6 trillion and the credit derivative market is worth $26 trillion. Financialization has increased the risk of financial instability (Glyn 2006).

In the Davos meetings of the World Economic Forum the American economy and the unstable dollar have been a major cause of concern. U.S. treasury debt at $7.6 trillion and net external debt at $4 trillion add up to an annual borrowing need of $1 trillion, or 10 percent of GDP (Buckler 2005) and interest payments of $300 billion a year and rising. The United States is deeply in the red to Asian central banks and relies on inflows of Asian capital and recycled oil dollars, and "what flows in could just as easily flow out" (Williams 2004). The dollar is now upheld more by fear of turbulence than by appeal.

For all these changes, the net financial drain from the global South is still ongoing. Poorer nations sustain American overconsumption and the overvalued dollar. The business press describes the world economy as a giant Ponzi scheme with massive debt that is sustained by vendor financing and dollar surpluses in China, Japan and East Asia. A tipping point is, however, that the financialization of economies (or the growing preponderance of financial instruments) and the hegemony of finance capital, the keynote of the nineties, backfires when finance follows the new money.

INSTITUTIONS

THE 1990s ARCHITECTURE of globalization is now fragile and the clout of emerging economies is growing.

The 1990s institutional architecture of globalization, built around the convergence of the IMF, World Bank and WTO, is increasingly fragile. Since its handling of the Asian crisis in 1997-98 and the Argentina crisis of 2001, the IMF has been nicknamed the "master of disaster." Argentina, Brazil, Venezuela, South Africa, Russia and other countries have repaid their debt to the IMF early, so the IMF has less financial leverage, also in view of the new flows of petro money. IMF lending is down from $70 billion in 2003 to $20 billion in 2006. The IMF has adopted marginal reforms (it now accepts capital controls and has increased the vote quota of four emerging economies) but faces financial constraints.

The World Bank has lost standing as well. In the 1990s the Bank shifted gear from neoliberalism to social liberalism and structural adjustment "with a human face" and an emphasis on poverty reduction. But the poverty reduction targets of the Bank and the

Millennium Development Goals are, as usual, not being met. Paul Wolfowitz's attempts as World Bank president to merge neoliberalism and neoconservatism have been counterproductive. Wolfowitz's anti-corruption campaign and focus on Iraq have been internally divisive.

The infrastructure of power has changed as well. The "Wall Street-Treasury-IMF complex" of the nineties has weakened because in the Bush II administration the Treasury played a weak and minor role (until Hank Paulson's appointment in 2006 which brought Wall Street back into the cockpit).

The 1990s architecture of globalization is now fragile for several reasons. The disciplinary regime of the Washington consensus is slipping away. Structural adjustment has shown a consistently high failure rate with casualties in sub-Saharan Africa, most of Latin America, and the 1997 Asian crisis and how it was handled by the IMF. Research indicates a correlation between IMF and World Bank involvement and negative economic performance, arguably for political reasons: since IMF involvement signals economic troubles, it attracts further troubles (McKenna 2005). Zigzag behavior by the hegemon—flaunting WTO rules, demonstrating lack of fiscal discipline and building a massive deficit—has further weakened the international institutions. Following the spate of financial crises in the nineties, crisis mismanagement and growing U.S. deficits, the macroeconomic dogmas of the Washington consensus have given way to a post-Washington no-consensus. Meanwhile increasing pressure from the global South is backed by greater economic weight and bargaining power.

HEGEMONY

RATHER THAN HEGEMONIC rivalry what is taking place is global repositioning and realignments toward growing multipolarity.

In general terms, the main possibilities in relation to hegemony are continued American hegemony, hegemonic rivalry, hegemonic transition, or multipolarity. The previous episode of hegemonic decline at the turn of the nineteenth century took the form of wars of hegemonic rivalry culminating in hegemonic transition. But the current transition looks to be structurally different from previous episodes. Economic and technological interdependence and cultural interplay are now far greater than at the *fin de siècle*. What is emerging is not just a decline of (American) hegemony and rise of (Asian) hegemony but a more complex multipolar field.

During the 1990s American hegemony was solvent, showed high growth and seemed to be dynamic. The United States followed a mixed uni-multipolar approach with cooperative security (as in the Gulf War) and humanitarian intervention (as in Bosnia, Kosovo and Kurdistan) as Leitmotivs. In brief, unilateralism with a multilateral face during the 1990s gave way to unilateralism with a unilateral face under the G. W. Bush administration (Nederveen Pieterse 2004a), a high risk approach that shows several weaknesses. By opting for unilateral "preventive war" the Bush II administration abandoned international law. The U.S. is now caught up in the new wars, particularly its "war of choice" in Iraq. In going to war in Iraq the U.S. overplayed its hand. After declaring an "axis of evil," the U.S. has few tools left in relation to Iran and North Korea.

The U.S. has been forced to give up its access to a base in Uzbekistan. In its first out-of-area operation in Afghanistan, NATO meets fierce resistance.

During the cold war, Muslims were cultivated as allies and partners on many fronts. Thus in the 1980s Ronald Reagan lauded the Mujahideen allies in the Afghan war as "the moral equivalent of our founding fathers." As the cold war waned these allies were sidelined. Samuel Huntington's "clash of civilizations" article in 1993 signaled a major turn by targeting the Islamic world (in fact, he warned against a Confucian-Islamic alliance and specifically referred to military cooperation between China and Pakistan). Thus erstwhile allies and partners were redefined as enemies and yesterday's freedom fighters were reclassified as today's terrorists.

In response to this policy shift and the continuing Israeli and American politics of tension in the Middle East, a militant Muslim backlash took shape of which the attacks of 9/11 2001 are a part. The cold war "green belt" and "arc of crisis" has become an "arc of extremism" with flashpoints in the Middle East and Central Asia. Satellite TV channels in the Arab world contribute to awareness among Muslims. Muslim organizations increasingly demonstrate high militancy and swift responses, for instance to the Danish cartoons and statements by Pope Benedict. The Lebanon war in 2006 has shown Israel's weakness and Hezbollah's strength as part of a regional realignment away from the American supported Sunni governments to Iran, Syria and Shiites.

New security axes and poles have emerged, notably the Shanghai Cooperation Organization (deemed a "counterweight to NATO") and the cooperation of China, Russia and Iran. Other emerging poles of influence are India, Brazil, Venezuela and South Africa.[1] The G77 makes its influence felt in international trade and diplomacy. For instance, it has blocked intervention in Darfur on the grounds of state sovereignty, in a strategic part of the world, and besides the sovereignty of an Islamic government, in part as a response to American expansion in the Middle East and Central Asia. China has generally backed G77 positions in UN Security Council negotiations (Traub 2006), a position that is now gradually changing.

On the military frontiers of hegemony, the United States spends 48 percent of world military spending (in 2005) and maintains a formidable "empire of bases." But the wars in Iraq and Afghanistan demonstrate the limits of American military power. As a traditional maritime and air power, the United States cannot win ground wars (Reifer 2005). On the economic front, the U.S. is import dependent and "Brand America" has lost points. Not only are U.S. levels of debt high, but manufacturing capacity is eroded, there are no reserves and the savings rate turned negative for the first time in 2005, so an adjustment seems inevitable. The aura of American power is fading too. Rising anti-Americanism affects the status of American products and American pop culture is no longer the edge of cool. An advertising executive notes growing resentment of American-led globalization.

> We know that in [the] Group of 8 countries, 18 percent of the population claim they are avoiding American brands, with the top brand being Marlboro in terms of

---

[1] In the background alternative options emerge, such as a comeback of the idea of a strategic triangle of China, Russia and India, which goes back to 1998 (Titarenko 2004).

avoidance. Barbie is another one. McDonald's is another. There is a cooling towards American culture generally across the globe. (Holstein 2005).

The main tipping points in relation to American hegemony are domestic and external. Domestic tipping points are the inflated housing market and credit card debt. If rising interest rates are necessary to sustain external borrowing, it will increase the pressure on domestic debt. If interest rates remain low, it will increase pressure on U.S. external borrowing. The external tipping points are fading dollar loyalty, financial markets following new money, the strategic debacles in Iraq and the Middle East, and the growing American legitimacy crisis.

There are generally three different responses to American hegemony. The fist is *continued support* — for a variety of reasons such as the appeal of the U.S. market, the role of the dollar, reliance on the American military umbrella, and lingering hope in the possibility of American self correction. The second is *soft balancing* — ranging from tacit non-cooperation (such as most European countries staying out of the Iraq war and declining genetically modified food) to establishing alternative institutions (such as the Kyoto Protocol and the International Criminal Court). And the third is *hard balancing* — only few countries can afford this, either because they have been branded as enemies of the U.S. already so they have nothing to lose (Iran, North Korea, Cuba, Venezuela), or because their bargaining power allows them maneuvering room (as in the case of China and the SCO).

An intriguing trend is that the number of countries that *combine* these different responses to American hegemony in different spheres is increasing. Thus China displays all three responses in different spheres — economic cooperation (WTO), non-cooperation in diplomacy (UN Security Council) and overt resistance in Central Asia (Wolfe 2005) and in relation to Iran.

American unilateralism and preventive war are gradually giving way to multipolarity if only because unilateralism is becoming too costly, militarily, politically and economically. New clusters and alignments are gradually taking shape around trade, energy and security. Sprawling and cross-zone global realignments point to growing multipolarity rather than hegemonic rivalry.

INEQUALITY AND STRUGGLE

THE FLASHPOINTS OF GLOBAL inequality are rural crises and urban poverty in emerging economies, chronic poverty in the least developed countries, and international migration.

Let us review these trends in a wider time frame. Postwar capitalism from 1950 to the 1970s combined growth and equity. Although overall North-South inequality widened, economic growth went together with growing equality among and in countries. Neoliberal "free market" economies during 1980-2000 produced a sharp trend break: now economic growth came with sharply increasing inequality within and among countries. The main exceptions to the trend were the East Asian tiger economies.

The trend in the 2000s is that overall inequality between advanced economies and emerging economies is narrowing while inequality in emerging societies is increasing. The pattern of rising inequality in neoliberal economies (the U.S. and to a significant degree the UK and New Zealand) continues and has begun to extend to Japan, South

Korea and Australia. International migration has become a major flashpoint of global inequality and produces growing conflicts and dilemmas around migration in many countries. Overall global inequality is staggering with 1 percent of the world population now owning 40 percent of the world's assets.

James Rosenau offers an optimistic assessment of global trends according to which rising human development indices, urbanization and growing social and communication densities are producing a general "skills revolution" (1999). However, the flipside of technological change and knowledge economies is that with rising skill levels come widening skills differentials and urban-rural disparities. The second general cause of growing inequality is unrestrained market forces, promoted by multinational corporations, international institutions and business media. Familiar short hands are *Wal-Mart capitalism* (low wages, low benefits and temp workers), *Las Vegas capitalism* (speculative capital) and *shareholder capitalism* (in contrast to stakeholder capitalism). The third general cause of inequality that affects developing countries are fast growth policies that reflect middle class and urban bias and aggravate rich-poor and urban-rural gaps.

Practically all emerging economies face major rural and agricultural crisis. In China this takes the form of pressure on land, deepening rural poverty, pollution, village-level corruption and urban migration. In Brazil and the Philippines, land reform drags because there is too weak a political coalition to confront landholding oligarchies. In South Africa, the apartheid legacy and the poor soil and weak agricultural base in the former Bantustans contribute to rural crisis.

This is a classic problem of modernization. In the past, failure to bring the peasant hinterland into modernity gave rise to fascism. A major failing of communism in Russia was the collectivization of agriculture. Emerging economies need balanced development and "walking on two legs," yet urban bias (low agriculture prices, inadequate support for agriculture) and the intrusion of transnational market forces in agriculture (land appropriations, multinational agribusiness) are crisis prone.

The impact of poor peoples' movements and social struggles during the 2000s is greater than during 1980-2000, notably in China and Latin America. In China where "a social protest erupts every five minutes," the social crisis is widely recognized and has led to the "harmonious society" policies adopted in 2005. In Latin America, poor peoples' movements have contributed to the election of leftwing governments in Venezuela, Bolivia, Ecuador and Nicaragua and to policy adjustments in Argentina and Chile.

The "Shanghai model" of fast growth policies that are geared to attract foreign investment has been abandoned in China, but is being pursued with fervor in India. What is the relationship between the India of Tom Friedman (*The world is flat*) and P. Sainath (*Everybody loves a good drought*), between celebrating growth and deepening poverty, between Gurgaon's Millennium City of Malls and abject poverty kilometers away, between dynamic "Cyberabad" and rising farmer suicides nearby in the same state of Andhra Pradesh? According to official figures, 100,248 farmers committed suicide between 1993 and 2003. Armed Maoist struggles have spread to 170 rural districts, affecting 16 states and 43 percent of the country's territory (Johnson 2006).

> For every swank mall that will spring up in a booming Indian city, a neglected village will explode in Naxalite rage; for every child who will take wings to study in a

foreign university there will be 10 who fall off the map without even the raft of a basic alphabet to keep them afloat; for every new Italian eatery that will serve up fettuccine there will be a debt-ridden farmer hanging himself and his hopes by a rope. (Tejpal 2006)

India's economic growth benefits a top stratum of 4 percent in the urban areas with little or negative spin off for 80 percent of the population in the countryside. The software sector rewards the well educated middle class. The IT sector has an upper caste aura—brainy, requiring good education, English language—and continues upper caste privileges, now in the knowledge economy, with low cost services from the majority population in the informal sector. Public awareness is split between middle class hype and recognition of social problems, but there are no major policies in place to address the problems of rural majorities and the urban poor.

In addition to rural crisis, the emerging powers face profound urban poverty, creating a "planet of slums" (Davis 2005). The rural crisis feeds into the world of the favelas, bidonvilles, shanty towns and shacks. Urban policies are at best ambivalent to the poor and often negligent. For instance, Bangkok's monorail mass transit system connects shopping areas, but not the outlying suburbs. A trend in India is that in a scissor operation the rural poor are driven out of agriculture so they flock to the cities, while the urban poor are being squeezed out of the cities by land appropriations and clampdowns on illegal settlements, vagrancy and hawking and illegal stores, so the poor have nowhere to go.

TRENDS IN TWENTY-FIRST CENTURY GLOBALIZATION

IS THE CUSP OF the millennium, 1980-2000 and 2000-present, a significant enough period to monitor significant changes in globalization? Why, in a short period of decades, would be there significant trend breaks? My argument is essentially that two projects that defined the 1980-2000 period, American hegemony and neoliberalism—themselves the culminating expressions of longer trends—are now over their peak. They are not gone from the stage, but they gather no new adherents and face mounting problems (indebtedness, military overstretch, rising inequality, legitimacy crises), and new forces are rising. The new forces stand in an ambiguous relationship to neoliberalism and American hegemony.

In sum, the overall picture shows distinct new trends in trade, institutions, finance and hegemony. Table 1 reviews the main trends in current globalization. The trend break with the old patterns is undeniable, but it is too early to speak of a new pattern. We can also reflect on these changes in a longer time frame. According to the thesis of Oriental globalization (Hobson 2005, Nederveen Pieterse 2006), early globalization was centered in the Middle East (500-1100 CE) and between 1100 and 1800 was centered in China, India and Southeast Asia. Now, as a Shanghai economist remarks, after "a few hundred bad years" (Prestowitz 2005) China and India are back as the world's leading manufacturing center and information processing center.

Table 1: Trends in Twenty-First Century Globalization

Pattern 1990s	Pattern 2000s
Trade	
North-South trade dominates	Growing East-South trade
US-led trade pacts dominate	FTAA, APEC, WTO: passé or in impasse
Trend to regional/global trade pacts	Shift to bilateral FTAs (in North-South trade)
Finance	
Finance capital leads, crisis prone	Emerging economies hold dollar surpluses
IMF and World Bank discipline developing economies	IMF warns US its policies threaten economic stability
US dollar leads	Decline of dollar as world reserve currency
US top destination of FDI	China top destination of FDI
IMF blocks Asian monetary fund	Thai Asian Bond Fund; Bank of the South
Western financial markets dominate	New financial flows outside the West
Investment banks	Hedge funds, new financial instrument
Institutions	
Convergence IMF-WB-WTO	IMF lending down ($70bn 2003, $20bn 2006)
Social liberalism, poverty reduction	World Bank lost standing
'Wall Street-Treasury-IMF complex'	Weak Treasury
Washington consensus	(Post)Washington no-consensus
Hegemony	
US hegemony solvent and dynamic	US in deficit and cornered in new wars
'Clash of civilizations'	Muslim backlash
US led security	New security axes and poles
Inequality	
Growth & increasing inequality (except East Asia)	Inequality between North and NIEs decreases
Deepening rural and urban poverty	while inequality in NIEs increases
	Deepening rural and urban poverty
	International migration as flashpoint of global inequality

Thus in a historical sense twenty-first century globalization is reverting to normal, considering that Asia has been at the center of the world economy through most of long-term globalization. In this light, two hundred years of western hegemony have been a historical interlude.

Note, for instance, that it is not the first time that China is in the position of having accumulated the lion's share of the world's financial reserves. During "several periods of rapid growth in international commerce — from A.D. 600 to 750, from 1000 to 1300 and from 1500 to 1800 — China again tended to run very large trade surpluses." Between 1500 and 1800 China accumulated most of the world's silver and gold (Bradsher 2006, Frank 1998). So it is not the first time in history that China faces the "trillion dollar question" of holding the world's largest financial surplus.

Now however, Asia resumes its normal role in a world that is shaped and imprinted by two hundred years of western hegemony — in politics, military affairs, corporate networks, intellectual property rights and patents, institutions, styles and images. Asia makes its comeback in a world that, unlike in 1800, is deeply interconnected socially, politically and culturally, a world that is undergoing rapid technological change, more rapid than in 1800.

The West followed Asia and transcended it by introducing new modes of production (industrialism, mass production, Fordism), and now Asia follows the West and transcends it, and the question is which of the modes of production and regulation it has introduced (Japan pioneered flexible accumulation, East Asian development states, the Beijing consensus) will prove to be sustainable.

TOWARDS THE TWENTY-FIRST CENTURY
INTERNATIONAL DIVISION OF LABOR

IN CLOSING I REFLECT on the relations between advanced and emerging economies, particularly between the United States and East Asia, and on trends in emerging economies. Together these make up notes towards the twenty-first century international division of labor in the making.

A sketch of relations between advanced economies and emerging economies includes that manufacturing and service jobs lost in the U.S. lead to rising wages in East and South Asia. In the U.S. productivity has risen and corporate profits are up, but wages have been stagnant since the 1970s (with a brief upward blip in the late 1990s). Corporate profits, the Dow Jones and CEO remuneration are up because American corporations reap high yields from offshoring—rather than investing inward and innovating, as in Germany, the EU and emerging economies. Cheap Asian imports compensate for stagnant wages in the U.S., but over time the emerging skills squeeze and gradually rising wages in emerging economies will raise the cost of imports and will make offshoring marginally less attractive. At the same time, lagging inward investment and innovation undermine the competitiveness of American products. Financial services are the largest sector in the U.S. service economy, but, as mentioned earlier, finance follows the new money. Asian vendor financing will continue until alternative markets emerge—domestic and regional markets in Asia and new markets in east-south trade and trade with the euro zone.

Table 2 presents a working sketch of the uneven relations between American and East Asian economies including China. These relations are unstable for American trade and current account deficits cannot continue to rise indefinitely. Tipping points include the weak dollar, the eventual limits to American purchasing power (in view of stagnant wages) and the development of alternative markets for Asian products.

Table 2: Relations between United States and East Asian economies

UNITED STATES	EAST ASIA
Decline manufacturing	Rise manufacturing
Import oriented deindustrialization	Export oriented industrialization
Rising productivity, stagnant wages	Rising productivity, rising wages
Reduction in R&D and education	Technological upgrading, innovation
No national economic strategy	National economic strategies
Trade and external deficits	Trade and financial surplus
Shrinking middle class	Growing middle class
High concentration of income, rising inequality	Relatively egalitarian, rising inequality
Bilateral free trade agreements	Regional trade combinations

Twenty-first century globalization is both enabled by and transcends neoliberal globalization. Arguably twenty-first century globalization shows the frailty of neoliberal economies and the resilience of mixed economies. In the nineties economic growth was most rapid in the U.S. and East Asian exporting countries. For some time growth has been faster in the global South than in the North and most rapid in Asia and emerging economies. Growth has been moderate in the EU and Japan and medium in the U.S., but burdened by mounting debt.

As the advanced countries are undergoing a transition from industrial to post-industrial service economies, the countries best placed to make this transition without deepening social inequality and social pathologies are the social market economies with substantial public investments in education, health care, social services and ecological innovation.

If we look at the world as a whole, the majority economic form is the mixed economy with the social market in the EU, bureaucratically coordinated market economies (Japan) and developmental states (with different leanings in Asia, Latin America and Africa). In addition, on balance mixed economies are doing better and several are more sustainable, also in terms of energy use.

It has become difficult to uphold American capitalism as the norm because it relies on cheap Asian imports and Asian vendor financing.

> The calls for structural reform in Japan and Europe stem from the belief that the Americans and the other 'Anglo-Saxon' economies have the sort of flexibility that breeds success. Yet that hardly squares with the IMF's notion that the U.S. economy could be going down the pan at any moment (Elliott 2005).

Thus neoliberalism was dominant in 1980-2000 and now mixed economies are the majority accumulation regime, but matters aren't that straightforward.

To begin with this discussion takes place in a battlefield of paradigms, an arena in which few statistics, diagnoses and policies are ideologically neutral. Economic success and failure don't come with radio silence but are immersed in ideological noise and filtered through representations. Thus the World Bank claimed the "East Asian miracle" as evidence of the wisdom of its policies of liberalization and export-led growth, whereas according to Japan it showed the virtues of capable government intervention (Wade 1996). According to Alan Greenspan, the Asian crisis of 1997 demonstrated that Anglo-American capitalism was the only viable economic model. Most others have drawn the opposite conclusion that American led finance capital is crisis prone, and this has been one of the spurs of the turn of the millennium trend break in globalization patterns.

If the Washington institutions have lost clout, the knowledge grid of financial markets remains intact with ideological ratings such as the Economic Freedom Index and Competitiveness Index. Business media (such as the *Wall Street Journal* and the *Economist*) and the media big six (such as Time Warner and Rupert Murdoch's conglomerate) echo the ideological impression management of conservative think tanks and corporate interests. In the game of perceptions, western media reports often blame social unrest in emerging societies on state authoritarianism (and emphasize "human rights"), pro-market economists lay the blame on government corruption and inefficiency, whereas state and social forces focus on capitalist excesses (and local government incompetence). International institutions and free trade agreements, multinationals, financial markets and World Bank economists weigh in on the debates. Thus neoliberalism remains a prevailing adapt-or-die logic whose influence is transmitted via financial markets, international institutions and free trade agreements.

In relation to trends in emerging economies I focus on the twin themes of neoliberalism and social inequality. Does the rise of China, India and other emerging economies validate or invalidate neoliberalism?

According to American conventional wisdom and authors like Thomas Friedman (2005), China's economic rise follows Deng's four modernizations and the subsequent liberalization, and India's economic rise dates from its 1991 liberalization. These views are ideology rather than research based because research indicates different itineraries. Rodrik's (2004) work on the "Hindu rate of growth" argues that the foundations of India's economic resurgence were laid during the 1970s and 1980s. Recent studies of China break the mold of Mao stigmatization and find that improvements in industrial production, rural modernization, literacy and health care during Mao's time laid the groundwork for the post-1978 transformation (Gittings 2005, Guthrie 2006).

Liberalization and export orientation—the Washington consensus and World Bank formula—have contributed to the rise of Asia. American offshoring and outsourcing and exports to the U.S. have spurred rapid growth (thus Wal-Mart's imports alone represent 15 percent of the U.S. trade deficit with China; Prestowitz 2005: 68). But this would not have been possible or produced sustainable growth without Asia's developmental states. Their development policies enable Asian societies and producers to upgrade technologically and to foster domestic, regional and alternative markets. China's spending on high tech research and development now ranks third after the United States and Japan.

If we consider the cultural politics of neoliberalism, emerging economies surely match neoliberal trends. Middle class consumerism with its attendant features—such as marketing, commercial media, malls and shopping culture—is a leading trend throughout in all emerging societies. A headline reads "Developing countries underpin boom in advertising spending": "Advertising spending is soaring in the developing world, suggesting that U.S.-style consumerism is alive and well from Brazil and Russia to Saudi Arabia and Indonesia" (Silverman 2005).

If we consider economic doctrine, market fundamentalism is widely rejected. If we focus on neoliberal economics, the picture is less clear. If neoliberalism refers to monetarism and fiscal conservatism (which is contentious), many developing countries are *more* neoliberal than the United States' fiscal profligacy. Monetarism and fiscal conservatism aim to counteract inflation and avoid a deficit and the risk of financial turbulence.

Emerging societies must strike a cautious balance. While throughout the global South it is a cliché that neoliberalism doesn't work, the international financial markets continue business as usual, so for developing countries diplomacy is in order. Deficit countries cannot afford to offend the hegemonic institutions and credit regimes. Most countries must walk the tightrope and remain on reasonably good terms with financial markets and credit rating agencies lest their cost of borrowing and doing business goes up.

These are different reasons than during the nineties. Then the main considerations were debt and dependence on the Washington institutions, which now applies to fewer countries, and a default belief in free market policies as the most dynamic, pro-growth form of regulation, which has lost adherents since the crises of the nineties and economic disarray in the United States. If American deficits are crisis prone and inequality in the U.S. is growing sharply, why follow this model? Now emerging economies follow neoliberal policies (in the sense of fiscal conservatism) to *escape* from neoliberalism (in the sense of the vagaries of the "free market").

If neoliberalism refers to high-exploitation capitalism, again the picture is mixed. It does not generally apply to the tiger economies, South Korea, Taiwan or Singapore, at least in the sense that they have sizeable public sectors. It does apply to China and India. In China migrants from the impoverished countryside have been an essential component in the razor sharp "China price." In India the low wage rural economy and the urban poor support the modern sector with cheap labor, services and produce.

Thus inequality has not been a just so circumstance or a minor quirk en route to development, but a fundamental factor in production and in establishing the international competitiveness of several emerging economies. In China this has begun to change since the adoption of the "harmonious society" policy in 2005. In India high-exploitation capitalism, buttressed by caste particularly in the countryside, continues unabated without major changes in government policy.

"Beating them at their own game" and using market forces to develop while keeping one's identity is a difficult balancing act for competitiveness means conforming to business standards in which, so far, neoliberalism remains a default policy and which rework existing structures of inequality such as caste or ethnicity. Besides, domestic politics weigh in, such as "governability" in Brazil where the PT governs with a slim margin and must make coalitions with conservative parties in parliament.

Of the two big stories of twenty-first century globalization, the gradual East-South turn is widely recognized, but the deepening rural and urban poverty in emerging societies is not. Business media and pro-market economists engage in emerging markets boosterism. But the key challenge for emerging societies is to take the peasantry and the urban poor along. Discussions in emerging societies are about rehabilitating and renewing the developmental state (where it has been away), but not an authoritarian development state but one that is democratic, inclusive and innovative.

Throughout the world, in a "structure of common differences," interests affiliated with state, market or society interests shape policy debates (for instance in China see Kang 1998, Hui 2003, Xin 2003, Mittelman 2006). This "structure of common differences" is crosscut by the varieties of capitalism and the transnational interaction of capitalisms (often referred to as "globalization"). Varieties of capitalism are different ways of distributing risk and different ways of understanding and negotiating inequality, evolving from historical and cultural legacies, such as caste and communalism in India and race in South Africa and Brazil.

The East-South turn introduces a different interaction of capitalisms. China as workshop of the world competes with other developing countries; not just the United States, Europe and Japan see manufacturing jobs go to China but so do Mexico, Kenya and Bangladesh. Thus garment workers from Bangladesh to South Africa are under pressure from Chinese textile exports. In 2005 trade unions in Africa issued a call for action against China, noting "250,000 jobs lost in African clothing, textile and leather industries."[2]

An emerging debate in China—which is not nearly as well developed as the harmonious society—concerns the "harmonious world" or the idea that China's rise should not come at the expense of other developing countries and the world's poor. This is new on the agenda of the "Beijing consensus" and is yet to take shape and find a balance with China's other priorities.

Alternatives that had been sidelined during the epoch of neoliberal hegemony have taken on new legitimacy and influence since the turn of the millennium. The Beijing consensus and the Bolivarian alternative (ALBA) are emerging alternatives in Asia and Latin America. The Beijing consensus is "a model for global development that is attracting adherents at almost the same speed that the US model is repelling them" (Ramo 2004). Countries that are financially independent and have relative maneuvering room such as China because of its size and Venezuela because of its oil wealth are in a strong position to articulate alternatives to neoliberalism. The social market and human development have come back on the agenda. Global emancipation involves a wide equation and hinges on rebalancing the big three of state, market and society and introducing social cohesion and sustainability into the growth equation. This means that each component changes: the state becomes a civic state, the market a social market, and growth turns green.

NOTE

Different versions of this paper have been presented at several institutions in fall 2006: Korean Sociological Association conference on Global Futures and the New Asia, Seoul; Chulalongkorn University (Bangkok); Yunnan University (Kunming), and the Chinese Academy of Social Sciences (Beijing); the Globalism Institute, Royal Melbourne Institute of Technology; and Jawaharlal Nehru University (New Delhi). I am indebted to participants' feedback and the advice of many colleagues.

REFERENCES

Agtmael, Antoine van. 2007. *The emerging markets century*. New York: Free Press.

Becker, E. and E. L. Andrews. 2004. "IMF Says Rise in U.S. Debts is Threat to World Economy," *New York Times*, August 1.

Bradsher, Keith. 2006. "From the Silk Road to the Superhighway, All Coin Leads to China," *New York Times*, February 26: WK4.

Buckler, William A. M. 2005. "Global report," *The Privateer*, 518, January: 1-12.

Davis, Mike. 2006. *Planet of slums*. London, Verso

Dawar, Niraj. 2005. "Prepare Now for a Sino-Indian Trade Boom," *Financial Times*, October 31: 11.

Duménil, G., and D. Lévy. 2001. "Costs and Benefits of Neoliberalism: A Class Analysis," *Review of International Political Economy* 8, 4: 578-607.

Elliott, Larry. 2005. "America's Tricky Balancing Act," *Guardian Weekly*, October 7-13: 16.

Ferguson, James. 1999. *Expectations of modernity*. Berkeley: University of California Press.

Ford, Glyn. 2005. "Forging an Alternative to U.S. Hegemony," *The Japan Times*, February 7.

Frank, A. G. 1998. *Re Orient: Global Economy in the Asian Age*. Berkeley: University of California Press.

Friedman, Thomas L. 2005. *The World is Flat*. New York: Farrar Straus and Giroux.

Gittings, John. 2005. *The Changing Face of China: From Mao to Market*. Oxford: Oxford University Press.

Glyn, Andrew. 2006. "Finance's Relentless Rise Threatens Economic Stability," *Financial Times*, April 27: 13.

Gosh, Parthya S. 2006. "Beyond the Rhetoric," *Frontline*, October 6: 7-9.

Guthrie, Doug. 2006. *China and Globalization: The Social, Economic and Political Transformation of Chinese Society*. New York: Routledge.

Hobson, John M. 2004. *The Eastern Origins of Western Civilisation*. Cambridge: Cambridge University Press.

Holstein, William J. 2005. "Erasing the Image of the Ugly American," *New York Times*, October 23: B9.

Hui, Wang. 2003. "The 1989 Movement and the Historical Origins of Neo-Liberalism in China." Pp. 211-223, in Chi and Pin (eds.), *China Reflected*, special issue *Asian Exchange*, 18, 2 and 19, 1.

Johnson, Jo. 2006. "Insurgency in India—How the Maoist Threat Reaches beyond Nepal," *Financial Times*, April 26: 13.

Johnson, Steve. 2005. "Indian and Chinese Banks Pulling Out of Ailing U.S. Dollar," *Financial Times*, March 7.

Kang, Liu. 1998. "Is There an Alternative to (Capitalist) Globalization? The Debate about Modernity in China." Pp. 164-188, in F. Jameson and M. Miyoshi (eds.), *The Cultures of Globalization*. Durham, NC: Duke University Press.

Kennedy, Paul. 2001. "Maintaining American Power: From Injury to Recovery." Pp. 53-80, in S. Talbott and N. Chanda (eds.), *The Age of Terror: America and the World After September 11*. New York: Basic Books.

Lind, Michael. 2005. "How the U.S. Became the World's Dispensable Nation," *Financial Times*, January 26.

Magnus, G. 2006. "The New Reserves of Economic Power," *Financial Times*, August 22: 11.

Marber, Peter. 1998. *From Third World to World Class: The Future of Emerging Markets in the Global Economy*. Reading, MA: Perseus.

McGregor, Richard. 2006. "Pressure Mounts on China Forex Management," *Financial Times*, November 28: 6.

McKenna, Barrie. 2005. "With Friends Like the IMF and the World Bank, Who Needs Loans," *The Globe and Mail*, August 16: B11.

Mearsheimer, John, and Stephen Walt. 2006. "The Israel Lobby," *London Review of Books*, March 23, 3-12.

Mittelman, James H. 2006. "Globalization and Development: Learning from Debates in China," *Globalizations* 3, 3: 377-392.

Nederveen Pieterse, Jan. 2004a. *Globalization or Empire?* New York. Routledge.

_____. 2004b. "Towards Global Democratization: To WTO or Not to WTO? *Development and Change* 35, 5: 1057-1063.

_____. 2006 "Oriental Globalization: Past and Present." Pp. 61-73, in G. Delanty (ed.), *Europe and Asia Beyond East and West: Towards a New Cosmopolitanism*. London: Routledge.

Parker, G., and A. Beattie. 2006. "Chinese Lenders 'undercutting' on Africa Loans, *Financial Times*, November 29: 3.

Peel, Quentin. 2005. "The South's Rise is Hindered at Home," *Financial Times*, November 17: 17.

Petras, James. 2006. *The Power of Israel in the United States*. Atlanta, GA: Clarity Press.

Prestowitz, Clyde. 2005. *Three Billion New Capitalists: The Great Shift of Wealth and Power to the East*. New York: Basic Books.

Ramo, Joshua Cooper. 2004. *The Beijing Consensus*. London: Foreign Policy Centre.

Reifer, T. E. 2005. "Globalization, Democratization, and Global Elite Formation in Hegemonic Cycles: A Geopolitical Economy." Pp. 183-203, in J. Friedman and C. Chase-Dunn (eds.), *Hegemonic Declines: Past and Present*. Boulder, CO: Paradigm.

Rodrik, Dani. 2000. "How Far Will International Economic Integration Go?" *The Journal of Economic Perspectives* 14, 1: 177-186.

_____. 2004. "Globalization and Growth: Looking in the Wrong Places," *Journal of Policy Modeling* 26: 513-517.

Rosenau, J. N. 1999. "The Future of Politics," *Futures* 31, 9-10: 1005-1016.

Sainath, P. 1996. *Everybody Loves a Good Drought*. New Delhi: Penguin.

Tejpal, Tarun J. 2006. "India's Future, Beyond Dogma," *Tehelka, The People's Paper*, 25 November: 3.

Timmons, H. 2006. "Asia Finding Rich Partners in Middle East," *New York Times*, December 1: C1-5.

Titarenko, Mikhail 2004 Russia, China and India: context for interaction, *World Affairs*, 8, 4: 22-33

Traub, J. 2006. "The World According to China," *New York Times Magazine*, September 3: 24-29.

Vatikiotis, Michael. 2005. "Why the Middle East is Turning to Asia," *International Herald Tribune*, June 24.

Wade, R. 1996. "Japan, the World Bank and the Art of Paradigm Maintenance: The East Asian Miracle in Political Perspective'" *New Left Review* 217: 336.

Weitzman, Hal. 2005. "Peru Takes Faltering Steps in Bid to Win China Prize," *Financial Times*, May 30.

Whelan, Caroline. 2004. "Developing Countries' Economic Clout Grows," *International Herald Tribune*, July 10-11: 15.

Williams, Ian. 2004. "The Real National Security Threat: The Bush Economy," *AlterNet*, January 13.

Wolfe, Adam. 2005. "The 'Great Game' Heats Up in Central Asia," *Power and Interest News Report*, August 3.

Xin, Chen. 2003. "New Development of Consumerism in Chinese Society in the Late 1990s." Pp. 162-175, in Lau Kin Chi and Huang Pin (eds.), *China Reflected, Asian Exchange*, 18, 2 and 19, 1.

❦ ❦ ❦ ❦ ❧ ❧ ❧ ❧

A COMMENT ON "NEW TRENDS IN GLOBALIZATION"

Ron Westrum

Eastern Michigan University

*T*HIS IS A VERY interesting essay, though I believe particular parts of it could be questioned. The most important point to question is the use of "manufacturing share" of the American economy as an index of productivity. We are increasingly moving toward a knowledge economy (Stewart and Stewart 1997; Edvinsson and Malone 1997). Even if the manufacturing sector in the United States is shrinking, this may be a sign of health. Many American products are intangible and might be considered more as "information" or "knowledge" products rather than physical things. As the knowledge economy advances, one of the key trends in globalization will become the degree to which economies are knowledge-oriented versus manufacturing-oriented. This is one area where India could potentially shine, although the ability to create software is only partly related to the ability to manipulate knowledge.

Another comment to make is related to the more one above. Universities are in many ways the "factories" of the knowledge economy, and their inability to innovate in terms of courses is a problem. However, I do not see it so much as a problem of labeling new areas of discourse, but as a more fundamental problem of bureaucracy itself. The creation of novel courses has to come through the Byzantine labyrinth of course approval and the system for crediting departments with enrollments. Like creating new models at General Motors, there is a long lead time between conception and realization. Most western countries would rather pay whatever penalties are involved in keeping the old structures rather than cut the various Gordian knots and develop universities that work on a different principle. Universities have been around a long time and don't like to do radically new things. Countries ready to start from scratch and develop interdisciplinary and flexible new programs of study will gain a premium for not sticking rigorously to the old system. My guess is that we can look to Scandinavia for useful models, and to some smaller companies where failure to innovate is a death sentence, for the new forms.

References

Edvinsson, Leif, and Michael S. Malone. 1997. *Intellectual Capital: Realizing Your Company's True Value by Finding Its Hidden Brainpower*. New York: Harper Collins.

Stewart, Thomas A., and Tom Stewart.1997. *Intellectual Capital*: The New Wealth of Organizations. New York: Doubleday.

Ron Westrum *is Professor of Sociology at Eastern Michigan University, and author of* Sidewinder: Creative Missile Development at China Lake.

❦ ❦ ❦ ❦ ❧ ❧ ❧ ❧

CONSIDERATION ON "NEW TRENDS IN GLOBALIZATION"

Melissa L. Rayner
Eastern Michigan University

*W*HILE DR. JAN NEDERVEEN PIETERSE is unarguably one of the leading scholars in the study of globalization, I find this essay, to be a bit simplistic in its analysis. The author approaches the topic quite thoroughly and from many different angles, offering a wealth of conclusions. Few would contest his points or ignore the fact that the global economy is changing and that the advanced economies are not growing as rapidly as the developing economies. I agree with many of the arguments made whole-heartedly. However, it is my belief that the data used to support these conclusions is a bit callow in its reach.

The author's first and greatest oversight was his exclusion of cultural change from his review. The logic behind this decision was due to Nederveen Pieterse's belief that cultural changes "generally follow slower time lines than trends in political economy." I would argue that it is the cultural changes that fuel these trends, not lag behind them. Furthermore, cultural change, while perhaps more difficult to measure, would provide much more meaningful insights to the evolving face of globalization. Looking more closely at the cultures of the emerging powerhouse economies as well as those of the current hegemonic leaders, would perhaps answer the ever-plaguing question of *why* in addition to telling us *what* and *when*.

The missing cultural component would further aide in the understanding of complacency among the so-called "old winners." Do the western powers possess an inability to embrace change and adapt to the new political and economic world climate? Do the rising economies of the East and South possess a trait that enables them to implicitly not only understand change, but to also harness it and use it to their advantage? Are the answers to these questions embedded within the simple orientation of these cultures as either individualistic or collectivist in nature? I would argue *yes, yes* and *maybe* in response to these queries. Additionally, I would like to reference the Marxist concept of the dialectic of defeat, which posits that strength ultimately becomes weakness, in that it becomes a roadblock to innovations and thus stifles positive change. The dialectic of defeat provides a concise, theoretical explanation of the alleged decline of the current economic powers. On the flip side of this notion is the dialectic of triumph, which implies that failure breeds success through a greater willingness to innovate (Weinstein 1984).

In his review of hegemony, Dr. Nederveen Pieterse briefly turns his attention towards the declining popularity of American culture abroad. If the outside appeal of America is lessening than how can we make sense of the growing number of international students who want to study in American universities? Even with a decline in foreign admissions due to tighter and prolonged scrutiny of applications for student visas implemented in the wake of post 9/11, the total number of foreign students (primarily graduate students from Asia and Europe) who entered American universities that year was 572,509 (Baber 2006). On December 9, 2005, the *Chronicle of Higher Education* reported that foreign students accounted for over 61 percent of doctoral degrees awarded in engineering and over 46 percent of those awarded in the physical sciences, a majority of the recipients coming from Third World countries. Additionally, American movies, music, television, literature, fashion and dance are ubiquitous all across the globe. This certainly does not reflect a lack of appeal.

Dr. Nederveen Pieterse has defined American culture primarily in terms of market trends and the popularity of "Brand America." I surely would not choose to define American culture as McDonald's, Barbie, Marlboro or any other mega-brand. Buying, selling, and advertising are all certainly components of culture, but none of them can accurately define it. Culture is much more pervasive than all of that. Social scientists commonly define culture as the "shared beliefs, values, customs, behaviors, and artifacts that the members of society use to cope with their world and with one another, and that are transmitted from generation to generation through learning" (Bates and Plog 1990).

Most non social scientists would probably think of culture in a different way. The average consumer, which the author cites in his review of rising anti-Americanism, would, I doubt, consider American culture to be McDonald's and Barbie either. Culture to the common man is an ambiguous term at best; many people would probably define it as tradition or high society. Beyond the multiple interpretations of culture, another problem that arises is defining culture through the mega corporations that exist within it. Often super conglomerates, such as those cited above, are considered to be beyond the boundaries or allegiance of a single nation, rather becoming entities of and for themselves.

My other point of contention is much more general. The current mode of studying change, which applies old standards to new concepts, is inherently flawed. It can lead to inaccurate and misleading conclusions. Globalization, a process of which we are currently in the midst, will be best understood in hindsight. I well understand that we do not have the convenience of studying globalization in this manner and that we are limited to either studying it through projection or to not studying it at all. I would simply like to point out that no matter how believable the data we produce on this matter, it is merely a snapshot of the phenomenon, not a complete narrative.

Another reference that the author makes is to past globalization as an unequalizing process. Does this mean that the globalization of the present and future will become an equalizing process or will the roles remain constant, but the players change? Dr. Nederveen Pieterse seems to imply the latter, pointing out that inequality between countries is being replaced by inequality within countries. What he does not state is that the rise in skill levels that is becoming prominent across the world has not been accompanied by a rise in access to these skills. The already skilled are becoming even more skilled, while those with no skills are falling even further down the social ladder.

Professor Nederveen Pieterse ends his review of the changing face of globalization by asking whether the new models of the East and South or the old model of the West will prove to be sustainable. The answer to this query is most likely neither. Change is always occurring; therefore, almost nothing is lasting. After all, according to the heraclitean fashion, "everything changes but change itself." We must accept that the old model will be replaced by the new model, which in turn will be replaced by a newer model, as Dr. Nederveen Pieterse has so clearly shown us through his article.

References

Baber, Zaheer. 2006. "Globalization, Nostalgia, and the University," *Society* 43, 4 (May/June): 44-47.
Bates, Daniel G., and Fred Plog. 1990. *Cultural Anthropology*. New York: McGraw-Hill.
Weinstein, Jay. 1984. *The Grammar of Social Relations: The Major Essays of Louis Schneider*. New Brunswick: Transactions Books.

Melissa L. Rayner is a Sociology graduate student at Eastern Michigan University. Her research interests include cultural and racial studies, the effects of globalization on the Third World, research methodology, and India.

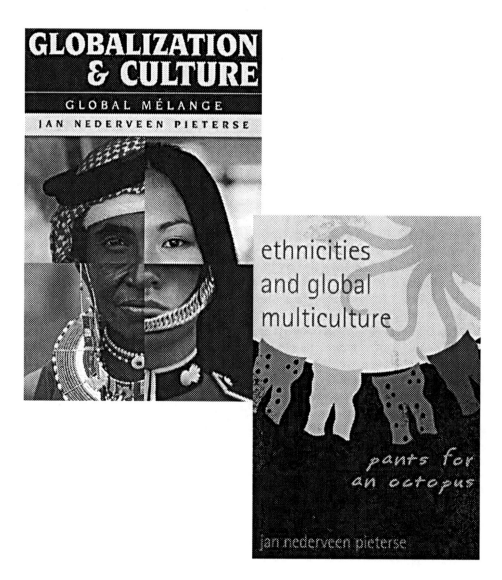

Of Mice, Men, and Mountains:
Justice Albanian Style

By FATOS TARIFA

Abstract

Northern Albanians have often been depicted as "a turbulent race of mountaineers, whose principal occupation has been to fight among themselves when not engaged in fighting against some one else." Their tribal customary law—particularly the norm of vengeance—continue to this day to be a subject of historical, sociological, anthropological, and juridical interest. Unlike most accounts that have been written about the customary law and vengeance among northern Albanians, many of which attributed them to the "Homeric condition" in which they lived and to their "epic ideas," this paper does not approach the "heroic" ethic of vengeance as a bit of exotica, or as an example of noble savagery. Instead, it aims to provide a detailed historical account of blood feud as it has been practiced for centuries among northern Albanians, a critical examination of some of the most popular interpretations of vengeance, as well as a sociological perspective on how avenging personal honor, from a sporadic, negligible, unreflective behavior became a biding social norm among the mountaineers of northern Albania.

*T*HERE IS NO WAY to approach—and deal with—the subject of vengeance and its economic, cultural and political workings and ramifications among northern Albanians without reference to a traditional body of customary law by which the life of the mountaineers' communities of northern Albania has been regulated for centuries up until the end of World War II. This corpus of customary law, known as the "Code of Lekë Dukagjini" (in Albanian: *Kanuni* i Lekë Dukagjinit), represents a series of injunctions, which were passed down by word of mouth for many generations. They were reputedly originally formulated by Lekë Dukagjini—an Albanian prince who ruled the territory of a narrow rugged valley in northern Albania that bears his name, and companion in arms to Albania's national hero, George Kastriot Skanderbeg—who lived in the fifteenth century.

Before the Ottoman Turks invaded Albania in the fifteenth century, the country was split up into a number of principalities, none of which was strong enough for long to subject a neighbor to its rule. Faced with the danger of Ottoman invasion, Skanderbeg

FATOS TARIFA is a former Albanian Ambassador to the Netherlands and the United States and currently a Visiting Scholar at the Department of Sociology at Eastern Michigan University. His most recent books include Europe Adrift on the Wine-Dark Sea *(2007), and* To Albania, with Love *(2007).*

was able to unite, under his leadership, all of the Albanian princes and their territories in a single state. They both fought against the Ottoman armies and kept Albania free for a quarter of a century. Although the Ottomans finally conquered Albania after Skanderbeg's death, they were unable to exert more than a nominal authority outside the main towns, certainly not in the remote highlands of northern Albania; hence they barely bothered with them. A number of authors point to the fact that there were no roads along which the Ottoman forces, strong enough to be effective, could march in order to reduce the Albanian mountaineers to real submission.

> The conquering arm of the Turk reduced the Bulgarian inhabitants of open plains to complete subjection within a comparatively short time; but a century and a quarter was required to secure a less firm hold upon the mountains of Serbia, while the inaccessible wilds of Albania and Montenegro were never completely subjected to Turkish power (Johnson 1916: 36).

As Margaret Hasluck points out, "The Turkish government, unable to enforce its will, accepted the situation and left the mountaineers to govern themselves, as they had presumably done under their native princes and chiefs" (1954: 9).

In reading the *Kanun*, Lekë Dukagjini appears as a kind of Albanian Moses, whose teachings were recorded in the memories of a tribal elite and Elders in the mountains of northern Albania in the form of proverbs and rites. In point of fact what Princ Dukagjini really did was codifying and adding to the existing customary law as well as introducing and enforcing it more rigidly to the territories under his control (Whitaker 1968).

THE ORIGIN OF THE *KANUN*

EVERY SOCIAL SYSTEM, or document, in which a given system is embodied, has a history, even though its beginnings may be shrouded in antiquity (Gouldner 1960). Like all documents of uncertain origin, however, the question of the origin of the *Kanun* can readily bog down in a metaphysical morass. Some believe that its origin can be traced in some measure to the ancient Illyrians, whose direct descendants the Albanians are and from whom they inherited their language, various traditions, customs and certain aspects of their legal system. Others believe that parts of the *Kanun* are adaptations from Roman law; other parts very likely do go back to the Bronze Age. Hutton (1954) observes that Albanian customary law is "primitive enough in many ways to be compared with the customary law of tribes much less civilized than the Albanians," whereas Ismail Kadare (1988a), Albania's most celebrated writer, argues that the *Kanun* probably predates Aeschylus.

Although the *Kanun* of Lekë Dukagjini has no identifiable origin, the striking similarities between the common laws of Homeric Greece and the *Kanun* make it possible to imagine that this corpus of unwritten law—practiced in various forms also in other parts of the Balkans, in southern Italy, and among the northern Caucasian peoples—could have well originated in Illyria. This might also explain why, of all other societies, in northern Albania customary law persisted well into the mid twentieth century as the only, or a "parallel", informal legal system and to some degree it remains valid in various areas even today.

Of Mice, Men, and Mountains: Justice Albanian Style

Like Émile Durkheim, who believed that by studying the religious beliefs and practices of the Aboriginal populations of Australia one could understand all religion in its most elementary form (Durkheim 1968 [1912]), the British anthropologist Edith Durham, studying Albania's customary law and writing about it at the same time as Durkheim, believed that she had discovered "the land of the living past." Durham, like her contemporary historian Robert Seton-Watson, started from the assumption that the key to understanding the past is the understanding of the present.

> The past as a key to the present—this is true of every country and period. The present as a key to the past—this is peculiarly true of Central and South Eastern Europe (Seton-Watson 1923: 16).

Durham felt that she had found that past in northern Albania and that the Balkans could be approached as an *in vivo* tableau of a society functioning on the basis of tribal customary law, a sort of "living laboratory"—or reservation—for the study of Europe's distant tribal past and the origins of the European civilization. In her renowned book *High Albania*, published in 1909, Durham wrote:

> The wanderer from the West stands awestruck amongst them [the Albanians], filled with vague memories of the cradle of his race, saying: 'This did I do some thousands of years ago; thus did I lie in wait for mine enemy; so thought I and so acted I in the beginning of Time' (1985 [1909]: 1).

There is little doubt that the *Kanun* of Lekë Dukagjini, in its codified form in which we know it today, is not quite the same tribal customary law that has habitually been practiced throughout the centuries. It has surely had its "spontaneous development," to use Henry Maine's (1861) language in his *Ancient Law*, but it has also changed purposefully by human agency "to suit the purposes of those who transmitted the oral law." Hasluck observed that "every type of unwritten law has been constantly recast, added to, and restarted down the centuries by a body of experts drawn from the rank of rulers" (1954: 9). Each new era made modifications to the code, which are to be attributed to "a conscious desire for alternation" (Hutton 1954). It is most certain, for example, that the *Kanun*, especially that part of it which spells out the rules regulating vengeance, has undergone important changes when the Ottomans introduced the firearms as weapons of offence and defense. Because firearms made murder easier than before, new rules must have been adopted to prevent the great loss of life inflicted by their use (Hutton 1954).

The *Kanun* was not written and recorded for centuries. The code remained in the verbal custody of the village or tribal elders and subject to modification or reinterpretation from time to time by assemblies of clans or villages. And just as the application of the traditional *Kanun* varied somewhat from one to another of the relatively isolated mountain communities so, no doubt, "in the same community the centuries brought some changes in its interpretation and application, since both of these depended considerably on the memory and wisdom of the local chieftains and elders" (Kastrati 1955: 124). As to the accuracy of the northern tribesman's memory Durham (1910) observed that he possess "an extraordinary memory," and has handed down "quantities of oral traditions, most of which remain to be collected."

Analysis of the traditional Albanian epic songs (*këngë trimërie*) of the Homeric style show significantly that in the absence of a literate society in the highlands of northern Albania they served as a repository of collective memory about their national history, the lives and traditions of their ancestors, and the norms and institutions regulating their remote communities. Martin Camaj draws a parallel between the *Kanun* of Lekë Dukagjini and the Albanian epic songs, "the *true natural form* of which is not written but *sung,* and hence in eternal wandering from mouth to mouth and from generation to generation" (Camaj 1989: xv). Writing in 1923, Rose Wilder Lane provides an interesting account of a conversation with a clansman from the northernmost Albanian village of Thethi, in which he said:

> I am an old man, and I have seen that when men go down to the cities to learn what is in books they come back scorning the wisdom of their fathers and remembering nothing of it, and they speak foolishly, words which do not agree with one another. But the things that a man knows because he has seen them, the things he considers while he walks on the trails and while he sits by the fires, these things are not many, but they are sound. Then when a man is lonely he puts words to these things and the words become a song, and the song stays as it was said, in the memories of those that hear it (Lane 1923: 180).

It wasn't until the mid-1930s that the *Kanun* of Lekë Dukagjini, which until then was handed down orally from father to son and from generation to generation for who knows how many hundred of years, was meticulously transcribed in its fullest form and published integrally in Albanian. The author of the text was Shtjefën Konstantin Gjeçov, a Franciscan priest, born in Kosovo in 1874. Gjeçov began his labors in 1913 collecting, sifting out and writing ancient stories as preserved in the repository of collective memory of the chieftains and the elderly in northern Albania and Kosovo. He provided "the best and the most trustworthy version of the [customary] law as remembered, interpreted and applied in a given community at the time he himself studied it" (Kastrati 1955: 124).

Indeed, in the form it is compiled, Gjeçov's work is genuinely a professional piece of ethnographic anthropology. His approach to this "unwritten Torah" is that of the Talmudist: he surrounds quotes from the *Kanun* with his own interpretations and reconstructs the "ancient law" on the basis of his own empirical observations. In numerous footnotes he draws parallels with the Laws of Manu, Roman law, Greek Public law, and the Ten Commandments. By the time of his death in 1929 the final text was not ready. The document, as it is known to us today[1] was completed by priests from his order, using Gjeçov's manuscripts and notes, and published in book form under Gjeçov's name in 1933.

Leonard Fox (1989), the English translator of the *Kanun*, points to "an astonishing resemblance between the customary law of the northern Albanians and that of the peoples of the North Caucasus." Quoting the German anthropologist of the earlier part of the twentieth century Adolf Dirr, Fox informs us that the two systems of customary law may be considered practically interchangeable: "The analogies are so strong, that one immediately asks oneself the questions that always arise in ethnography: Borrowing?

[1] *The Code of Lekë Dukagjini* by Shtjefën Gjeçov. New York: Gjonlekaj Publishing Co., 1989. Hereafter the *Kanun.*

Common origin? Basic similarity of thought?" Although Dirr gave numerous examples, particularly those involving hospitality and the blood-feud, he made no attempt to explain the striking similarities between the two systems (Fox 1989: xix).

THE BEDROCK, SCOPE, AND POWER OF THE *KANUN*

THE *KANUN* WAS about all aspects of life of northern Albanian society and the relations among its members. The cornerstone of the *Kanun* was the concept of *Besa*—the oath or the word of honor—as was honor the primary and most important cohesive institution of Albanian social fabric. Inseparably connected with this was the high value placed by the Albanian mountaineers upon the lineage honor. Family honor was a supreme value among them to the extent that, as Whitaker (1968) points out, any explanation of the extended family system among the Ghegs[2] must take account of this "cosmo-philosophical element." Honor was the principal value of traditional northern Albanian society, something prized above personal liberty, or even life itself. For "what profit is life to a man if his honor be not clean? To cleanse his honor no price is too great" (Dako 1919).

In this extremely remote cosmo-philosophical reality of northern Albania, Honor (*Nderi*), the Word of Honor (*Besa*, a term very rich in meaning and use, which means also faith, trust, protection, truce, or all of these together), and Hospitality (*Mikpritja*) were indissoluble elements of people's lives. Honor represented their *supreme moral value*; Besa was their *true religion*,[3] and Hospitality their *most sublime virtue*.

Hospitality

NUMEROUS FOREIGN TRAVELERS testify to the hospitality of the Albanians, both in northern and southern Albania. In the highlands of northernmost Albania, however, their hospitality has been solemnized, romanticized and glorified by foreign travelers and a number of renowned poets, anthropologists, historians as well as diplomats.[4] At the end

---

[2] The traditional name commonly used to refer to northern Albanians vis-à-vis the Tosks of the southern part of the country.

[3] "La Besa c'est la religion albanaise, c'est la religion du people" (Godart 1922: 75). As a sacred promise and obligation to keep one's given word, *Besa* was idolized and romanticized in the rhapsodies of the Albanians who immigrated to southern Italy after the death of their national hero George Kastriot Skanderbeg. In the famous song *Kostantini e Doruntina*, the mother reminds her son, now in his grave, of his *besa*, and she summons him to arise in order to fulfill his promise to bring her daughter back from a foreign land: *"Kostantin biri im/ku ësht besa që më dhe/të më sillje Doruntinën/Doruntnën t'ët motër?/Besa jote ësht nën dhee!"* (*Konstantin, my son/where is the besa you gave me/ that you would bring Doruntina back to me/Doruntina, your sister? Your besa is under the earth!"*). In the course of this rhapsody, the motif of which occurs among other Balkan peoples as well, Kostantin rise from the dead, fulfills his promise, and returns to the grave. The motif of this rhapsody has been captured masterfully and restyled as a fascinating story by Ismail Kadare (1988b) in his novel *Doruntina*.

[4] There is an extensive literature, much of it written by early foreign travelers to the area in the nineteenth and twentieth centuries and up to World War II. For a detailed information see Mema (1987a, 1987b), and Allcock and Young (1991). Among the most well-known figures who traveled to Albania were Lord Byron, J.C. Hobhouse, and Edward Lear. Other renowned figures include Baron Franz Nopsca, Edith M. Durham, etc.

of the nineteenth century, Cozens-Hardy admitted that in northern Albania there was "every element of romance to fascinate the traveler" (1894: 401). His confession is indicative to what Paul Fussell (1980) calls the "Western bourgeois vogue or romantic primitivism," to which the Balkan lands were subjected at the turn of the twentieth century and during the interwar period.

Be that as it may, the glorification of Albanian hospitality by foreigners could be explained by at least six specific reasons: (1) the remarkable forms and rituals in which hospitality was expressed among the mountaineers of northern Albania; (2) the universality of its reach, involving uncompromising protection of one's guest, even one with whom the host is in a state of blood feud; (3) its profound power in society and on each individual's life—both as a constitutive principle of morality and as a central element of their day-to-day life; (4) its unparalleled altruistic appeal and application; (5) the unusually scarce material resources as well as the extremely remote, harsh, and inhospitable geographical setting—amounting to an almost absolute isolation—in which people conferred such hospitality that is beyond any description; and (6) and equally important, the way in which hospitality was sanctified in the *Kanun* as a basic institution of society. Edith Durham (1910) noted that hospitality was "the law of the mountains" and she accepted it even when meager, since "the tribesman gave freely and of his best: he offers you 'bread and salt and my heart.'"

This sublime virtue in the moral world of northern Albanians was best expressed in the *Kanun*'s definition of the house of the mountaineer: "The house of the Albanian belongs to God and the guest" (Gjeçov 1989: 132). So before it was the house of its master, it was the house of one's guest. "The guest, in an Albanian's life represents the supreme ethical category" (Kadare 1990: 76); it is more important than blood relations.

A rigid set of rules prescribed in the *Kanun* graciously honored and protected the guest in a mountaineer's house. In a strikingly similar way with the Laws of Manu,[5] yet in much more—and incredibly meticulous—details, the *Kanun* describes the richness and the unassailable nature of the social rules honoring and protecting a guest. A benighted traveler, for example, could claim supper and shelter from any house he wished. The *Kanun* compelled that "at any time of the day or night one must be ready to receive a guest with bread and salt and an open heart, with a fire, a log of wood, and a bed (Gjeçov 1989: 132).

With hospitality went protection.[6] If a traveler had slept under the roof of an Albanian, the host was obligated to declare a blood feud against any person who insulted or harmed his visitor. The *Kanun* demanded that "if someone mocks your guest or abuses him, you must defend your guest's honor, even if your own life is in danger" (*ibid.*:

---

[5] *Manava Dharmasastra*, Book III, 99 and 101.

[6] One of the most important rules of hospitality was taking the weapon of a guest upon entering someone else's house. His weapon was hung on a hook, and the guest was escorted to the place of honor near the hearth. Gjeçov maintains that the very act of taking and holding his weapon had a threefold symbolic meaning and significance. It was at once (a) a sign of *valor* and *honor*, as well as an indication of the host's pleasure that a guest has come to him; (b) a sign of *guardianship*, since after the host has said "Welcome," the guest must have no fear and know that his host is ready to defend him against any danger; and (c) a sign of *prudence*, since, if the host holds his weapon, even if his guest has some bad intention, he is unable to accomplish it since he is disarmed (Gjeçov 1989: 132-134).

136). A man, who did not avenge his guest, if the latter was inadvertently killed, would be universally despised.

Furthermore, the duty of protection applied not only while the guest was in one's house, but within a certain length of time after he had been entertained, usually until he received hospitality from another man, or until sundown of the day on which he left, whichever was [the] sooner. After a guest had left one's house, the host was obliged by the *Kanun* to accompany him "as far as he requests to be accompanied" (*ibid.*: 134). The guest could also be accompanied by a child—whether a boy or a girl—who was considered to be a man or a woman in terms of the continued protection of their house.[7] The rationale behind this was that a guest should be accompanied both lest he became the victim of some wicked act and lest he harmed someone while under one's protection since, according to the *Kanun*, "if your guest commits some evil act while under your protection, you are responsible for it" (ibid.). The *Kanun* therefore stated that "the person dishonored or harmed is not obliged to pursue the one who committed the act of dishonor or damage, but knocks at the door of whoever gave him shelter and food" (*ibid.*). According to the *Kanun*, "Just as you are obliged to answer for an offence to your guest, so you are also obliged to answer for an offence to someone else by your guest" (*ibid.*).[8]

The *Kanun* advised that a guest who was attacked should call out the name of his host, sanctioning that "a person falls under your protection even by simply calling out your name: 'I am so-and-so's guest.' Although you may no longer be at home, if someone bothers that person, he is considered to be your guest and your honor is sullied" (*ibid.*: 136). Because of this concern for the safety of one's guests, nobody could enter the house of another person when the occupants were not at home or without giving notice of his presence in the courtyard.[9] The safety bestowed on the stranger was equally inviolate. "No Albanian in his senses ever threw a friend lightly away" (Hasluck 1954: 212).

For the violation of the hospitality the *Kanun* gave a choice of two paths: [potential] ruin or dishonor. To a person whose hospitality had been violated, everything was given with the left hand and passed under the knee. According to the *Kanun*, the left hand was considered dishonorable—it takes and does not give, and it is not used to greet friends. The left hand was used to remind one that he should have avenged the blood of his guest, since "it was a settled thing that one could atone for the blood of a father, of a brother—even one's child—but never for the blood of a guest" (Kadare 1990: 42).

Formerly, the *Kanun* sentenced traitors to be driven away with a club, and they were not permitted among honorable men. A house that had broken the laws of hospitality or violated the *Besa*—the most serious crimes in the Highlands—was burned down, the murderer shot by the assembled men of the village and his blood went unavenged for it was declared unworthy of being avenged (see Gjeçov 1989: 136). If the people who lived in the house were not guilty of the murder, that house, in which a guest had been

---

[7] The *Kanun* demanded that "if you accompany your guest on his way, you are responsible for any dishonor that someone may cause him" (Gjeçov 1989: 134). It prescribed, however, that "If you have accompanied your guest to the place he wanted to go, and you have turned your back to attend to your own affairs, and he is shot by a riffle and killed, you are not responsible for his blood" (*ibid.*).

[8] In a more laconic way, the *Kanun* states: "The bread pays for the damage" (Gjeçov 1989: 134), hence "Hospitality honors you, but also creates problems for you" (*ibid.*).

[9] "Call out and, if no one replies, either stand and wait or go about your business" (Gjeçov 1989: 60).

killed in violation of the *Besa*, was burned to ground (*ibid.*: 210). However, since the betrayal or murder of one's guest was most unusual in highland Albania, so was the burning of houses.

Besa

THE RULES AND the power of the *Kanun* extended uncompromisingly beyond the household and the obligation to honor and protect the guest. The *Kanun* sanctioned the inviolability of private property and accorded *Besa* a central role in all property relations.

One of the most powerful manifestations of *Besa* was the "truce of livestock and the herdsman."[10] This was a truce mutually agreed upon by two or more villages or Banners, determining routes for the travelers, messengers, and herdsmen with their flock through the Alpine pastures and valleys and guaranteeing their protection. The guarantors of the truce of livestock and the herdsman were the Standard-Bearers, the Chiefs, and the men of Banners united in this truce. If some mishap occurred to the traveler, the messenger, or the herdsman before leaving the other Banner or while pasturing flocks within the designated areas, the truce of livestock and the herdsman was considered violated (*ibid.*: 168).

The violation of this truce incurred a number of penalties, varying from fines paid to the family of the victim to the destruction of the murderer's property, together with his crops and land, his livestock, and everything else he possessed.[11] The *Kanun* imposed the punishment of communal burning, destruction and execution of someone by his village, or his expulsion from the region, for certain well defined crimes. They were: (a) killing a guest under your protection; (b) committing serious slander, or beating or killing a priest; (c) killing a member of your own clan; (d) committing murder after the reconciliation of

---

[10] Described in much detail in Book 10 (Chapter 22, CXXIII) of the *Kanun* (see Gjeçov 1989: 168-70).

[11] The *Kanun* ordered that the Banner of the murderer burned down three *kulla* [stone towers used as dwellings] belonging to the murderer. If he did not own three *kulla*, his own *kullë* was burned, along with two other belonging to his close relatives. If he did not have close relatives, two belonging to his distant relatives—even those a hundred times removed—should be burned" (*ibid.*: 170). In 1987, while trekking in the footsteps of Edith Durham in the mountains and valleys of northern Albania along with my friend Peter Lucas, a veteran Boston journalist, we visited the village of Thethi, which we found as remote and isolated as it was back in 1908, when the British anthropologist traveled through that area. "There are not too many places like it left in the world, unchanged after hundreds of years," Lucas (1991) wrote. Upon entering the village, we met herders Mark Luku, 98, and Gjergj Preka, 82, both from Thethi, and sat down with them to hold a conversation about the *Kanun* and the blood feud. Mark Luku recalled a story when he, alongside other men of Thethi—a man from every house—burned down the kulla of a fellow villager, since he had violated the truce of livestock and the herdsman, negotiated between two villages, by stealing a few sheep from the flock of someone from a neighboring village. "His disgraceful and dishonorable act enraged the entire village of Thethi and brought upon him the hatred of all," Mark Luku said, adding that "anyone from Thethi who stole the flock of a herder from another village protected by the truce violated the besa of all of Thethi." When asked about the time when this story took place, Mark Luku said coolly: "Ohu! That happened some eighty years ago." In 1987, eighty years ago meant the first decade of the twentieth century. Shtjefën Gjeçov confirms that the truce of livestock and herdsman was still in force in the early twentieth century in the mountains of Gjakovë: in Nikaj-Mërtur, Gash, Krasniq and elsewhere, as well as in the mountains of Dukagjin: in Shalë, Theth, Shosh, Kir, Gjaj, Plan, and Toplanë.

blood; (e) committing a murder and then concealing it; (f) killing a murderer during a truce; (g) killing a cousin in order to become the owner of his property; or (h) permitting the malefactors of the Banner to enter your home (*ibid.*: 210). In *all* these cases the house of the perpetrator was burned by the entire village. For the most awful offences—such as those described in points a, b, f, and g—the perpetrator himself was executed, or, if not— for crimes related to points c, d, e, and h—his family was fined and his survivors were all expelled from the village for 5 to 15 years (*ibid.*: 210-12). The *Kanun* summarizes it all in Article 1195 as follows:

> If someone commits these crimes, he is executed by the village, his family is fined, his house is burned, his trees are cut down, his garden and vineyards are destroyed, and his survivors are expelled from the country with their belongings (ibid.: 210-212).

THE *KANUN* IS NOT a religious document. It was binding for Christians and Muslims alike, but it was sacred nonetheless. It so much influenced the mountaineers of northern Albania that, with Lekë Dukagjini cast in the role of the Marquees of Queensberry, the words "Lekë said so" obtained, one could say, far more obedience than the Ten Commandments. Special rituals common to members of both religions restored equilibrium after crisis of birth, marriage, and death. As Carleton Coon observed,

> All of those rituals, which reinforced their social habits, were of much greater importance to the mountaineers than the rites of church or mosque, which were not as well adjusted to this particular form of society (Coon 1950: 30).

In short, the teaching of Islam and of Christianity all had to yield to the *Kanun*. It was precisely this Durkheimian sort of sacred authority of the *Kanun*—or the "collective conscience"—that accounts for the universal conformity given to it.

With its 1,263 articles the *Kanun* was comprehensive, universal, and inescapable for any family or clan member or the broader community of people in the areas in which it was introduced and enforced with rigidity. It was devised literally as a legal framework to govern every aspect of their life and it had not forgotten a single aspect of economics or ethics, or the slightest human action. As Kadare points out, "its power reached everywhere, covering lands, the boundaries of fields. It made its way into the foundations of houses, into tombs, to churches, to roads, to markets, to weddings" (1990: 27). It sanctioned—for Christians as well as Muslims—the attitude toward marriage, the selection of wives, the rites to be conducted during wedding ceremonies and birth, people's roles in family and society, the rigid gender division of labor, the forms of punishment, the rules of blood-feud, and the customs to be followed when a person died. In a word, the *Kanun* was the law that governed everything in peoples' lives—from cradle to grave. It contained statutory, criminal, civil, and family laws as well as procedural rules for both criminal and civil courts. As such, it took care of all of these subjects "once and forever," and it served to shape up rigorously patterned forms of behavior while inhibiting change in a society whose members were "trained from childhood to believe in its infallible authority" (Coon 1950: 37).

Whitaker (1968) suggests that for its comprehensiveness, its clarity and logic the *Kanun* of Lekë Dukagjini, in its codified version that has come down to us, "deserves to be ranked among the great legal documents of the world." Kadare, on his part, maintains that the *Kanun* was not merely a constitution; it is also "a colossal myth that has taken on the form of a constitution. Universal riches compared to which the Code of Hammurabi and the other legal structures of those regions look like children's toys" (Kadare 1990: 73).

CAUSES, RULES, AND RITUALS OF VENGEANCE

THE MOST PECULIAR law of the *Kanun* is probably the one that compels a family to avenge a crime by killing an adult male member of the perpetrator's family, which must then in turn take revenge, resulting in incessant struggles whose fullest ramifications could be the decimation and even the demise of entire families.

Northern Albania, much more than Montenegro, the Caucasus region, Sicily or Corsica, is the land where "blood feud" (*gjakmarrje*—literally translated as *blood taking*) still holds the greatest sway in our days. In the past, similar systems of honor and blood vengeance were also found in Scotland,[12] medieval Iceland, in Japan,[13] and in the U.S. region of Appalachia, as with the famous feud between the Hatfields and McCoys. They are still to be found in various Mediterranean societies, such as Corsica, Sicily, Barbagia in central Sardinia, Andalusian sierras, and Kabylia in northern Algeria (see Blok 1981) despite the complexity of the Mediterranean Basin as a geographical and "culture area." The *Kanun*, however, goes far beyond the Hatfield and McCoy notion of "an eye for an eye" and "a tooth for a tooth." In northern Albania compensation could be obtained by killing *any* member of the original offender's family and the newly spilt blood then cried out for yet more compensation. The result was a natural tendency toward escalation. Writing in the late 1950s about his native Montenegro, Milovan Djilas illustrates how compelling the need to take revenge was to the Montenegrins:

> Vengeance—this is a breath of life one shares from the cradle with one's fellow clansmen, in both good fortune and bad, vengeance from eternity. Vengeance was the debt we paid for the love and sacrifice our forebears and fellow clansmen bore for us. It was the defense of our honor and good name and the guarantee of our maidens. It was our pride before others; our blood was not water that anyone could spill. It was, moreover, our pastures and springs—more beautiful than any-

---

[12] Several authors have emphasized a number of similarities between the Albanian highlands and medieval Scotland. Writing in the early twentieth century, John Foster Fraser, for example, has noted: "The condition of Albania is not unlike that of the Highlands of Scotland in the sixteenth century, when the clans were at constant feud with one another. Many times I thought of similarities between Albania and Scotland....The alertness of the Scottish Highlander to resent insult is only equaled by the quickness of the Albanian to shoot anyone who may disagree with him. The quilted petticoat of the Albanian is certainly similar to the Highlander's kilt. And if you could hear the wail of Albanian music in the hills you might, without much stretch of the imagination, fancy you were listening to the skirl of the bagpipes (Fraser 1912 [1906]: 246).

[13] In feudal Japan the Samurai class upheld the honor of their family, clan, or their lord by *katakiuchi* or revenge killings. These killings could also involve the relatives of an offender.

one else's—our family feasts and births. It was the glow in our eyes, the flame in our cheeks, the pounding in our temples, the word that turned to stone in our throats on hearing that our blood had been shed. It was centuries of manly pride and heroism, survival, a mother's milk and a sister's vow, bereaved parents and children in black, joy and songs turned into silence and wailing. It was all, all (Djilas 1958: 107).

THE LIFE OF THE mountaineers in northern Albania has been—and to a large extent remains—organized in terms of kinship and descent, where the social pressure of the *fis* (kinfolk or tribe) asserted a major influence. According to the *Kanun*, "For the Albanian of the mountains, the chain of relationships of blood and kinship are endless....Relationships of brotherhood and clan are claimed with all those descended from common ancestors, up to the present...[and] even if the family of an Albanian is divided into four hundred branches, no intermarriages among its members occur" (Gjeçov 1989: 142).

The family (*familja*), according to the definition given by the *Kanun*, "consists of the people of the house; as these increase, they are divided into brotherhoods [*vllazni*], brotherhoods into kinship groups [*gjini*], kinship groups into clans [*fis*], clans into banners [*flamur*], and all together constitute one widespread family called a nation, which has one homeland, common blood, a common language, and common customs" (*ibid.*: 14).[14] The household (*shtëpi*) formed the basic unit of northern Albanian society. The extended family consisted of several brothers and their descendants, who would form a single residential and economic unit.[15] In the past, this system was common to much of the Balkans—the south Slav term *zadruga* being generally used in the sociological and anthropological literature to indicate this type of organization. The unity of the household—resulting from patrimonial lineage, common ownership of the means of production, and a perpetual need for common defense in a war-ridden society—was essential for the survival of this large family unit. Durham (1931) observed that in such society, the genealogies of individual persons would be carefully remembered, showing a link by male descent with the founder of the clan, who might have lived thirteen or fourteen generations earlier. The clan of Berisha, for example, claimed the longest genealogy, stretching back to 1370, and perhaps 1270, according to estimations provided by Baron Nopcsa (1912).

Northern Albanian society, as Ismail Kadare metaphorically describes it, is one in which life has always been only a hair's breadth away from death. Indeed, the laws of death have, for most of its history, prevailed over the laws of life. Even marriage, such a sublime symbol of life, was often accompanied by a veil of death. In many regions of northern Albania the bride's parents would give the young husband a "trousseau bullet"—part of her dowry—with which the bridegroom had the right to kill his wife should she attempt to leave him or if she betrayed him. Article 43 of the Kanun reads:

---

[14] A similar tribal system existed in Montenegro and in other parts of the western Balkans, such as Herzegovina and parts of the Sandzak (see Calhoun 2000).

[15] As late as 1987 the author encountered a household with 48 members in the village of Dragobi (Tropojë) in northern Albania.

If the girl does not submit and marry the husband chosen for her by her father, she should be handed over to him by force, together with a cartridge; and if the girl tries to flee, her husband may kill her with her parents' cartridge, and the girl's blood is lost [remains unavenged], because it was with their cartridge that she was killed (Gjeçov 1989: 28).

The cartridge was given to the groom by his wife's father as protection for "two acts (for which) a woman may be shot in the back...(a) for adultery; (b) for betrayal of hospitality (to any guest). For these two acts of infidelity the husband kills his wife, without requiring protection or a truce and without incurring a blood feud, since the parents of his killed wife received the price of her blood, gave him a cartridge, and guaranteed her conduct" (*ibid*.: 40).[16]

The *Kanun* was especially unforgiving—and very specific—about certain "evil acts," such as adultery. In strict similarity with the *Old Testament*,[17] the *Kanun* asserts that "if two people are caught together committing adultery and are killed, their blood remains unavenged" (*ibid*.: 176). The adulterous man and woman, however, remained unavenged only if they were killed in the act and with a single shot. If this was indeed the case, the parents of the adulterous pair could not seek vengeance, but should give the murderer a new cartridge with the words "Blessed be your hand" (*ibid*.). The *Kanun* demanded that a guarantee was given that vengeance for the blood of the adulterous pair would never be sought. If the parents of the victims doubted in their hearts that the murderer killed the pair in the shameful act, the jurors administered the oath to the murderer, in accordance with the *Kanun*. If the jurors found him guilty, the murderer incurred two blood-feuds and was also obliged to pay the fine specified by the *Kanun* (*ibid*.).

The death-toll exacted by the blood feud has historically been heavy for men in northern Albania. By the turn of the twentieth century, August Degrand, the French Consul in the city of Shkodër, northern Albania, reported that there were forty two murders in one month in a single village in the region of Mirditë (Degrand 1901: 159n). Writing at about the same time, Don Ernesto Cozzi (1910), estimated that the percentage of Albanian males dying in the feud ranged from five percent of the total male deaths in Reç to forty two percent in Toptanaj. In 1909, one of the Franciscan priests of Shoshi told Ludwig Edlinger (1910: 84) that as many as eighty percent of male deaths there were from the feud. Noel Malcolm claims that by 1912, the year that marked the end of the Ottoman domination in Albania, nineteen percent of all adult male deaths in the highlands of northern Albania were blood-feud murders and that in an area of western Kosovo with 50,000 inhabitants, 600 died in blood feuds every year (Malcolm 1998: 19-20). So fatal were these feuds in some remote areas that an old man was seldom to be encountered,

---

[16] This precept of the *Kanun* is in many ways similar to the "honor killings" of women that pervasively occur in the Muslim world, primarily in the Middle East, but frequently also in Pakistan (*karo-kari*), Bangladesh, India, Morocco, etc. In these societies, an "honor killing" of a woman today may occur because of her actual or perceived immoral behavior, such as marital infidelity, refusing to submit to an arranged marriage, demanding a divorce, flirting with or receiving phone calls from men, failing to serve a meal on time, or, grotesquely, "allowing herself" to be raped (see Hassan 1999).

[17] "If a man sleeps with the wife of another man, let each die, that is the adulterer and the adulteress; thus you will take this evil from Israel" (*Deuteronomy* 22: 22; *Leviticus* 20: 21).

in spite of the traditional longevity of the Albanian mountaineers; the men were killed off before they attained patriarchal years (Scriven 1918). According to Ronald Matthews (1937), in 1934 only thirty percent of the men in the highlands of northern Albania died in their beds. During the first forty years of the twentieth century forty percent of male deaths in those regions were attributed to homicide (Sestini 1943). Pietro Quaroni (1966), an Italian diplomat who served in Albania in the inter-war period, reported that vendetta, together with malaria, were the principal causes of the falling birthrate in upland Albania before World War II.

NUMEROUS FOREIGN commentators who have traveled through northern Albania or have written about it during the nineteenth century or in the earlier decades of the twentieth century referred to the Albanian mountaineers (*malsorë*) as being utterly lawless. This belief derived generally from the observation that, rejecting the Islamic law (*shariah*), which the Ottoman invaders failed to establish during five centuries of occupation, the Albanian mountaineers had no legal system and no state authority to which to obey. Like its neighboring Montenegro, northern Albania became, to use the language of Christopher Boehm, a "refuge-area warrior society" (Boehm 1984: 41). The rugged terrain on both sides of the border provided distinct defense or escape advantages whereas the tribal system was flexible enough for a variety of military actions, from small raids to larger territorial defense involving thousands of warriors as was particularly manifested in two distinct—but equally important—historical movements in Albania: the League of Prizren (1879-1882) and its military effort to protect the Albanian territories from annexation to Serbia, and the armed uprising in northern Albania and Kosovo (1910-1912) that eventually led to the formal independence of Albania from Ottoman rule.

It is precisely the absence of sanctions by any formal law that could be enforced by a settled government—or even merely by continuity in administration of a single ruling family—that can possibly explain the firm establishment of vendetta as the real sanction of Albanian customary law. Based on a distinctive sense of personal and collective dignity and a complete absence of a formalized punitive state apparatus, the *Kanun* conferred the power of exacting justice on the individual and the family.

> As they live under no laws, and each individual is the redresser of his own wrongs, bloodshed cannot but frequently occur. A blow is revenged, by the meanest among them, with the instant death of the offender (Broughton 1858 [1813]: 134).

Having said this, northern Albania was hardly unique in possessing a stateless society, one in which individuals and families were responsible for resolving disputes without written legislation and without an executive body to administer the law. Other societies too, like medieval Iceland, Corsica and Montenegro at certain periods of their national histories, have typically practiced a variety of methods—vengeance being one of them—to resolve disputes, with people taking the law into their hands,[18] but under a highly developed—albeit unwritten—set of *ethical norms* and *procedural rules*, which have helped them survive.

---

[18] Middleton and Tait (1958) as well as Bohannan (1977) describe this state of affairs as "self-help".

Durham (1910) observed that it was usual for writers who did not know the Albanian tribesman to denounce him as "a vulgar murderer, who kills wantonly for the sake of killing." Tragic and ruinous as it was vengeance in northern Albania was *not* disorderly and anarchic, as one might think. Nor was religion a part of it. Colonel George Scriven of the U.S. Army, who rummaged through northern Albania at the end of World War I, observed that the actions of the Albanian mountaineer toward his fellow-men were "based upon the strictest possible observance of law," albeit a tribal law founded upon "a most distorted idea of personal and family honor" (Scriven 1918). As far as religion is concern, Durham (1910) observed that it has not been more of an excuse for fighting than have other things; hence feuding took place not between Moslems and Catholics, but between Christian and Christian or Moslem and Moslem.

Durham (1910) suggested also that in order to understand a custom one must see it through the eyes of the natives. There is "a tragic grandeur," she wrote, about the man who was ready to sacrifice all he had, all that he held dear, even life itself, in order that he could do what he believed to be right—cleaning his and his family's honor. For the Albanian highlander honor was more important than life. Honor was the embodiment and the real meaning of life, since, according to the *Kanun*, a dishonored man was considered a dead person.[19]

Bearing in mind this central fact in the world of the Albanian tribesmen, Durham (1910) has suggested that blood feud could be regarded "not so much a punishment which they inflict, as an act performed for self purification, and as much a solemn and necessary act." It was, thus, "not merely vengeance but, most importantly, an offering to the soul of a dead man" (Durham 1928: 162). For there were certain offences that "blacken not merely the honor of the man against whom they have been committed, but blacken also the honor of his whole house and even of his tribe" (*ibid.*), hence only blood can cleanse the strain and satisfy justice.

> The man whose honor is blackened is obsessed with the idea of his own impurity. It gives him no rest. Blood he must have...[so that] his honor is clean, and if he must die he dies happy" (Durham 1910).[20]

BECAUSE BLOOD WAS such a central element of the tribesmen' cosmogony, the norms regulating vengeance, as we shall see later in more detail, were very *cautiously observed* and *coercively imposed*.

The *Kanun* describes numerous offenses for which a man could spill blood. Descriptions of northern Albania are full of accounts showing that it did not take much to give an offence to a mountaineer which eventually led to the taking of people's lives for what often appeared at first sight as trivial reasons. They ranged from major offenses such

---

[19] The idea that honor can be more important than life is by no means unique among the tribesmen of northern Albania. It has been known since antiquity, as shown in Tacitus's *Agricola* (Ch. 33): "An honorable death would be better than a disgraceful attempt to save our lives." See also Walcot (1978: 15-16).

[20] On the point of honor, Durham (1910) wrote: "When you meet a tribesman and he drinks to you *Tu ngjat jeta* (long life to thee), remember to drink *Tu ngjat me ner* (long honor to the) in return; for honor is better than life—in Albania."

as seduction, theft of women, elopement, cattle-stealing, and general raiding to the smallest infraction of custom, such as, a blow struck in anger, an unwitting shove in a crowd, a harsh word, a cruel joke, or even a play on words which is very easy in Albanian.[21] These offenses were not paid for in property or by fines but "by the spilling of blood." On the odd occasion and in very specific situations, however, the *Kanun* allowed exemption from being avenged in exchange for compensation in fines or property, provided that "a magnanimous pardon (through the mediation of good friends)" was asked before (Gjeçov 1989: 130-132). Jon Elster (1989) points out that, "Whenever there is a norm, there are often a set of adjunct norms defining legitimate exceptions," although these are often "less explicit than the main norm, and rely heavily on judgments and discretion."

The slightest reflection on a man's family, either on his kinsmen or his ancestors, was especially an offence against honor, which inevitably led to the declaration of a blood feud since the one really satisfactory revenge was murder. The *Kanun* ordered: "There is no fine for an offense to honor. An offence to honor is never forgiven" (Gjeçov 1989: 130). Family honor and prestige helped thus to perpetuate the blood feud. Whitaker (1968) has noted that the mountaineers of northern Albania were "always ready to defend their honor, and in its defense to shoot at the slightest provocation."

According to the *Kanun*, "a man who had been dishonored is considered dead" (Gjeçov 1989: 130), hence the terrible social pressure to avenge against the offender in order to restore honor for himself and his family. The honor of the injured party was sullied until he had slain either the actual offender or a male member of his family. The relatives of the slain individual were then compelled to take up the main hunt, and thus the feud spread. Such deaths invariably gave rise to a blood feud between two clans or families that could go on for decades, a life being exacted first on one side then on the other. In the tradition of northern Albania blood could be wiped out only with blood. The *Kanun* made it very clear that the drops of blood shed by a murderer demand other blood. In its prescripts, "Blood in never unavenged" (*ibid.*: 174).

Impairment of one's personal or family honor and the obligation to settle scores with the offender were blended as the most natural and perpetual thing in the everyday life of the mountaineers although this was contrary to everybody's *self-interest*. Vengeance appears to be one of those social norms, which, as Elster (1989) has convincingly argued, overrides self-interest. "Who sees not that vengeance, from the force alone of passion, may be so eagerly pursued as to make us knowingly neglect every consideration of ease, interest, or safety?"[22]

An offense to one's family and the person who caused it or his family could be neither forgiven nor forgotten. Men, who had it from their fathers, told their children the story of their enmity with the other family. The time that elapsed between a crime and its being avenged could be considerable, yet it did not whither away the memory of—or the

---

[21] The *Kanun* counts these major offenses to personal and family honor which could eventually start a blood feud: (1) violating one's hospitality; (2) calling a man a liar in front of other men; (3) insulting one's wife, or if she runs off with someone else; (4) taking the weapons a man carries on his shoulder or in his belt; (5) breaking into one's house, his sheepfold, his silo, or his milk-shed in his courtyard; (6) spitting at him, threatening him, pushing him, or striking him; (7) reneging on one's promise of mediation or on his pledged word; (8) not repaying him a debt or obligation (see Gjeçov 1989: 130-132).

[22] David Hume (1751), Appendix 11.

urge for—revenge. Whitaker (1968) for example, reports that in 1909 the Shalë clan avenged themselves by killing a man from Shkreli for a crime committed 65 years before.

> Mostly, the members of a family remembered from generation to generation every failure to avenge blood with blood. They were the living memory of the clan, and forgetting such things could only occur because of quite extraordinary events with long-lasting effects, like natural catastrophes, wars, migrations, plagues, when death was devaluated, losing its grandeur, its rules, its loneliness, becoming something common and familiar, ordinary, insignificant….In times of such flood of death, drear and turbid, it could happen that a debt of vengeance was forgotten. But even if that happened, the book was always there, under lock and key in the *Kulla* of Orosh, and the years might pass, the family flourish and put out new shoots, and then one day the doubt would arise, the rumor, or the mad dream that would bring everything to life again (Kadare 1990: 137-38).

Regardless of the accuracy and effectiveness of collective memory as a "mechanism" of social restrain and corrective behavior, I believe that just as it is possible that some of the *Kanun*'s precepts were forgotten or mutated when passed down orally, either due to the passing of time or deliberately by those in control, so it was possible also that, in many cases, the original cause that started a blood feud several decades earlier—what Boehm (1987) refers to as the "opening move"—was forgotten or distorted by future generations. It is possible that in many cases, all that a man, or his family, who carried it on knew was that a male member of the adversary family should be killed. It often happened that an absolutely innocent man, who was ignorant of the cause of offence, was sacrificed and his blood cleansed the other's honor, who, triumphant, announced his deed (see Durham 1910). When this occurred, the rival family would, in turn, concentrate on the task of retaliation. The murderer himself, another male member of his family, or even a quite distant cousin was liable to be shot. Thus the inter-family warfare would continue for generations. When it would eventually end no one knew. And because "successive generations had been accustomed to the feuds from their cradles, and so, not being able to conceive of life without them, it never entered their minds to try to free themselves from their destined end" (Kadare 1990: 144-145). Scott Anderson (1999) informs us that the longest reported blood feud in the highlands of northern Albania lasted 240 years and left scores dead.

SEVERAL AUTHORS HAVE pointed out that the rules regulating revenge are often highly elaborate (see Hasluck 1954; Boehm 1984; Elster 1989; 1990; Miller 1996). Even though revenge behavior might seem extremely impulsive and erratic, it is regulated by a number of curious and very well understood—even if unwritten—rules, principles and customs. In northern Albania these rules were carefully prescribed and compliantly observed by customary law. They were highly *codified* and *ritualized*, so that single killings were *not* seen as murder, but as the avenger's greatest merit in saving his personal honor and the dignity and honor of his family—even when he knew it would result shortly in his own death, or in the death of his close kin.

Anyone who carefully reads the *Kanun* will readily note that taking revenge for the murder of one's family member or kin was indeed the strictest procedural ritual of all customs in the everyday life of the Albanian mountaineers. A set of rules, all of which are meticulously described in the *Kanun*, became binding norms that were habitually and universally accepted and enforced in the highlands. The inventory of such elaborate rules is incredible for its consistency and details.

First and foremost, because the *law of hospitality* was stronger than the *law of vengeance*, no murder could be committed in a guest's presence.

One could only kill *one* person from the murderer's family in avenging the blood of a single individual, not more. However, the *Kanun* provided that certain crimes were judged so heinous that they mandated a 2-for-1 payback.

Under no circumstances could a woman or a child be killed. Only adult males were targeted for vengeance. A male child was considered a grownup as soon as he was able to carry a rifle. According to the *Kanun*, it is a duty of the father "to buy arms for his sons when they reach the proper age" (Gjeçov 1989: 44). The *Kanun* granted blanket exemption from blood feud to females, the killing of whom was seen as a profound violation of a *man*'s personal honor. One of the main precepts of the *Kanun* was that "Blood follows the finger" [i.e. the person who commits a murder incurs a blood-feud], but this law did not include women, since a woman did not incur blood, even if she happened to kill someone.

> If a woman kills her husband or anyone else, her parents incur that blood. Her husband purchases a woman's labor and cohabitation, but not her life….If a woman kills her husband and is then killed in turn by her brother-in-law, because she killed his brother, this latter act is not permitted by the *Kanun*. The blood of a woman is not equal to the blood of a man; the parents of the wife therefore incur the blood of her husband (Gjeçov 1989: 38).[23]

The *Kanun* strictly prohibited an ambusher to fire his gun at women, children, a house, or livestock. Even a man could not be ambushed or attacked if accompanied by a woman—his own wife, daughter, sister or a female relative. Frequently women accompanied their men when they traveled in order, by their presence, to furnish protection to them from an implacable foe.[24] Malcolm observes that the murder of a woman in northern Albania was the strongest taboo, adding that "any woman could walk through raging gunfire in the knowledge that she would never be shot at….This was very much a man's world. Women had their honor, but it existed through, and was defended by, men" (1998: 19-20).

If an ambusher fired at women, children, a house or livestock he violated the *Kanun*,

[23] Article 897 of the *Kanun* upholds: "The family of the victim may not take vengeance on the women of the murderer's family, because 'A woman and a priest do not incur the blood-feud'" (Gjeçov 1989: 172).

[24] In his study of the blood feud in Montenegro, Boehm describes a similar condition with respect to the sanctity of women. He reports that it was even possible for women to enter directly into combat during the first stage of a feud, when the killer's clan shut itself in and the victim's clan attacked the fortified stone farmhouse, which had loopholes [for firing rifles] everywhere. With no fear of being harmed, women could carry straw and firebrands up to the house to try to burn it. Also, women of a besieged house could go outside at night carrying torches, to light up the enemy so that their own men could shoot at them. This exemplifies the strength of these particular rules—to shoot a woman was a source of shame (*sramota*) for the entire clan (*Boehm* 1984: 111-12).

and if he was not punished by his Banner for this disgrace, the armed conflict could extend "from house to house, then from clan to clan, from village to village, and finally from Banner to Banner" (Gjeçov 1989: 164).

When a violent death occurred, the *natural* avenger was the dead man's brother. Originally customary law had sanctioned that "the family of the victim could not pursue or kill any of the brothers, nephews or cousins of the murderer, but only the actual perpetrator" (*ibid.*: 172). Later on it was permitted that the in the absence of a victim's brother, another male member of the family or the closest male relative could take the mantle. By allowing this it was assumed that the responsibility for a murder was held to be collective, therefore, in seeking vengeance a man could wipe out the blot on his family honor by killing the brother of the perpetrator (see Coon 1950: 30). With the passing of time the *Kanun* extended the blood-feud to all males in the family of the murderer as well as to his cousins and close nephews.[25]

According to the *Kanun*, revenge could be effected at a meeting deliberately sought, or in ambush. Occasionally a group of friends could accompany the avenger on his mission of revenge, but any death caused by these persons would be "credited" to the man who had asked them to accompany him, and who was obliged by the *Kanun* to pronounce the following words: "All the guns that are fired are mine" (Gjeçov 1989: 162). The *Kanun* provided, however, that if a person went to ambush a fellow-villager, taking with him other villagers as accomplices, and he killed that person, both the leader and his accomplices incurred blood with the victim's family (*ibid.*: 164). The *Kanun* also provided that if a person entered a house, before occupying a place of ambush, and had coffee, ate bread, or took bread from there with him, then lied in ambush and killed someone, the family of the murdered man sought blood from the household that gave him food" (*ibid.*). The *Kanun* was very explicit: "A gun or bread given with knowledge of the murder brings blood on the one who gave it" (*ibid.*).

It was a strict rule than nobody could kill surreptitiously without leaving some article to identify himself as the author of the murder. Nobody, of course, would normally wish to kill anonymously, since one of the main purposes of the blood-feud—the public retrieving of family honor—would thereby be thwarted. The *Kanun* obliged the avenger to call out his enemy by name, say the right words before he fired,[26] and shoot him dead—if possible using one bullet.[27] That was the main thing. Then the avenger should turn the victim over on his back, put his hands crossed on his chest, his weapon

---

[25] It is not quite clear, however, as to how far vengeance was extended in the mountains of northern Albania. It seems that different rules have applied in different areas. In the examples of the application of the *Kanun*, which he appended to the publication of the *Kanun* of Lekë Dukagjini, Gjeçov informs that in the territory governed by Skanderbeg, the law remained in force that vengeance for blood could be taken on any member of the brotherhood, the clan, and the progeny: "Pursue the clan for blood," "Fire your gun at a member of the clan." In the territory governed by Lekë Dukagjini, however, the law that remained in force was: "Blood follows the finger," that is vengeance could be taken only on the murderer, and "after twenty-four hours following the murder, vengeance may not be taken on the relatives of the murderer" (see Gjeçov 1989: 242n).

[26] "Words spoken during a murderous attack have significance and force, i.e. the "spoken pledge" at the time when the situation leading to the murder is developing" (Gjeçov 1989: 118n).

[27] Gjeçov points out that the use of a chisel, a club, or anything made of iron, such as knives or axes, were forbidden, for they were considered fit only for cattle.

near his head and cover his face by a kerchief. In any case, to leave a dead man face-down or his weapon far off, was an unforgivable disgrace (see Kadare 1990: 27). "The murderer may not dare to take the victim's weapon. If he commits such a dishonorable act, he incurs two blood-feuds" (Gjeçov 1989: 164).

The first thing the avenger had to do after killing someone was to send word to the victim's family so that there was no confusion regarding his identity (ibid.). He would then hide in the *kulla*—a two- to three-story grim stone tower built as a "neutral corner" and used for sanctuary for a feuding clansman with fresh blood on his hands—to avoid the immediate vengeance of the victim's family. The *Kanun* demanded that the relatives of the murderer should protect him during the first 24 hours after killing because, if he was killed by someone from the victim's family, that person was simply avenging blood and did not incur punishment (*ibid*.: 168).[28] Meanwhile, his family would send someone to the parents and the relatives of the victim to request and negotiate a twenty-four hour *besa* (the short truce) for the avenger and the entire family, so that they could immediately prepare to defend themselves.[29]

From that moment, the doors of the houses of the avenger's clan, of kinsfolk—near and distant—would all close, for this was the moment of danger, before the victim's family had granted the short truce. After a murder was committed, within 24 hours any member of the murderer's family could be killed in revenge "whilst the blood was boiling." "Blinded" by the newly shed blood, the victim's family had the right to take revenge on any member of the avenger's family or clan. Thereafter, the feud lay between the two households, or clans, although this restriction was never too strictly observed. As soon as another clansman became involved, the feud between the two clans became general and any member of the one could fall a victim to vengeance taken by any member of the other. The ideal was to exact vengeance as quickly as possible since public opinion spurred the avenger (Whitaker 1968).

The *Kanun* defined the truce as "a period of freedom and security which the family of the victim gives to the murderer and his family, temporarily suspending pursuit of vengeance in the blood-feud until the end of the specified term" (Gjeçov 1989: 166). No one was paid for being a guarantor, or a truce negotiator, since "based on the principle of reciprocal need," the *Kanun* did not permit payment to those who acted as guarantors, or to those who obtained a truce for someone (*ibid*.). As for the avenger, he would remain in the *kulla* awaiting the judgment of the victim's family. The twenty-four hours truce was usually granted by the victim's family, since according to the Kanun, "to agree to a truce is the obligation of an honorable man" (*ibid*.).

The long truce (the thirty-day *besa*), was granted only by the village's elders since only they could ask for it the victim's family in the name of the village. It was also the elders' entitlement and responsibility to judge whether the murderer could be pardoned, or fined, or his feud for could formally end. In any case, the thirty-day truce could not be requested until after the burial of the last victim. If the killing had been performed in

---

[28] According to the *Kanun* "after 24 hours, the family of the murderer no longer guards him" (Gjeçov 1989: 168).

[29] If a member of the victim's family, or one of his relatives, killed the murderer after 24 hours had passed, that person was no longer avenging blood, but was incurring blood (*ibid*.: 166, 168).

accordance with the rules, if the *gjaks* (the murderer) had killed "like a man" and had behaved properly at his victim's burial and at the funeral dinner and everything else had been carried out with scrupulous obedience to the *Kanun*, the long truce was mediated and, in most cases, granted by the elders.[30]

A tower of refuge (*kulla*) in the northernmost village of Thethi,
Albania (1987). Courtesy of Peter Lucas.

If the family of the victim had agreed to a truce with the murderer, the latter, even though he was the one responsible for the death, was obliged by the *Kanun* to go to the funeral of his victim, accompany the body to the cemetery and attend the wake to honor the man's soul. If there was one man who could *not* be excused from the burial and the wake, this was the murderer of the victim. According to the *Kanun*, "if the murderer does not go to the funeral and the wake after the truce has been given, it is not considered dishonorable for the family of the victim to withdraw the truce, since the murderer has added insult to injury" (Gjeçov 1989: 166). However absurd this situation, the avenger knew that he was better protected by the twenty-four hours truce than by the loophole of the *kulla*. And if the village asked for the thirty-day truce on his behalf and the truce was agreed upon by the victim's family, the murderer would be at peace for another four weeks. The truce was also extended to the entire clan of the murderer in its village, regardless of how many people this comprised. If the family of the victim was obstinate

---

[30] If the elders of the village could not reach an agreement on certain complex cases, those cases were settled by the interpreters of the *Kanun* who enjoyed unrivaled standing in the highlands of northern Albania.

and did not agree to give the village a truce, the murderer, together with his entire family and all his relatives, should remain indoors. After that, death would lurk all around him. He could move around only at night, hiding from the sun, the moonlight, and the flicker of torches, but at the first light of day he would have to flee and conceal himself (*ibid.*: 164, 168).

Symbolism

IT IS INTERESTING to see how much symbolism was blended in the norms and rituals of vengeance. Symbolic elements were not things in themselves but forms of expression for relationships within a given tribe or among tribes. In some areas, for example, when the mountaineers had to avenge a violation of hospitality or a murder, they would not shave their beards until the vengeance was accomplished. After that, they would shave their beards, give a feast, and enjoy themselves with their friends and fellow-villagers, just as at a wedding (see Gjeçov 1989: 218n).

Similarly, to remind one that he should have avenged the blood of his guest—or a murder in his family—so that he could return the honor back to his family and tribe, the left hand was used by all the members of the community to "greet" him in public.[31] It was a sort of theatrical performance played out in front of others to disgrace him publicly, very similar to what Pierre Bourdieu (1979: 141) found among the Kabyles in Algeria. To a man that had failed to avenge the blood of a guest, or that of a family member, everything was given with the left hand and passed under the knee until he avenged him. As in other Mediterranean societies, in Albania, too, *honor* acquired its meaning in relation to *shame*. Public disgrace and shame were reserved for those who failed to restore personal or family honor.

The centrality of blood as a symbol finds particularly striking parallels in various feuding societies, as it revolves around proverbs, such as "blood does not become water" (in Albania); "blood is no water" (in Montenegro, see Djilas 1958: 107); or "blood is not for sale" (in Corsica, see Knudsen 1985). In houses that had a death to avenge, the custom required that they hung up the victim's bloodstained shirt at the upper store of the house, or a corner of their *kulla*, and they should not take it down until the blood had been avenged. In his acclaimed novel *Broken April*, Ismail Kadare suggests that "when bloodstains began to yellow, people said, it was a sure sign that the dead man was in torment; he had found no rest and was crying out for vengeance" (1990: 111). Here, too, parallels abound, and not just from the Mediterranean. Keith Brown reports the significance of blood symbolism in sixteenth-century Scottish feuding, in part because blood could stand for a man's life, in part because it could stand for the bond of kinship (*ibid.*: 28). Brown goes on adding that bloodstained clothes were sometimes even brought before courts—such was the "visual impact [of blood] in a society where symbol and ritual were important means of communication (1986: 29). In Montenegro, as we are told by Boehm, a mother "repeatedly showed a container of her dead husband's blood to her

---

31 A very similar tradition has been described by Höeg (1925: 20) as part of the Mediterranean code of honor. Henslin (2007: 41) also reports that in some cultures offering someone food or a gift with the left hand would be a great insult.

young sons to remind them, as they grew up, that since there was no one else to do the job, they must avenge him" (Boehm 1987: 63).

As noted before, the rules of the blood feud were only a small part of the *Kanun*, just a chapter (Chapter 22). But they dominated the whole life of the tribesman since, as Edith Durham (1910) put it, "everything turns on *gjak* (blood)." The other part, which had to do with everyday life and was not soaked with blood, was inextricably bound to the bloody part, so much so that, as Kadare splendidly describes in his *Broken April*, no one could really tell where one part left off and the other began. "The whole was so conceived that one begat the other, the stainless giving birth to the bloody, and the second to the first, and so on forever, from generation to generation" (Kadare 1990: 27).

MAKING SENSE OF BLOOD TAKING: FRAMES OF REFERENCE

IT IS INTERESTING from a sociological perspective to ask—at some level of abstraction—how did avenging personal honor, from a sporadic, negligible, unreflective behavior become a biding social norm universally shared and sustained among the mountaineers of northern Albania for centuries, leading to a deliberate, predictable, norm-guided behavior—hence a control system—as was codified in the *Kanun* of Lekë Dukagjini. Is it simply because, as Djilas puts it, the irrationality and the feelings enacting the norms of vengeance resemble "the wildest, sweetest kind of drunkenness" (Djilas 1958: 107)? Or, is it something else, and much more substantial and complex than this?

In this closing section I consider a number of old and recent interpretations of vengeance, particularly as it was codified in the *Kanun* of Lekë Dukagjini and practiced in northern Albania over the centuries. I do not intend to offer an alternative interpretation; what I shall try to do is better described as pointing toward the direction in which a better understanding of vengeance and the *Kanun*—and probably a more informed and complex explanation—might be found.

Of all interpretations attempting to explain vengeance in northern Albania, the one that has very little appeal among sociologists and anthropologists alike is the "theory" that feuding among northern Albanians is virtually a natural characteristic of them, a distinctive state of nature reflecting their primitive tribalism, or even a primordial attribute of their "unique" race. As W.H. Cozens-Hardy put it, northern Albanians, like their neighboring Montenegrins, have been described as a people for whom "every occupation, except fighting, is beneath the dignity of a man" (1894: 397). In light of this "theory", war has always been "their chief occupation and their first thought" (*ibid.*), and their society was one in which "men channeled their energies into murderous aggression against each other" (Schwartz 1955: 570). Hence, the craving for revenge among Albanian tribesmen is seen as a cultural given and a natural affinity, like kinship sentiments. It allegedly has an overpowering emotional and non-rational quality. For an Albanian man, according to Coon, his "first loyalty is to his 'blood', that is, his extended family," and "the very act of vengeance is a ritual, as is the constant repetition of the need for vengeance" (Coon 1950: 37).

Of Mice, Men, and Mountains: Justice Albanian Style

The argument that violence and blood feuds are a remnant of — or reversion to — tribalism has been profusely used by some authors aiming to explain the ethnic conflicts and fratricidal wars in the Balkans, particularly those between Serbs and Kosovo Albanians. In his *Balkan Ghosts*, Robert Kaplan (1993) conveys this view most explicitly, maintaining that these people had been killing each other in tribal and religious wars for centuries.

Describing the mountaineers of northern Albania in the early twentieth century, George Scriven (1918) argued that having spent their lives "in constant conflict with nature in its most unfriendly aspects, they have been taught from infancy to fight against man as readily as against the warring elements of the air." While hardly any clearer than Scriven, Gabriele Annan is equally certain about this primordial imperative of and urge for revenge among northern Albanians. She writes: "The tribal highlanders had only one interest and one hobby: blood feud," adding that "almost anything could be taken as an insult, to be avenged by the death of the perpetrator, or a member of his family....Almost every family was 'in blood' with two or three others" (Annan 1988).

Contrary to this view, studies on [collective] violence show that kinship sentiments are very real social facts — and they can become extremely salient and emotional — but in ordinary times they are only one of several roles and identities that matter (Oberschall 1998). There is a lot of variance in a population on kinship attachments and identities. Such identities are "less primordial and fixed than contingent and changing" (Linz and Stepan 1996: 366). They are amenable to being constructed or eroded by human agency and political choices.

Another poor interpretation is the neo-Malthusian explanation that considers blood feud in upland Albania as "a characteristic mechanism of population control" (Coon 1950: 40). According to Coon, among the tribes of northern Albania blood feuds and warfare were incessant and their underlying cause was "population pressure." This author goes on arguing that feuds and sudden death, just like emigration, are "necessary safety valves" for the survival of a population (*ibid.*: 32, 21). Stephen Wilson makes a similar claim with regard to nineteenth century Corsica where, in his words, "the idiom of honor was used to justify the violence and the deadly spiral of vengeance" among families resulting from competition for "scarce resources" as an "economic imperative" (Wilson 1988a; 1988b).

Coon and Wilson are not alone in trying to argue for a neo-Malthusian "theoretical" justification of modern-day feuding. Writing on the blood feud in Montenegro, Christopher Boehm also believes that feuding serves as a form of population control (1987: 175-80). The basic rationale behind this claim, in his view, is that feuding is particularly suited to *ecologies* in which people compete for limited resources, as in the mountains of Montenegro or Albania, in Appalachia, the highlands of Scotland or the hills and lava fields of Iceland — anywhere, as Boehm puts it, were "groups regularly came into contact in situations were avoidance could not easily resolve intergroup conflicts" (*ibid.*: 240).

This interpretation is inadequate. I will constrain myself by making only two brief remarks. First, the population of the mountainous regions in northern Albania, where revenge taking was practiced most frequently and austerely, has always been very sparse even though poverty in those areas has not been more significantly pronounced than in some more densely populated—but equally remote—areas in eastern and southernmost Albania. Second, this interpretation ignores the wisdom that demographic imperatives do not work in isolation; they are always combined with social and cultural factors (Weinstein 2005: 55-6).

A third interpretation falls into the old philosophical doctrine of geographical determinism as was formulated in the eighteenth century by Montesquieu in his *De l'esprit des lois* (*The Spirit of the Laws*). Coon, for example, refers to "the land forms, the climate, the geographical position away from main routes of travel and migration," which combined made the mountains and the forests of northern Albania "one of the most marginal and isolated regions of Europe...a true refuge area, comparable to the Caucasus and the western Himalayan reaches" (Coon 1950). Writing in the same vein, Hasluck points to the "fantastic physical features which have molded the way of life of the mountaineers," arguing that such geographical characteristics have influenced the tribal cleft which still survives in the population, especially in the main valleys in the north, such as Shalë, Shkrel and Orosh (Hasluck 1954: 1, 2).

This argument is popular, but weak. While few would deny that "little tradition" cultures, to use the language of the Chicago anthropologist Robert Redfield (1947), have evolved and survived in response to specific and unique environments, enabling them to remain relatively unaffected by the evolution of other cultures, anthropologists and social historians have, by and large, exaggerated the salience of the geographical environment to specific cultural traditions among various peoples. In our case, environmental conditions alone do not suffice to explain the "little" and isolated tradition or the culture of blood feud in northern Albania.

Oddly enough, there are also those who think that blood feud is quite an *irrational* behavior and can be explained only with the feelings and the emotional state of the individual who practice it. Such a "theory" is very superficial. Although emotions and feelings certainly have their own part, they alone can not explain the unremitting chain of revengeful behavior from generation to generation. For how could anger motivate the killing of someone for a perceived insult to one's personal or family honor, or even a murder that took place long before anybody in either family had been born? Most revenge actions in northern Albania usually occurred after a relatively long time from the previous murder.

There is, of course, no denial of the strong emotions of grief, pain, or hate that the murder of a member of one's family can trigger. Such emotions are part of the human experience. With the passing of time, however, those emotions will, more likely than not, lose both their *intensity* and the *propensity* to seek revenge if they were not stirred by a sense of *moral duty* or *social obligation*—hence the fear of shame if failing—to do so. Here is where social norms come to play with all of their binding authority, enabling us, among others, to understand the Durkheimian world of *homo sociologicus* in northern Albania and in other Mediterranean societies, such as Montenegro, Corsica or Sicily, where notions of honor and shame have been of central cultural significance (Peristiany 1966; Davis 1977: 89-101).

Social norms do not become binding overnight but in the course of extensive and prolonged social interaction and frequently recurring events that bestow them enough power to become almost universally acknowledged, accepted and obeyed, so much so that in the event of breaking them, the ramifications will be inevitably highly undesirable. I agree with what I believe to be Elster's major argument, that *social norms* are shared and sustained "by the feelings of embarrassment, anxiety, guilt and shame that a person suffers at the prospect of violating them" (Elster 1989). Hence, as Elster points out, however impulsive or irrational vengeance might seem it is the inescapable outcome resulting from the infringement of this norm-guided behavior—awfully merciless social sanctions and punishment ranging from public humiliation to ostracism—that makes it a *rational* behavior based on a specific cost-benefit analysis. In other words, the rationality of following the norms and obeying the rules of the *Kanun* when it came to avenge one's personal or family honor resulted from the necessity to avoid the embarrassment and the shame for failing to do so as well as the economic and social sanctions associated with it. For, as Elster (1989) maintains, whenever there is a norm to do X, there is also a "meta-norm" to sanction people who fail to do X.

One of the most popular theories about the *Kanun* of Lekë Dukagjini and the blood feud as its central part and punitive apparatus is that this corpus of customary law was meant to prevent endless feuding by urging the swiftest vengeance and a rough, follow-up justice. I do not know of explicit statements of this view. Several writers, however, have taken this position, believing that the *Kanun*, although it permitted killing, effectively regulated retribution, preventing general mayhem. Lord Broughton, for example, who traveled with his life-long friend Lord Byron on his famous journey to Albania, Greece and Turkey in the early nineteenth century, considered instant private retaliation among the mountaineers of Albania an effective deterrent. He wrote: "The custom of wearing arms openly…instead of increasing diminishes the instances of murder, for it is not probable that a man will often hazard an offence for which he may instantly lose his life" (Broughton 1858 [1813]: 134).

The general argument here is that norms of retribution serve the social function of resolving conflicts and reducing the level of violence below what it would otherwise have been.[32] Boehm, for example, maintains that there will be fewer quarrels in societies regulated by codes of honor, since everybody knows that they can have disastrous consequences (1984: 88). Rightly, Elster does not think so. As he points out, it is not clear that there is less violence in a vendetta-ridden society than in an unregulated state of nature, since in the state of nature there might be less violence because people would not harm others just to get even (Elster 1989).

This "deterrent" theory is hard to evaluate. I shall, however, adduce three arguments against it. First, it falls short of explaining why the practice of blood feud existed in the first place or, when, where, why, and how it began. Second, it does not account for why blood feud was a common phenomena and, indeed, the law of the land in northern Albania, but virtually nonexistent in the south.[33] Third, if the prevention of endless feuds was its goal,

---

[32] For a provocative account on this issue see Elster (1989).

[33] Unlike other British travelers, Lord Broughton did not have first-hand acquaintance with northern Albania. He traveled only through a limited area in the southernmost part of the country neighboring Greece—as is shown, among others, in his statement that "there are very few of them [Albanians] who cannot speak Greek" (1858 [1813]: 135)—and his description of the southern *banditti* mountaineers bears no resemblance whatsoever with the highlanders of northern Albania. Hence his deterrent argument is irrelevant in light of our discussion.

why then the urge to even the score as soon as possible and the universal disgrace if retaliation was delayed? The very high death-toll exacted by the blood feud seems to contradict the "central point" of such a theory.

I have reasonable doubts about all of these "theories". They are essentially inadequate since ignoring the importance of symbolism and separating the code of honor and vengeance from their historical, economic and cultural context, none of them adds up to a strong claim of explaining the endless blood feuds in northern Albania. An explanation provided by Shtjefën Gjeçov in a footnote on Paragraph CLVII (Book 11) of the *Kanun* seems much more reliable to me. The man who assembled and masterfully edited the *Kanun* of Lekë Dukagjini brings into focus a very important aspect, which has surprisingly passed unnoticed to all of those who have studied the *Kanun*. According to Gjeçov, just like the burning of houses for certain crimes was a late development, promulgated by the Ottoman government and put into effect by certain powerful families in the mountains of northern Albania, so did the custom of seeking blood in vengeance from the *entire* family of the murderer not occur in earlier days. That practice, too, was a late development, since originally the *Kanun* applied the principle "Blood follows the finger." Contrary to the "theory" that the *Kanun* aimed at preventing endless feuding by urging the swiftest vengeance in order to control the practice of blood feud and prevent general havoc, Gjeçov pointed out that the inclusion of any male members from the murderer's family—even of those not living in the same house—as targets for retaliation, indeed intended "to make it easier to exact vengeance" (Gjeçov 1989: 212n).

Because in most cases "blood money" was involved—fines (up to 500 grosh) were to be paid by the murderer's family to the powerful House of Gjomarkaj in Mirditë, the Chiefs of clans, or the representatives of Banners—there was a vested interest in expanding the pool of males against whom vengeance could be taken. The larger the number of males eligible for murder, the more money for the powerful families, who, in the name of the *Kanun*, or the "Law of Lekë," maintained political, social, and economic control over such a vengeance-ridden society. In Gjeçov's own words,

> The greed for money on the part of some Chiefs and representatives of Banners, in association with the Elders, caused certain customs to increase and develop for the purpose of filling wallets and stomachs (Gjeçov 1989: 212n).

At the very least, I believe that this account, provided by the man who was the first to collect, organize and publish the *Kanun*, definitely proves Hasluck's point, to which I referred earlier in this paper, that like any type of customary law, the *Kanun* of Lekë Dukagjini has been constantly recast and added to by a body of experts drawn from the rank of rulers.

We know very little about the real origin of blood feud in northern Albania to evaluate the "theories" discussed above. However, none of them offers a clear-cut set of explanations. They seem to add little to our understanding of the blood feud and its sociological and psychodynamic significance as a particular—but very rigorous, pervasive, and judiciously prescribed—pattern of human behavior, a corrective institution, and an almost universally shared pattern of beliefs and social arrangements in the highlands of northern Albania.

Against this background, I think it is useful to consider, as a plausible frame of reference or, at least as a useful intellectual exercise, how the institution of blood feud can be approached from the standpoint of the functional theory, which I am inclined to favor above the rest. The reader is encouraged to think of other possible sociological frameworks.

Functionalism, as Alvin Gouldner (1959) maintains, explains "the persistence of social patterns in terms of their ongoing consequences for existent social systems." It may be assumed, as a first approximation, that because the main rule of vengeance is reciprocity at any given case—a man for a man; a soul for a soul, or a life for a life, as was also found in the *Old Testament*[34]—the concept of reciprocity assumes *central* importance in explaining the blood feud.

If we start from this assumption, then Hobhouse (1956 [1906]) and Thurnwald (1932) were right in considering reciprocity in every relation of primitive life as a key intervening variable through which shared social rules were enabled to yield stability in society. This, in Thurnwald's view, is the basis on which the entire social and ethical life of primitive civilizations presumably rests (Thurnwald 1932: 137). George Simmel's remarks take us a step further since, in his view, not only in primitive societies but in *every* society, all relations among men "rest on the schema of giving and returning the equivalence" (Simmel 1950: 387). The concept of reciprocity is thus tacitly involved in *all* human behavior, whereas in the case of blood feud it was overtly prescribed in the *Kanun* and very rigorously observed in practice.

Contrary to some cultural relativists, Gouldner (1960) suggests that the norm of reciprocity is universal; it is "no less universal and important an element of culture than the incest taboo, although, similarly, its concrete formulations may vary with time and place." Because blood was reciprocated only with blood, that is to say that the exchange was correctly alike, or identical in form, Gouldner would call this kind of reciprocity "homeomorphic" in comparison with what he calls "heteromorphic" reciprocity, that is when the things exchanged are "concretely different although equal in *value*" (*ibid.*).

It must be emphasized, however, that from the standpoint of functional theory the norm of reciprocity can only serve to explain the preservation of the custom of blood feud as a mechanism for the stability of the social system that invented it and relied on it, but *not* as a "starting mechanism" for the establishment of that particular system. Functionalist theory, as Gouldner points out, is applicable to already established, on-

---

[34] In the original Hebrew, paragraphs 17-22 of Chapter 24 read: "17. If anyone takes the life of a human being, he must be put to death; 18...life for life; 19. If anyone injures his neighbor, whatever he has done must be done to him; 20. fracture for fracture, eye for eye, tooth for tooth. As he has injured the other, so he is to be injured" (Leviticus 24: 17-22). In a remarkably similar way, a number of articles of the *Kanun* of Lekë Dukagjini affirm that "all are equal" (Gjeçov 1989: 170); "On his own scale, each man weights the same as everyone else" (*ibid.*: 130); "the value of a man's life is the same, whether he is handsome or ugly" (*ibid.*: 170); "all men have the same value" (*ibid.*); "Leka [Dukagjini] considered all blood equal; the good are born from the bad and bad from the good. 'Soul for soul, all are equal before God'" (ibid.: 130); and "whoever kills a human being...must pay the same penalty" (*ibid.*: 170). Hence, articles 901, 902, and 903 of the *Kanun* spell out that "if two men kill each other in the course of an argument, the law that states "a head for a head or blood for blood" has been fulfilled, since both are dead" (*ibid.*: 172) and "the families of the murdered men have no claims on each other, nor may they demand compensation from each other. They must guarantee a truce, in accordance with the Kanun" (*ibid.*); and "if one is killed and the other is wounded, then the wounded man must pay the balance of the blood-money for the murdered man" (*ibid.*: 172-4).

going systems. Its focus is *not* on "starting mechanisms" that create a given social system but in mechanisms by means of which an already established system is enabled to maintain itself.

In light of this discussion, the norm of reciprocity is of little help in explaining when and why blood feuds started to become a common practice in northern Albania, or in any other society for that matter. Yet, it helps to understand why, once it became a common practice, the blood feud was codified in all of its meticulous details and rules, which helped to preserve the system and maintain its stability for hundreds—if not thousands—of years, even though it did not benefit anyone.

We may never be able to know when, why and how the mountaineers of northern Albania began to avenge blood for blood, making it a universally accepted and practiced—and fastidiously observed—social norm that became central to the customary law that ruled their lives for centuries. Certainly it was not a sort of "primordial urge" in them, and not either their "unique" psychology or character. Furthermore, it was not any sort of population pressure, nor where climate, terrain or other geographical factors those that established and/or maintained the widespread practice of blood feud. Although functionalist theory may not be able to provide an explanation for the origin of vendettas, it certainly provides insights on the rationale behind the perpetual existence of blood feuds through the rule of "reciprocity" as a norm that maintained and safeguarded the existing social system.

Functionalist theory also provides certain answers as to how individual members of a given society are prepared through socialization to play a role in maintaining their social system. Even though we may never be able to determine what served as a "starting mechanism" or, to use Boehm's term, as an "opening move" of the blood feud, once revenge was instigated and reciprocity was sanctioned as the most appropriate norm, it was gradually internalized in both parties (the murderer and his family and the victim's family) as the norm *obligating* the party that had first suffered injury to avenge it in the *same* way. Boehm (1983) employs the notion that "attitudes, like genes", are likely to be transmitted intergenerationally through socialization and in this way may become culturally routinized. Routinization of vengeful practices and collectively learned, internalized and obeyed norms and rules accompanying them helped shape the behavior of the mountaineers, making them believe—individually as well as in group—that such rules were for *everyone* binding *in their own right*.

Through such a process of socialization the norm of reciprocity, applied with extreme rigor especially in the practice of vengeance, gradually gained what Gouldner (1959) would call "a kind of *prima facie* legitimacy for properly socialized group members." Internalized as such, the norm of reciprocity, as I understand it here, performed an important function of preserving the tribal social system in northern Albania and its customary law that remained unchallenged by outside influences for a very long time. It became, to use Sugden's (1989) language, the "convention equilibria" of northern Albanian society. Because the rights and obligations of parties were internalized as *socially* and *juridically* binding norms for all the members of the community, they *readily* and *fully* assumed responsible participation in the social system as defined and sanctioned in the *Kanun*. Here Gouldner (1959) provides a reasonable proposition that "not only does the norm of reciprocity play a stabilizing role in human relations in the *absence* of a well developed system of specific status duties, but it contributes to social stability even when these are present and well established."

REFERENCES

Allcock, John B., and Antonia Young (eds.). 1991. *Black Lambs and Grey Falcons: Women Travelers in the Balkans*. Bradford: Bradford University Press.

Anderson, Scott. 1999. "The Curse of Blood and Vengeance." *New York Times Magazine*, December 16.

Annan, Gabriele. 1988. "Roughing it." *The New York Review of Books*, December 22.

Blok, Anton. 1981. "Rams and Billy-Goats: A Key to the Mediterranean Code of Honour." *Man* 16, 3: 427-440.

Boehm, Christopher. 1983. *Montenegrin Social Organization and Values: Political Ethnography of a Refuge Area Tribal Adaptation*. New York: AMS Press.

_____. 1984. *Blood Revenge: The Anthropology of Feuding in Montenegro and Other Tribal Societies*. Lawrence: University Press of Kansas.

_____. 1987. *Blood Revenge: The Enactment and Management of Conflict in Montenegro and Other Tribal Societies*. Philadelphia: University of Pennsylvania Press.

Bohannan, Paul J. 1977. "Anthropology and the Law. Pp. 290-299, in Sol Tax and Leslie G. Freeman (eds.), *Horizons of Anthropology*. Chicago: Aldine Publishing.

Bourdieu, Pierre. 1979. "The Kabyle House or the World Reversed," in *Algeria 1960: Essays by Pierre Bourdieu*. Cambridge: Cambridge University Press.

Broughton, Lord, G.C.B. 1858 [1813]. *Travels in Albania and Other Provinces of Turkey in 1809 & 1810*. London: John Murray.

Brown, Keith. M. 1986. *Bloodfeud in Scotland 1573-1625: Violence, Justice and Politics in an Early Modern Society*. Edinburgh: John Donald.

Calhoun, Steven C. 2000. "Montenegro's Tribal Legacy." *Military Review*, July-August.

Camaj, Martin. 1989. "Foreward." Pp. xiii-xv, in Shtjefën Gjeçov, *The Code of Lekë Dukagjini*. New York: Gjonlekaj Publishing Company.

Coon, Carleton. 1950. *The Mountains of Giants: A Racial and Cultural Study of the North Albanian Mountain Ghegs*. Papers of the Peabody Museum of American Archeology and Ethnology XXIII, 13. Cambridge, MA: Harvard University, Peabody Museum.

Cozens-Hardy, W.H. 1894. "Montenegro and its Borderlands." *The Geographical Journal* 4, 5: 385-405.

Cozzi, Ernesto. 1910. "La vendetta del sangue nelle montagne dell'alta Albania." *Anthropos* 5: 654-687.

Dako, Christo. A. 1919. *Albania: The Master Key to the Near East*. Boston: Grimes.

Davis, John. 1977. *People of the Mediterranean: An Essay in Comparative Social Anthropology*. London: Routledge & Kegan Paul.

Degrand, August. 1901. *Souvenirs de la Haute-Albanie*. Paris.

Djilas, Milovan. 1958. *Land without Justice*. London: Methuen.

Durham, Edith M. 1910. "High Albania and its Customs in 1908." *The Journal of the Royal Anthropological Institute of Great Britain and Ireland* 40: 453-72.

_____. 1928. *Some Tribal Origins, Laws, and Customs of the Balkans*. London: Allen & Unwin.

_____. 1931. "Preservation of Pedigrees and Commemoration of Ancestors in Montenegro." *Man* 31, 163: 154-155.

_____. 1985 [1909]. *High Albania*. Boston: Bacon Press.

Durkheim, Emil. 1968 [1912]. *The Elementary Forms of the Religious Life*, trans. Joseph Ward Swain. London: George Allen & Unwin.

Edlinger, Ludwig. 1910. "Wanderungen durch das östliche Bosnien, Montenegro und Albanien." *Mitteilungen des Vereins für Erdkunde zu Leipzig*, 1909: 63-88.

Elster, Jon. 1989. "Social Norms and Economic Theory," *Journal of Economic Perspectives* 3, 4: 99-117.

_____. 1990. "Norms of Revenge." *Ethics* 100, 4: 862-85.

Fox, Leonard. 1989. "Introduction." Pp. cvi-xix, in Shtjefën Gjeçov, *The Code of Lekë Dukagjini*. New York: Gjonlekaj Publishing Company.

Fraser, John Foster. 1912 [1906]. *Pictures from the Balkans*. London: Cassell & Co.

Fussell, Paul. 1980. *Abroad: British Literary Traveling Between the Wars*. Oxford: Oxford University Press.

Gjeçov, Shtjefën. 1989. *The Code of Lekë Dukagjini*. New York: Gjonlekaj Publishing Company.

Godart, Justin. 1922. *L'Albanie en 1921*. Paris: Presses Universitaires de France.

Gouldner, Alvin W. 1959. "Organizational Analysis," in Robert K. Merton *et al.* (eds.), *Sociology Today*. New York: Basic Books.

_____. 1960. "The Norm of Reciprocity: A Preliminary Statement." *American Sociological Review* 25: 161-178.

Hasluck, Margaret. 1954. *The Unwritten Law in Albania*. Cambridge: Cambridge University Press.

Hassan, Yasmeen. 1999. "The Fate of Pakistani Women." *International Herald Tribune*, May 25.

Henslin, James M. 2007. *Sociology: A Down-to-Earth Approach*. Eight Edition. Boston: Allyn and Bacon.

Hobhouse, L.T. 1956 [1906]. *Morals in Evolution: A Study in Comparative Ethics*. London: Chapman & Hall.

Höeg, Carsten. 1925. *Les Sarakatsans: une tribu nomade grecque. Vol. 1*. Paris: Edouard Champion.

Hume, David. 1751. *An Enquiry Concerning the Principles of Morals*.

Hutton, J.H. 1954. "Introduction." Pp. xi-xv, in Margaret Hasluck, *The Unwritten Law in Albania*. New York: Cambridge University Press.

Johnson, Douglas Wilson. 1916. "The Balkan Campaign." *Geographical Review* 2, 1: 27-47.

Kadare, Ismail. 1988a. *Eschyle ou l'eternel perdant*. Paris: Fayard.

_____. 1988b. *Doruntine*. New York: New Amsterdam Books.

_____. 1990. *Broken April*. New York: New Amsterdam Books.

Kaplan, Robert. 1993. *Balkan Ghosts*. New York: St. Martin Press.

Kastrati, Qazim. 1955. "Some Sources of the Unwritten Law in Albania." *Man* 55, 8: 124-27.

Knudsen, Anne. 1985. "Internal Unrest: Corsican Vendetta — A Structured Catastrophe." *Folk* 27: 65-87.

Lane, Rose Wilder. 1923. *Peaks of Shala*. New York: Harper & Brothers.

Linz, Juan J., and Alfred Stepan. 1996. *Problems of Democratic Consolidation*. Baltimore: John Hopkins University Press.

Lucas, Peter. 1991. "In Albania: A Trek in the Footsteps of an Amazing English Author." *Boston Globe*, September 29.

Maine, Henry Sumner. 1861. *Ancient Law: Its Conception with the Early History of Society and Its Relations to Modern Ideas*. London: John Murray.

Malcolm, Noel. 1998. *Kosovo: A Short History*. New York: New York University Press.

Matthews, Ronald. 1937. *Sons of the Eagle*. London: Methuen.

Mema, Shpëtim. 1987a. *Albanica I*. Tirana: Biblioteka Kombëtare, Sektori i Albanologjisë.

_____. 1987b. *Albanica II*. Tirana: Biblioteka Kombëtare, Sektori i Albanologjisë.

Middleton, John, and Davis Tait (eds.). 1958. *Tribes without Rulers: Studies in African Segmentary Systems*. London: Routledge & Kegan Paul.

Miller, William Ian. 1996. *Bloodtaking and Peacemaking: Feud, Law, and Society in Saga Iceland*. Chicago: University of Chicago Press.

Nopcsa, Baron Franz. 1912. "Beiträge zum Vorgeschichte und Ethnologie Nordalbaniens,"

Wissenschaftliche Mitteilungen aus Bosnien und der Herzegowina (Wien) 12: 168-253.

Oberschall, Anthony. 1998. "Theories and Realities of Ethnic Violence: Bosnia." *Sociological Analysis* 1, 3: 1-25.

Peristiany, J.G. (ed.). 1966. *Honor and Shame. The Values of Mediterranean Society.* London: Weidenfeld & Nicolson.

Quaroni, Pietro. 1966. *Diplomatic Bags: An Ambassador's Memoirs*, Trans. and ed. Anthony Rhodes. New York, D. White Co.

Redfield, Robert. 1947. "The Folk Society." *American Journal of Sociology* 52, 1: 293-308.

Schwartz, Richard D. 1955. Review of *The Unwritten Law in Albania. Stanford Law Review* 7, 4: 566-571.

Scriven, George P. 1918. "Recent Observations in Albania." *The National Geographic Magazine* 34, 1: 90-114.

Sestini, Aldo. 1943. "La regioni dell'Albania." Pp. 253-412, in *Reale Società Geografica Italiana* (comp.): L'Albania. Bologna: Zanichelli.

Seton-Watson, Robert W. 1923. *The Historian as a Political Force in Central Europe.* London: School of Slavonic Studies at the University of London, King's College.

Simmel, Georg. 1950. *The Sociology of Georg Simmel.* Trans. and ed. Kurt H. Wolff. Glencoe, Ill: Free Press.

Sugden, Robert. 1989. "Spontaneous Order." *Journal of Economic Perspective*, 3, 4: 85-97.

Thurnwald, Richard. 1932. *Economics in Primitive Communities.* London: Oxford University Press.

Walcot, Peter. 1978. *Envy and the Greeks: A Study of Human Behaviour.* Warminster: Aris & Philips.

Weinstein, Jay. 2005. *Social and Cultural Change: Social Science for a Dynamic World.* Second Edition. Lanham: Rowman & Littlefield Publishers, Inc.

Whitaker, Ian. 1968. "Tribal Structure and National Politics in Albania, 1910-1950." Pp. 253-293, in I.M. Lewis (ed.), *History and Social Anthropology.* London: Tavistock Publications.

Wilson, Stephen. 1988a. *Feuding, Conflict and Banditry in Nineteenth-Century Corsica.* Cambridge: Cambridge University Press.

_____. 1988b. "Infanticide, Child Abandonment, and Female Honour in Nineteenth-Century Corsica." *Comparative Studies in Society and* History 30, 4: 762-783.

☙ ☙ ☙ ☙ ❧ ❧ ❧ ❧

TARIFA'S EXPOSITION OF THE *KANUN*: SOMETHING FOR SOCIOLOGISTS AND PHILOSOPHERS ALIKE

Rory J. Conces
University of Nebraska at Omaha

*T*O BE ASKED TO provide a commentary on a work is often to be asked to provide a set of criticisms, criticisms that hopefully run deep and generate an exchange between the author and his or her readers. Accordingly, my success as a commentator would depend on the intensity of this exchange. But this approach is not one that I will take while commentating on Fatos Tarifa's informative and insightful work "Of Mice, Men, and Mountains: Justice Albanian Style." I will allow those from within the ranks of the sociologists, those who are most familiar with the ethnography of northern Albania, to begin the debate. Since I am a philosopher, and a different sort of philosopher at that, I plan to follow K. Anthony Appiah's lead when he refers to philosophy as "kibitizing plus attending to the big picture" (Appiah 2001: 104).

The big picture has to do with the *Kanun* as a legal and moral framework that governed for centuries every aspect of people's lives in northern Albania. Tarifa does a painstaking job in laying out the fundamental elements of this framework by exploring the origin of the *Kanun*; examining the key concepts of Honor (*Nderi*), the Word of Honor (*Besa*), and Hospitality (*Mikpritja*); linking the rituals of vengeance within this conceptual web; and juxtaposing a more informed and complex explanation with other "theories" that manifest serious deficiencies in explaining the blood feuds in northern Albania.

As customary law composed of a set of injunctions governing the everyday lives of the mountaineers of northern Albania and codified into a set of 1,263 articles by Lekë Dukagjini—a fifteenth-century Albanian prince and ally of Albania's liberator, Skanderbeg—and transcribed and published in the mid-1930s, the *Kanun* is an extraordinary legal and moral framework that functioned to keep order and create a certain amount of cohesiveness among Christians and Muslims in that part of Albania. In his detailed discussion of the rules governing vengeance, Tarifa makes it clear that though blood letting was indeed regulated, the regulation was such that it often led to its escalation. Granted, vengeance was not allowed in certain instances, and these instances were spelled out in great detail, such as in the case of adultery when the adulterous pair are "killed in the act and with a single shot." Yet the blood feuds took a heavy toll on the male population of northern Albania. The numbers given are staggering.

"Of Mice, Men, and Mountains" is not short on references to those knowledgeable of northern Albania, including the famed British anthropologist Edith Durham. One such reference is to her claim that customs must be understood through the eyes of the people who live them. This is an important facet of ethnographic work because neglecting such an approach has led many to interpret the northern Albanian mountaineers as a lawless people. But Tarifa reminds his readers that the *Kanun* tells a very different story. The situation of those people is anything but unregulated murder and mayhem.

Seen through the eyes of modern moral theorists, however, the *Kanun* and some of its fundamental elements can be placed within an on-going philosophical debate. For all the order and stability that the *Kanun* provided the mountaineer communities, the framework's crucial components of honor and the word of honor confound one of the complaints issued by contemporary critics against morality, which is that morality is an exclusively other-regarding affair rather than a self-regarding project (Louden 1992: 13-14). As Tarifa notes, "for the Albanian highlander honor was more important than life [and liberty]. Honor was the embodiment and the real meaning of life, since, according to the *Kanun*, a dishonored man was considered a dead person." Of course, the honor of the family or the tribe can also be blackened, and not to seek vengeance in this case would be regarded as a disgrace to the family or tribe. Yet in a very real sense, inaction would be an unbearable disgrace to the individual, and so to seek blood letting in this case is, in part, a self-regarding act. If it would be difficult, if not impossible, to live with oneself, then to avenge one's family member (or even a guest in one's dwelling) is in a very meaningful sense a self-regarding affair. So it appears that the "lived morality" of the northern Albanian mountaineer (and I contend, that of many other peoples) was not exclusively other-regarding.

Moreover, it is this unrelenting obligation to settle scores that represents the weakness of the *Kanun* as a moral framework that provides efficacious guidance to practice. Although honor is part of a virtuous character, and character should not go unnoticed in a complete moral framework, honor is taken to such an extreme in the *Kanun* that, as Tarifa notes, it is "contrary to everybody's [including the community's] *self-interest*." Even the traditional models of morality—Kantian, utilitarian, and virtue theory—would find such an outcome to be troubling. With the forces of modernity approaching northern Albania, it was only a matter of time before this weakness of the *Kanun* would lead to its abandonment by many.

Yet in other ways the *Kanun* is in keeping with the traditional model of morality as one that requires moral agents to adopt an other-regarding point of view. This is demonstrated by the practice of hospitality, what Tarifa calls the "most sublime virtue" of the people of northern Albania. Tarifa notes that this is best captured in the *Kanun*'s definition of the mountaineer's house: "The house of the Albanian belongs to God and the guest" (citing Gjeçov 1989: 132). Interesting enough, the obligation to care for the guest was true even when the guest was in a state of blood feud with the one who was giving shelter and protection. So the guest for the northern Albanian took on an even greater importance than blood relations.

What is particularly interesting about hospitality is that while this practice was an other-regarding affair within the lived-world of the Albanian, even to the point of placing one's own life in danger for the sake of the guest, Tarifa does not give us any reason to believe that this practice took on the additional meaning that it has acquired today, which is one of risk taking in the hope of generating empathy. For those who work in the area of conflict prevention, the empathic response and finding ways to invoke such a response are extremely important. It is often difficult to bring disgruntled parties to interact in close proximity in order for an empathetic response to take hold. One way to achieve this closeness is for one of the parties to show hospitality towards the other. This means, according to the theologian Martin Marty, that there should be "a call that at least one party begin to effect change by risking hospitality toward the other" 2005: 1). This amounts to receiving a stranger into one's home, a stranger who may be liked or even hated, so that barriers can be disassembled and a relationship either initiated or restored. But there is no indication that hospitality had such a function in the case of the mountaineers, which suggests that hospitality as practiced by the Albanians was limited insofar as it had little, if any, impact on subduing the endless blood feuds.

The value of Tarifa's "Of Mice, Men, and Mountains: Justice Albanian Style" does not lie solely in giving us a better understanding of the *Kanun* and the code of vengeance, as well as in offering explanations for the origin and maintenance of vengeance in northern Albania. It also surfaces in how his discussion of the *Kanun* finds its way into a bigger picture, one that is not so obvious and that is well beyond the scope of Tarifa's work. Although "Of Mice, Men, and Mountains" will no doubt generate a discussion among sociologists, including one that exposes the limits of the *Kanun*, it has already helped this philosopher to empirically inform the ongoing debate among his colleagues over competing models of morality.

References

Appiah, K. Anthony. 2001. "Grounding Human Rights," In Michael Ignatieff (ed.), *Human Rights as Politics and Idolatry*. Princeton, N.J.: Princeton University Press.

Gjeçov, Shtjefën. 1989. *The Code of Lekë Dukagjini*. New York: Gjonlekaj Publishing Company.

Louden, Robert B. 1992. *Morality and Moral Theory: A Reappraisal and Reaffirmation*. New York: Oxford University Press.

Marty, Martin. 2005. *When Faiths Collide*. Malden, MA.: Blackwell.

Rory J. Conces is Associate Professor of Philosophy and Religion at the University of Nebraska at Omaha. He is the author of Blurred Visions: Philosophy, Science, and Ideology in a Troubled World, *and the founding Editor of* International Dialogue: A Multidisciplinary Journal of World Affairs. *He has traveled extensively in the Balkans and some of his work has been translated into Albanian and Bosnian.*

❦ ❦ ❦ ❦ ❦ ❦ ❦ ❦

BLOOD FOR BLOOD:
CUSTOMARY LAW, COLLECTIVE RIGHTS, AND SURVIVAL IN NORTHERN ALBANIA

Marisa O. Ensor
Eastern Michigan University

*I*N THE EARLY 1930s Malinowski lamented that social anthropology had neglected the study of the law "to an extent which the layman would find unbelievable and which the specialist realizes with shock" (1934: xi). While these reflections on the initial focus of the discipline might have been justified, the growing body of socio-anthropological scholarship explicitly concerned with legal issues, and with broader questions of order in society, suggests that any early oversights have long been remedied. Fatos Tarifa's ethnohistorical analysis of the role of northern Albanian traditional customary law in general, and the *Kanun*—its formal codified version—in particular, as the primary frameworks governing community life in this Balkan region, is an exemplary illustration of social science's valuable contribution to the study of the legal systems of historical and contemporary societies worldwide.

Tarifa refers to the *Kanun* as a corpus of traditional customary law, associated with tribal life in the remote highlands of northern Albania. Customary law is generally derived from custom and tradition—that is, long-established practices that have acquired the force of law by common adoption or acquiescence; it is frequently defined in opposition to authoritarian law, which is established and imposed from above by coercive sources of authority such as rulers, powerful secular or religious elites, or court systems (Benson 1990). The formulation of the *Kanun* is popularly attributed to Lekë Dukagjini, an Albanian prince who lived in the fifteenth century. Although, as Tarifa reminds us, Prince Dukagjini's contribution was probably limited to expanding the already existing customary injunctions, as well as imposing them more strictly on the territories under his control (Whitaker 1968), the admittedly artificial boundary between customary and authoritarian law became blurred as the *Kanun*'s source of legitimacy switched from the force of custom and tradition to the authority of a powerful, almost mythical ruler.

Distinctions on the sources of legitimacy and authority, while sometimes arbitrary, can nonetheless be important as regulations imposed from above—or perceived as such—tend to require more force and coercion than those seen as originating from community practice through mutual recognition and acceptance. Whatever the particular balance between consensus and coercion in securing compliance, order in any society must entail a certain level of understanding among the members as to what are the acceptable and unacceptable forms of conduct in a given context. In the absence of such shared assumptions, social life could scarcely exist (Roberts 1979: 31). Although not really discussed in Tarifa's analysis, it would be enlightening to ascertain which source of legitimacy was favored by those who followed the *Kanun* themselves, particularly women and other groups whose ascribed roles in patriarchal highland Albanian society were so clearly subordinated. Gender issues also frame an interesting discrepancy regarding the alleged "universal conformity" to this body of law of a society whose members were "trained from childhood to believe in its infallible authority" (Coon 1950: 37). Given that the code was handed down orally "from father to son," remaining in the verbal custody of male elders and "northern tribesmen"—females appear to have been excluded from acquiring this knowledge—it is not clear how women, entrusted with the upbringing and socialization of the next generation of compliant mountaineers, managed to inculcate in their children the need to conform with a large, complex and all-encompassing body of law with whose specifics they were apparently unacquainted.

Commentary

Indeed, another striking characteristic of the *Kanun* is its systematic thoroughness, expressed in 1,263 strictly enforced articles which governed in astounding detail every aspect of people's lives. It is worth noting that this ancient legal code had been handed down orally for centuries, and was not written down until the mid-1930s. It has been argued that enshrining a given set of indigenous customary practices in a written code tends to privilege some practices over others, often reflecting the priorities of the ruling elites, creating an artificial "tradition" — or distorted customary law — that then becomes identified as part of indigenous culture (Bonvillain 2006: 433). Tarifa acknowledges that the modern written version of the *Kanun* is unlikely to be quite the same customary law that had habitually been practiced by tribal groups for many generations. The code was subject to modification and reinterpretation over time, and was somewhat differently applied among the relatively isolated mountain communities where it constituted the primary source of law. Under these circumstances, one wonders how many of the written 1,263 articles were literally "remembered" by the chiefs and elders consulted by the Shtjefën Gjeçovi; which ones might have been reinterpreted, deleted or added, to better reflect the social conditions of the time — or the informants' own personal priorities; and what effect did being filtered through a Franciscan-trained lens have on the teachings preserved in the collective memory of the Albanian highlanders of the early 20th Century.

Although comprising only a single chapter of the code, the aspect of the *Kanun* that has most firmly gripped the scholarly and popular imagination is undoubtedly the compulsory retaliatory killings or "blood feuds". Revenge-driven violence, whether in the form of blood feud, or individual acts of revenge, is by no means unique to the mountain dwellers of northern Albania. Indeed, cross-cultural studies reveal that some version of this practice has been part of the cultural repertoire of societies as diverse as ancient Greece, Medieval Iceland, Renaissance England, the Jibaro Indians of eastern Ecuador, contemporary Corsica and Egypt, and the Balkan societies of Albania, Montenegro, Serbia and Macedonia. Based on his own fieldwork in Montenegro supplemented with accounts of other societies, Boehm defined blood feud as "a pattern of homicidal conflict that simultaneously involved the ideas or scorekeeping and alternating retaliation and that is theoretically interminable but generally is pacifiable thorough the payment of compensation for blood" (1984: 222), an interpretation consistent with Tarifa's ethnohistorical account.

The remote and inaccessible highlands of Albania, Tarifa observes, were never completely subjected by the Ottoman Turks. Loosely organized in largely autonomous tribal and patrilineal clan units, and lacking an official authoritarian legal system and a state authority to administer the law — Islamic *shariah* law was never successfully imposed in the region — Albanian highlanders were responsible for devising and enforcing their own methods of conflict resolution. Interpersonal conflict could too easily escalate in such a warrior society, threatening to spread throughout the entire region. Feuding, however, was not unconstrained, and rules regulating blood feuding were modified and made more strict after the Ottomans introduced firearms with greater killing potential than the local weapons traditionally used in the region. "By subjecting to rules the conflicts that [did] arise and keeping them between lower social units such as families or clans, they [could] be kept from disrupting the entire society" (Hayden 1985: 717). Tribal cohesion was thus maintained despite the disruptive tendencies of the proclivity to feud. In other words, the regulations surrounding vengeance served to limit blood feuds' spread and duration, provided a rational, if violent, solution to the potential problem of the ramification of honor-based conflicts throughout the society, and contributed to the survival of the community as a whole. The *Kanun*'s prominence as an informal legal system in several regions of Albania has persisted to some degree until the present suggesting that, whatever its limitations, this body of law is perceived as performing an important function in the communities where it has been implemented.

From a legal anthropology standpoint the implications of retaliatory killings — both a threat to the individual right to life, and an affirmation of community survival — are illustrative of the dialectical relationship between the rights of the individual and the collective rights of certain groups. Human rights are largely based on the liberal tradition of the protection of the individual, and most international human right instruments are expressed in the language of individual rights. The term "collective rights" remains rather ambiguous, although various definitions of "collective" or "group rights" have been proposed. Theodoor van Boven, for instance, defines collective rights as those pertaining a collectivity of persons who share special and distinct characteristics a racial, ethnological, national, linguistic, or religious nature and/or who find themselves in specific situations or conditions (1982: 55). So defined, the rights of highland Albanian groups seem to conform to this category. Although Tarifa's analysis does not explicitly use a human rights framework—a relatively modern concept whose prominence postdates the Kanun—I would argue that human rights considerations do nonetheless provide an additional vantage points from which to examine the individual and collective dimensions of life in northern Albania.

Many legal scholars and human rights advocates currently highlight the interdependence between individual and collective rights, rejecting an excessively sharp distinction between them. Article 29 of the Universal Declaration, which states that "everyone has duties to the communities in which alone the free and full development of his personality is possible", is pointed out as an illustration of modern global conceptions of rights as encompassing both aspects of this dialectic (Brownlie 1981: 26). On the other hand, there is a clear possibility of conflict between collective and individual rights. Those who oppose the concept of collective rights often ground their arguments on the problematic issue of representation (Jovanovic 2005: 643). In effect, "most groups are not homogeneous at any given moment", resulting in "conflict[s] of interests within groups", with those "between masses and elites"—subordinated and dominant groups—being the most important ones (Kukathas 1995: 269). Or, as Laura Nader reminds us "law is often not a neutral regulator of power but instead the vehicle by which different parties attempt to gain and maintain control and legitimization of a given social unit (2002: 117). Furthermore, prioritizing collective rights over the rights of individuals may fix collective identities too rigidly, and thus, oppressively, given that "group rights strengthen dominant subgroups within each culture and privilege conservative interpretations of culture over reformative and innovative ones (Tamir 1999: 163).

Tarifa suggests that the "perpetual need for common defense in this war-ridden society" made preservation of the unity and stability of highland Albanian families, organized in terms of extended patrilineal households, "essential for survival". The *Kanun,* a set of laws "that governed everything in people's lives—from cradle to grave"—is seen as a method of maintaining this social structure, thus ensuring the collective survival of the community. In this rigid code individual rights and freedoms are clearly subordinated to local understandings of collective rights. The burdens imposed on some members, however, are considerably more onerous than those expected of others. For instance, the stability of marriage appears to have been enforced by giving the husband the right to kill his wife if she betrayed him or attempted to leave him, even if she had not voluntarily consented to the marriage and had been forcefully handed over to her husband by her father. There does not seem to have been a comparable arrangement for wives. Females were exempted from blood feud, as their "blood" was not seen as equal to that of men, and it was prohibited for ambushers to fire their gun at women. Tarifa refers to this attitude as "the sanctity of women". Some would argue that the fact that the proscription also extended to children, houses and livestock—that is, men's property—suggests that women were objectified, rather than sanctified, in northern Albanian society. In fact, Tarifa admits that "this was very much a man's world" and, I would add, an illustration of the often cited adage arguing that "the dominant view is the view of the dominant".

While the rigid enforcement of the *Kanun* may have indeed contributed to the survival of generations of highland Albanian households under extremely demanding circumstances, the need for doing so in such a violent way and at the expense of women's autonomy—and possibly that of other subordinated groups—remains a topic for further discussion. Overall, Tarifa's thoughtful analysis serves to increase our knowledge of the role of customary law in traditional societies,

Commentary

and points to the need to establish culturally-sensitive methods for balancing the interests of individuals, the collective rights of social and cultural groups, and the state. It also makes the case for a more integrated understanding of law and social science as not just compatible, but mutually constitutive, disciplines. As the American jurist Oliver Wendell Holmes once reflected, the law is "one big anthropological document" (1920: 212).

References

Benson, Bruce L. 1990. *The Enterprise of the Law: Justice without the Law*. San Francisco, CA: Pacific Research Institute for Public Policy.

Boehm, Christopher. 1984. *Blood Revenge: The Anthropology of Feuding in Montenegro and Other Tribal Societies*. Lawrence, KS: University Press of Kansas.

Bonvillain, Nancy. 2006. *Cultural Anthropology*. Upper Saddle River, NJ: Pearson, Prentice Hall.

Brownlie, Ian. 1981. *Basic Documents on Human Rights*. Oxford, UK: Clarendon Press.

Coon, Carleton. 1950. *The Mountains of Giants: A Racial and Cultural Study of the North Albanian Mountain Ghegs*. Papers of the Peabody Museum of American Archaeology and Ethnology XXIII, 13. Cambridge, MA: Harvard University, Peabody Museum.

Hayden, Robert. 1985. "Reviewed Work(s): Blood Revenge: The Anthropology of Feuding in Montenegro and other Tribal Societies, by Christopher Boehm". *American Anthropologist*, New Series, 87, 3: 716-717. Berkley: University of California Press.

Holmes, Oliver Wendell. 1920. "Law in Science—Science in Law." In *Collected Legal Papers*. New York: Harcourt, Brace and Co.

Jovanovic, Miodrag A. 2005. "Recognizing Minority Identities through Collective Rights," *Human Rights Quarterly* 27: 625-651.

Kukathas, Chandran. 1995. "Are There Any Cultural Rights?" In Julia Stapleton (ed.), *Group Rights: Perspectives Since 1900*. Bristol, UK: Thoemmes Press.

Malinowski, Bronislaw. 1934. "Introduction." In H. Ian Hogbin (ed.), *Law and Order in Polynesia*. New York: Harcourt, Brace & Co.

Nader, Laura. 2002. *The Life of the Law: Anthropological Projects*. Berkley: University of California Press.

Roberts, Simon. 1979. *Order and Dispute: An Introduction to Legal Anthropology*. New York: St. Martin's Press.

Tamir, Yael. 1999. "Against Collective Rights." In Christian Joppke and Steven Lukes (eds.), *Multicultural Questions*. Oxford: Oxford University Press.

Van Boven, Theodor C. 1982. "Distinguishing Criteria of Human Rights." In Karel Vasek (ed.), *The International Dimensions of Human Rights*. Westport, CT: Greenwood Press.

Whitaker, Ian. 1968 "Tribal Structure and National Politics in Albania, 1910-1950." Pp. 253-293, in I. M. Lewis (ed.), *History and Social Anthropology*. London: Tavistock Publications.

Marisa O. Ensor is Assistant Professor of Cultural, Applied and Legal Anthropology at Eastern Michigan University. Her research examines the experiences of vulnerable groups in situations of conflict-, disaster- and development-induced displacement, focusing on socio-cultural rights issues.

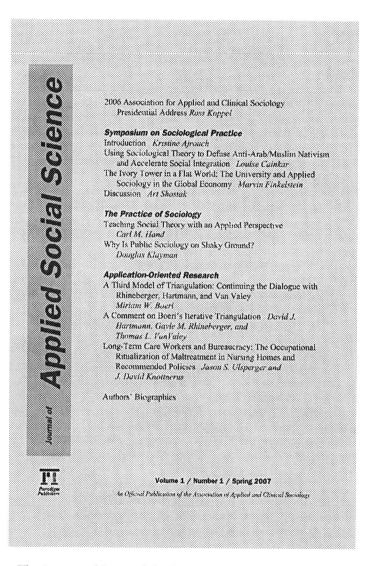

Volume 1 / Number 1 / Spring 2007
An Official Publication of the Association of Applied and Clinical Sociology

The inaugural issue of the *Journal of Applied Social Science,*
the official publication of the Association
of Applied and Clinical Sociology

Public Attitudes toward Bribery in Albania and Their Determinants

By LIQUN CAO AND STEVEN STACK

Abstract

This paper focuses on the public attitudes toward bribery in postcommunist Albania, a country that has, arguably, experienced the most protracted and painful transition of all Eastern European countries. Today Albania faces a serious problem with corruption, of wich bribery is an important part. We examine the data from *World Values Surveys* and investigate the extent to which bribery is accepted in Albania as a corrupt practice, comparing this with public attitudes towards bribery in other neighboring countries. We have found that public acceptance of bribery is significantly higher in Albania than elsewhere in the Balkans. The social determinants of public tolerance towards bribery are explored and their implications are discussed within the limitation of data.

*W*HILE THERE IS much debate on the trajectory of value change in the most advanced societies (Inglehart 1997; Weinstein 1982), there is general agreement that cultural, economic and political changes in the democratic transitional societies are moving toward being more consistent with the cultural, economic and political system in Western European societies (Fukuyama 1992; Henisz et al. 2006; King and Sznajder 2006; Murzaku and Dervishi 2003; Tarifa 1998).

The debate of whether it is the economic system that determines the cultural and value systems of a society, or it is the cultural value system that determines the economic system has been ongoing for over a hundred years. But that cultural and economic changes go together in coherent ways has been generally established. Democratic theory posits that participation in the decision-making process by the public is essential to the well being of society (Rousseau 1762; Bentham 1843; Mill 1849; Fukuyama 1992; Weinstein 1982). Collection of public opinions and monitoring of its shift are very important parts of contemporary democratic society. The current study investigates the public attitude toward bribery in Albania and its surrounding societies and the determinants of the public attitude toward bribery.

LIQUN CAO is Professor of Sociology and Criminology at Eastern Michigan University and an Honorary Member of the Albanian Institute of Sociology. STEVEN STACK is Professor of Sociology and Criminal Justice at Wayne State University.

Albania is a unique case for studying the democratic transition for several reasons. First, it is an anomaly in the European landscape. To outsiders, its geographic location makes it a European society. To Europeans, its religious affiliation makes it a foreign society. The communist rule from 1944 to 1991 did not fundamentally change this perception. The nation adopted a constitution in 1976 that did not allow any foreign credit, aid or investment, further isolating itself from all major nations in the world (Doja 2000; Tarifa 1995; 1998). Second, a successful transition to a democratic society will set up a precedent for the rest of Muslim societies. Because democracy has spread as a part of modernization and because all Muslim societies are so far not entirely part of this group with Turkey as an exception, there has been speculation that there is a problem of compatibility between a Muslim society and democracy. Third, it is possible that the process may simply illustrate the difficulty of democratic transition in a largely agricultural society, regardless of the religious affiliation.

In 1991 Albania ended 46 years of xenophobic Communist rule and established a multiparty democracy. The transition, however, is incomplete and has proven to be stressful for its people and for its successive governments due to the lack of democratic tradition and of civil society. The central government is reluctant to devolve power, civil society has not been functional, and multiparty politics is perceived as a struggle to achieve power for personal ends. Although Albania has made some progress in its democratic development and in its reestablishment of legitimacy, its transition into a full-fledged democracy with transparency and accountability of government institutions and a market economy remains difficult (Saltmarshe 2000; Tarifa 1995; 1998; Tarifa and Weinstein 1995/96; Tarifa and Fortman 1998).

In the mid-1990s, the International Monetary Fund forced the state to liberalize banking practices. Many citizens, however, were naive and ill-prepared to the workings of a market economy. They put their entire savings into fraudulent pyramid banking schemes. In a short while, $2 billion (80 percent of the country's GDP) had been moved into the hands of just a few pyramid scheme owners, causing severe economic troubles and civil unrest after the collapse of pyramid schemes (CIA 2006; Tarifa 2007b; Tarifa and Lucas 2006).

King and Sznajder (2006) have found that international coercion, normative emulation, and competitive mimicry are three basic mechanisms driving policy diffusion in the democratic transitional societies above and beyond the domestic political, economic, and technological factors. Citizens in a country pressured into market-oriented infrastructure reform when poor industry-performance does not create demands for such reform, or when the national policy-making apparatus lacks sufficient checks and balances to support a well-organized market, may fare worse than those in a country adopting reform as the result of clear performance shortfalls and in the presence of domestic institutional support. The Albanian case with the pyramid scandals has further verified the finding.

Stability was far from being restored in the years after the 1997 riots spurred by the collapse of the pyramid schemes. Even though Albania experienced real progress in terms of GDP growth—41 percent increase from 1990 to 2003 (King and Sznajder 2006)—the general mood of falling expectation remained widespread. The power feuds inside the Socialist Party led to a series of short-lived Socialist governments. In addition, the country was flooded with refugees from neighboring Kosovo in 1998 and 1999. The government of Fatos Nano as well its successor led by Sali Berisha have been plagued by a series of corruption scandals. In the 2005 general elections, the Democratic Party and its allies won a victory on the promises of reducing crime and corruption, promoting economic growth, and decreasing the size of government, yet in the past two years there have been no signs of improvement.

Corruption has emerged as a top concern for Albanian society (Saltmarshe 2000; Transparency International 2007). The word, however, has proven to be an ambiguous term and its usage in the society is not well established. For example, once the Democratic Party was elected to power in 1992, the former President Ramiz Alia and Fatos Nano, the head of the principal opposition Socialist Party, were accused of corruption and were both imprisoned. To many observers, the cases were not supported and the accusation was politically motivated (Tarifa 1995; Tarifa and Weinstein 1996).

In a democratic society, the study of public opinion is important for at least three reasons (Browning and Cao 1992; Cao et al. 1998; Cullen et al. 1996). First, policy decisions by public officials should reflect public opinion (Shapiro 2003; Wasserman 2006). A democratic government relies on citizens' cooperation in implementing public policy that is supposed to work for the well-being of an entire society. Second, a democratically elected government receives its mandate from the public and public opinion may not only yield important insights into citizens' needs, but also into the correlates of their attitudes. Third, public opinion plays a critical role in a society experiencing democratic transition (Cao and Burton 2006) because it tends to push political parities toward moderation on the most sensitive and divisive issues.

Furthermore, the study of cross-national public opinions is important for at least three reasons (Cao et al. 1998). First, comparative public opinion may serve as a barometer of a culture's contemporary sentiment and reflect the universality or differentiation of certain public moods. As such, the information from these surveys may be useful in the attempt to understand the behavior of the public and the differential responses of various segments of a society. Second, the expressed attitudes may foreshadow any popular changes within a society over time. Moreover, comparative public opinion in different societies may reveal certain persistent cultural variations. Last but not least, comprehension of international public opinions may help us appreciate the cultures of different societies and further enlighten us on why and how things happen in that society.

The use of survey information to study public opinions in Albania is relatively new. There are few empirical assessment of that nation. Accordingly, the current study seeks to fill the void in the sociological literature in English regarding Albanian's public attitudes. Inconsistency may exist concerning a new democracy. For example, Albania has been and continues to be regarded as a Muslim society, but in fact it is not (Tarifa 2007a). Forty years of communist rule have largely destroyed the tradition. This is especially true in large cities, such as Tirana, where one tenth of its national population resides.

Corruption, of which bribery is a major part, is a politically and morally loaded word, referring to the use of one's position for illegitimate private gains, bearing in mind that these are shadowy fields of activity that often defy precise categorization.[1] All politicians are openly against such behavior, but few seem to be able to avoid it. The current government of Sali Berisha was elected partially by benefiting from the scandals of corrup-

---

[1] For a more detailed discussion on the definition of corruption see Genaux (2004).

tion perceived by the public about Nano's previous government and partially by bene-fiting from pledges that it would get rid of corruption.

Corruption has been a recognized social problem for a long time, although it has continued to be under-researched by sociologists. It is not an issue that exists only in a particular society, or in a few societies. Abuses of power are present in all societies where there are marked asymmetries of power. As Lord Acton's axiom suggests, power tends to corrupt and absolute power corrupts absolutely. The extent of corruption, how-ever, does vary from one nation to another. In general, it is more prevalent during the democratic transition. The lack of reliable and systematic data has kept the study of cor-ruption out of the research agenda of empirical sociologists. We will overcome the dif-ficulty by using data from *World Value Surveys.*

The survey was conducted in 2002. The country was a mystery throughout the years of communist domination and it is only recently that it was possible for outsiders to have access to survey data. With the rapid transformation to become a democratic state, like most other societies in transition, corruption has emerged to be one of the top concerns in the political arena (Saltmarshe 2000; Transparency International 2007). We will focus on one form of corruption: accepting a bribe in the course of one's duties.

According to the latest report from *Transparency International,* 66 percent of Albanians said that they paid a bribe in the last 12 months, which was the highest among all nations surveyed. The prevalence of bribery, however, may be related to the general acceptance of it in a given society. Peshkopia (2005) argues that the higher level of perceived bribery is partially driven by the sudden increased people smuggling – both across the Adriatic Sea to Italy and over the Albanian-Greek border. Postcommunist Albania was ill-prepared for being Europe's gatekeeper. The current research examines what extent the public agrees that bribery is acceptable and the social determinants of accepting a bribe in the course of their work.

Although the study of public opinion has a long tradition in the U.S., surveys of cit-izen perceptions have appeared to gain prominence in emerging democracies only in recent years (Cao et al. 1998; Cao and Burton 2006; Cao and Dai 2006; Davis, et al. 2004). Caution must be exercised when undertaking the comparative study of public opinion (Cao and Burton 2006). This type of scholarly inquiry raises two interrelated questions: (1) whether the public opinions mean the same in two different cultures and (2) why cit-izens rate the issue as they do. In dealing with these two issues, it is critical that researchers avoid two potential traps within in the comparative literature.

First, we should avoid comparing apples with oranges and realize that public opin-ions obtained from more stable democratic societies and from transitional countries are not always comparable. In a democratic transitional society, public opinion is inaccurate because people are alienated from the political decision-making process and because their quality of life is unstable. Expressed opinions under this situation are less reflective of true public sentiment. Second, it is easier to explain similarities between nations than to explain differences. In our view, public attitudes are formed in a larger socio-cultural con-text and nations with very different cultures and religions are more difficult to compare than countries with similar cultures and similar religious traditions (see Stack and Cao 1998). Thus, when research determines differences between two very different societies, it is often not possible to identify the exact sources, whether it is the culture or the religion, which has caused the difference (Cao 2001). To avoid this problem, we only include Albania's neighboring nations in our comparative analysis. These nations are Bosnia and Herzegovina, Croatia, Greece, Macedonia, Montenegro, Serbia, and Slovenia. Except for Greece, all of them were part of former Yugoslavia. All of them have experienced similar historical and current social changes, and have similar conditions as Albania.

METHOD

The Sample

THE CURRENT STUDY employs data from the European Values Study Group and the World Values Survey Association (*European and World Values Surveys Integrated Data File, 1999-2002* Release I 2004). This data set is the compilation of the *European Values Surveys* and *World Values Surveys*. It is a product of a collaboration of investigators from more than eighty countries. The contents within the surveys were designed to facilitate cross-national comparisons of basic values covering a wide range of issues. The surveys were conducted via face-to-face interviews with respondents. The wording of the questions, answer categories, and sequencing were supposed to be identical for all participating nations. Each survey collects data from representative samples of adult citizens aged eighteen and older. The quality of the surveys varies among different nations and they are quite compatible.

The Albanian sample was collected from February 17 to March 5, 2002, and the sample size is 1,000. Using a nationally representative multistage random probably sampling frame, the sample was designed to be representative of the entire adult population aged 18 years and older.[2]

The Dependent Variable

The dependent variable of tolerance of bribery is a scale of the extent to which people would tolerate the behavior. The respondents were asked, "Please tell me for each of the following statements whether you think it can always be justified, never be justified, or something in between." Then they were asked, if the knew "someone accepting a bribe in the course of their duties." The scenario clearly confines the behavior "in the course of their duties" and leaves no doubt that it involves accepting a bribe. The responses ranged from 1=never justifiable through 10=always justifiable. The higher the score, the more tolerant one is of bribery.

The Independent Variables

The independent variables are age, marriage, employment, social class, gender, ethnicity, and education. In addition, there are three attitudinal variables of satisfaction in life, confidence in the press and confidence in the police.

Age is measured as the respondent's actual age in years at the time of the survey.

---

[2] For further discussion of the surveys, see *European and World Values Surveys Integrated Data File, 1999-2002 Release I* (2004).

Marriage is a dummy variable where 1=married and widowed, and 0=all other non-marital statuses (single, living together as married, divorced, and separated). Social class is assessed with the subjective feeling about one's own relative standing among one's nation, where 5=lower class and 1=upper class for the socioeconomic class. Employment status is captured as a dummy variable where 1=full-timed employed and students, and 0=all others (part-time, self-employed, unemployed, housewives, retired, and others). It is expected that age, marriage, social class, employment are negatively associated with tolerance of bribery because these characteristics represent a *status quo* within a society and as control theory suggests people with intact or strong social bonds are less likely to be deviant (Hirschi 1969).

Gender is a binary variable where male=1 and female=0. Ethnicity is measured as a dummy variable coded "1" if minority (Greek, Macedonian and others), "0" otherwise. Gender and minority status may be positively related to tolerance of bribery. They represent the suppressed groups within a society according to feminist theory (Adler 1975). Education is a ten-category ordinal variable (1 to 8) with a higher score representing more education. It is a measure of liberalism, a global symbolic orientation that signifies one's openness to new concepts and trends. It may be positively related to accepting a bribe.

The attitudinal variables are satisfaction in life, confidence in the police and in the press. Satisfaction is a scale from 1=dissatisfied to 10=satisfied. It is expected to have a negative influence on tolerance of bribery because it also taps the concept of *status quo*. Confidence in the press and in the police are measured as ordinal variables with 1=a great deal, 2=quite a lot, 3=not very much, and 4=not at all. To reverse the order, we used 5 to minus the original item so that the higher score represents the higher confidence in the press and in the police. These two variables may have different effects on tolerance of bribery. The press, as the fourth power within a democratic society, was relatively new and to what extent the public understand its power remains uncertain. In the west, the public's confidence in the press should be related to the public intolerance of accepting bribery. It, however, may have a different effect on the tolerance of bribery in Albania because both phenomena are new. In contrast, confidence in the police may be negatively related to tolerance of bribery: the more confident one is, the less tolerant to bribery one will be.

Religiosity is a good predictor in many studies (Unnever et al. 2006), but the Albanian survey only contains a few items regarding religion. The preliminary correlation analysis indicates that none of them are related to accepting a bribe. This has confirmed Tarifa's (2007a) argument that Albania remains largely a society in which after more than forty years of ruthless communist rule a large part of the population do not identify themselves with any religious faith. Missing data are not a serious problem for this survey. In general, most missing values did not exceed five percent of the data. No effort was made to address the missing data. The listwise deletion was used in all regression analyses and the final sample size in the regression analysis was 912.

RESULTS

TABLE 1 PRESENTS the major characteristics of the Albanian sample. The mean age for the sample is 41 years old and it ranges from 18 to 81 years old. This distribution seems older than the actual population. The gender distribution, however, is very close. The

marriage looks reasonable. The percentage of minority in the sample is also reflective of the national population. According to CIA's *World Factbook*, the estimates of the Greek population ranged from 1 percent (official Albanian statistics) to 12 percent (from a Greek organization). Our sample's percentage of 1.7 is more consistent with the official estimate. For the unemployment rate, the official rate was 13.8 percent, but "may exceed 30 percent due to preponderance of near-subsistence farming" (CIA 2006). Even so, our sample's employment rate of 36 seemed to be really low. This should be kept in mind when the results of regression analysis are interpreted.

Table 1: Major Characteristics of the Sample
(N=1,000)

Mean Age	40.97 (range=18-81)
Marriage (yes=1)	.772
Employment (yes=1)	.358
Social Class	3.60
1=upper class	1.3%
2=upper middle class	7.7%
3=lower middle class	37.1%
4=working class	31.9%
5=lower class	18.1%
Gender (male=1)	.495
Ethnic Minority (yes=1)	.017
Education*	4.11
1=less than primary school	12.5%
2=primary school	26.4%
3=junior high	23.7%
4=high school	21.0%
5=college and more	16.4%

* The original coding is 1 to 8; here we re-organized the categories but used the original variable in the regression analysis.

Figure 1 presents the comparison of means for the publics' tolerance of bribery in seven societies around Albania. Except Greece, all other seven societies are in the process of democratic transition. Clearly, the level of tolerance for bribery is highest in Albania, followed by Greece, Slovenia, Croatia, Macedonia, Bosnia and Herzegovina, Montenegro, and Serbia. The t-test of mean difference indicates that there is a significant difference between Albania and Greece in their tolerance level of bribery. The level of tolerance for accepting a bribe is significantly higher in Albania than in Greece, which is the next highest mean in the tolerance of bribery. It should be noted that Greece has been a democratic society for a long time, but it also is one of nations that has the lowest standard of living among European Union nations.

Table 2 presents the results of the regression analysis on the public's tolerance of bribery. Age is associated with the tolerance of bribery as expected: the older one is, the less one would tolerate bribery. Social class and employment are also related to the tolerance of bribery as expected: the upper class people and those employed are less tolerant of accepting bribery in the course of work.

These variables have captured the concept of status quo in a society. Other socio-demographic characteristics of gender, education, marriage, and ethnic minority are not statistically significant in the regression model.

Figure 1: Tolerance of Bribery (means)

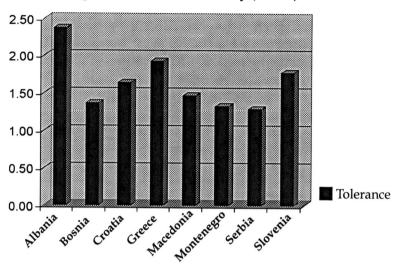

Table 2: Social Determinants of Tolerance towards Bribery

Variables	b (ß)
Age	–.015 (–.105)*
Marriage (yes=1)	–.085 (–.017)
Employment (yes=1)	–.375 (–.088)*
Social Class	–.192 (–.086)*
Gender (male=1)	.034 (.008)
Ethnic Minority	–.976 (.062)
Education	–.052 (–.057)
Satisfaction	–.082 (–.089)*
Confidence in the Press	.486 (.190)*
Confidence in the Police	–.311 (–.130)*
Constant	4.285*
F =	7.492
R Square =	.077

*p < .05; N = 1,000

For the attitudinal variables, all of them are statistically related to tolerance of bribery. Satisfaction in life and confidence in the police are negatively related to tolerance of bribery. Those who are more satisfied with their lives are less tolerant of bribery and those who are more confident in the police are less tolerant of bribery. Confidence in the press, however, is positively associated with tolerance of bribery. Those who are confident in the press are also more tolerant of bribery. This effect, however, is contradictory to our expectation. The entire model explains about 8 percent of variance of tolerance of bribery.

DISCUSSION

MORE THAN SIXTEEN years of political and economic changes in Albania have transformed the once self-isolated and underdeveloped nation into a new society. After the communist era, Albania moved from a decidedly introverted to an extroverted ideal in the context of a mix of Eastern and Western influences. Although it is considered the only European country with a majority Muslim population (with the exception of Bosnia and in the future Kosovo), it is argued that religious beliefs are not permanent features of human nature since the Albanian project of eliminating them from everyday practices was completed in fifty years. Regardless of which political party is in power, the social and political trajectory is set: the elite of Albania are determined to move the nation to be more democratic and to join the European Union.

The current analysis is pertinent because it was impossible to obtain the public's opinion in the past and the survey methods to collecting information remains new to the nation. Our study examines one of the important issues concerning the nation: accepting a bribe in the course of one's duties. Bribery as a part of corruption has been identified as one of the greatest obstacles to economic and social development (Fishman and Gatti 2002; Husted 1999). The two aspects of corruption are the tolerance of corruption in a society and the tolerance of the regime that is corrupted. The current study investigated the public's tolerance of bribery—a specific form of corruption—in Albania and its surrounding nations. We have found from the data of *World Values Surveys* that the level of tolerance toward bribery is significantly higher in Albania than among its neighboring nations. This is consistent with the previous research findings that the level of anomie is higher in societies experiencing democratic transition and rapid industrialization (Cao 2004). In that study, accepting a bribe in the course of one's duties was one component of anomie.

Although Albanian economic growth has not seemed to be affected by bribery, its long-term effects are unpredictable. From other more developed societies, we learn that corruption undermines development by distorting the rule of law and weakening the institutional foundation on which economic growth depends. Along with the growing reluctance of international investors and donors to allocate funds to countries lacking adequate rule of law, transparency and accountability in government administration, it has the greatest impact on the most vulnerable part of a country's population, the poor.

We cannot be certain whether the higher acceptance of bribery among the Albanian public is the result of the legal culture or the lack of civil society. Civil society, defined as those institutions, organizations, and practices that are not controlled by the state but which help to support and lend legitimacy to the political system, are beginning to form, albeit slowly, in Albania. The transition to democracy requires a civil society to bolster both democracy and legitimacy. Thus far, the development of civil society remains quite limited in Albania, mostly taking the form of political parties, while media, cultural, and educational organizations are forming much slower and more painfully. Greece stands out as an example of a country that has experienced a democratic system since 1974, but has been unable to develop fully its civil society for both historical and practical reasons, as patron clientelism continues to plague its political culture. Turkey has begun to witness the development of a civil society, but continues to be one of the worst offenders of human rights.

We further analyzed the social determinants of tolerance of bribery in Albania. Our model indicates that age and social class influence tolerance of bribery as we expected: older and upper class people, as part of the society's status quo, are less tolerant of bribery. In addition, satisfaction in life and confidence in the police predict the tolerance of bribery as we expected too: those who are more satisfied in life and those that have higher confidence in the police are less tolerant of bribery. Satisfaction in life also taps the concept of status quo in a society. Those who are more successful under the current system oppose bribery and corruption more strongly than those who are not doing well under the system, are trying to find loopholes and the most efficient ways to their success regardless of the means.

The effect of confidence in the press on the tolerance of bribery is different from our instinct. Higher confidence in the press is associated with more tolerance of bribery. This may be an indication that the legal culture has not really changed. The legal culture is the socially derived product comprised of interrelated concepts such as legitimacy and acceptance of authorities, preference for and beliefs about dispute arrangements, and authorities' use of discretionary power (Cao and Burton 2006). With regard to Albania, traditionally, the nation is a communist and a Muslim society with a distinct legal culture when compared to the West. In its recent move toward westernization, its overt legal structure has changed, yet the underlying legal substructure may remain largely unchanged. In addition, the linguistic influence in the interpretation of the questionnaire item cannot be completely ruled out. Since this is the first study of its kind and it is explorative in nature, future studies are needed to verify this effect.

In summary, Albania has experienced a fundamental change in economic, social and political structures. These changes have significant consequences for the national value system too. The current research examines the public attitudes toward accepting a bribe and has established a baseline of information for future comparison. Such a study is important because value change tends to move in tandem with the economic and political structures. If Albania is genuinely interested in joining the European Union, the economic and political structure as well as the value system should move toward the European integration. Since the survey is a relatively new method in collecting data in that society and since the linguistic compatibility is not established beyond doubt, we have to take the current results as tentative. Hopefully, our research will generate more interest in this regard and better surveys will be designed and collected, allowing more sophisticated data analysis.

REFERENCES

Adler, Freda. 1975. *Sisters in Crime: The Rise of the New Female Criminal*. New York: McGraw-Hill.

Bentham, Jeremy. 1843. *The Works of Jeremy Bentham*, ed. Jay Browning. Edinburgh: Tait.

Browning, Sandra Lee and Liqun Cao. 1992. "The Impact of Race on Criminal Justice Ideology," *Justice Quarterly* 9, 4: 685-701.

Cao, Liqun. 2001. "A Problem in No-Problem Policing in Germany: Confidence in the Police in Germany and USA," *European Journal of Crime, Criminal Law and Criminal Justice* 9, 3: 167-179.

_____. 2004. "Is American Society More Anomic? A Test of Merton's Theory with Cross-National Data," *International Journal of Comparative and Applied Criminal Justice* 28, 1: 15-31.

Cao, Liqun, and Velmer Burton, Jr. 2006. "Spanning the Continents: Assessing the Turkish Public Confidence in the Police," *Policing: An International Journal of Police Strategies and Management* 29, 3: 451-463

_____., and Mengyan Dai. 2006. "Confidence in the Police: Where Does Taiwan Rank in the World?" *Asian Journal of Criminology* 1: 71-84.

_____., Steven J. Stack, and Yi Sun. 1998. "Public Confidence in the Police: A Comparative Study between Japan and America," *Journal of Criminal Justice* 26, 4: 279-89.

CIA. 2000. *The World Factbook, 2007*. http://www.cia.gov/cia/publications/factbook/index.html

Cullen, Francis T., Liqun Cao, James Frank, Robert H. Langworthy, Sandra Lee Browning, Renee Kopache and Thomas J. Stevenson. 1996. "Stop or I'll Shoot": Racial Differences in Support for Police Use of Deadly Force," *American Behavioral Scientist* 39, 1: 451-63.

Davis, Robert C., Christopher W. Ortiz, Yakov Gilinskiy, Irina Ylesseva, and Vladimir Briller. 2004. "A Cross-National Comparison of Citizen Perceptions of the Police in New York City and St Petersburg, Russia," *Policing* 27, 1: 22-36.

Doja, Albert. 2000. "The Politics of Religion in the Reconstruction of Identities," *Critique of Anthropology* 20, 4: 421-438.

European Values Study Group and World Values Survey Association. 2004. *European and World Values Surveys Integrated Data File, 1999-2002 Release I*, Ann Arbor, MI: Inter-University Consortium for Political and Social Research.

Fishman, Raymond, and Roberta Gatti. 2002. "Decentralization and Corruption: Evidence Across Countries," *Journal of Public Economics* 83: 325-345.

Fukuyama, Francis. 1992. *The End of History and the Last Man*. New York: Free Press.

Genaux, Maryvonne. 2004. Social Sciences and the Evolving Concept of Corruption," *Crime, Law & Social Change* 42: 13-24.

Henisz, Witold J., Bennet A. Zelner, and Mauro F. Guillen. 2006. "The Worldwide Diffusion of Market-Oriented Infrastructure Reform, 1977-1999," *American Sociological Review* 70: 871-897.

Inglehart, Ronald. 1997. *Modernization and Postmodernization*. Princeton, NJ: Princeton University Press.

Hirschi, Travis. 1969. *Causes of Delinquency*. Berkeley: University of California Press.

Husted, Bryan W. 1999. "Wealth, Culture, and Corruption," *Journal of International Business Studies* 30: 339-359.

King, Lawrence P., and Alexksandra Sznajder. 2006. "The State-Led Transition to Liberal Capitalism: Neoliberal, Organizational, World-Systems, and Social Structural Explanations of Poland's Economic Success," *American Journal of Sociology* 112: 751-801.

Mill, John Stuart. 1965 [1849]. *Collected Works*, ed. J. M. Robson. Toronto: University of Toronto Press.

Murzaku, Ines A., and Zyhdi Dervishi. 2003. "Albanians' First Post communist Decade—Values in Transition: Traditional or liberal?" *East European Quarterly* 37, 2: 231-56.

Peshkopia, Ridvan. 2005. "Albania – Europe's Reluctant Gatekeeper," *Forced Migration Review* 23: 35-36.

Rousseau, Jean-Jacques. 1953 [1762]. *Rousseau, Political Writings*, ed. R. Watkins. London: Nelson.

Saltmarshe, Douglas. 2000. "Local Government in Practice: Evidence from Two Villages in Northern Albania," *Public Administration and Development* 20, 4: 327-337.

Shapiro, Ian. 2003. *The State of Democratic Theory*. Princeton, NJ: Princeton University Press.

Stack, Steven, and Liqun Cao. 1998. "Political Conservatism and Confidence in the Police: A Comparative Analysis," *Journal of Crime and Justice* 21, 1: 71-76.

Tarifa, Fatos. 1995. "Albania's Road from Communism: Political and Social Change, 1990-1993," *Development and Change* 26, 1: 133-162;

_____. 1998. "Disparities and Uncertainties: Reflections on Communist and Post-Communist Eastern Europe," *Journal of Social Sciences* 2, 2-3: 91-103;

_____. 2007a. *To Albania, with Love.* Lanham, MD: Hamilton Books.

_____. 2007b. *Acrimonies of Transition: Private and Public.* Ann Arbor, MI: Huron Valley Publishing Inc.

Tarifa, Fatos, and Jay Weinstein. 1995/96. "Overcoming the Past: De-Communization and Reconstruction of Post-Communist Societies," *Studies in Comparative International Development* 30, 4: 63-77;

_____., and Bas de Gay Fortman. 1998. "Vulnerable Democracies: Legitimation Challenges to Post-Communist Systems," *Journal of Social Sciences* 2, 2-3: 211-219.

_____., and Peter Lucas. 2006. "Albania: Authoritarianism without Oil," *Mediterranean Quarterly* 17, 2: 32-39.

Transparency International. 2006. *Report on the Transparency International Global Corruption Barometer 2006.* http://www.transparency.org/news_room/in_focus/2006/gcb_2006

Unnever, James, D., Francis T. Cullen, and John P. Bartkowski. 2006. "Images of Go and Public Support for Capital Punishment," *Criminology* 44: 835-866.

Wasserman, Ira. 2006. *How the American Media Packaged Lynching (1850-1940).* Lewiston, NY: The Edwin Mellen Press.

Weinstein, Jay. 1982. *Sociology/Technology: Foundations of Postacademic Social Science.* New Brunswick: Transaction Books.

❦ ❦ ❦ ❦ ❧ ❧ ❧ ❧

Public Attitudes toward Bribery in Albania
Further considerations on Cao and Stack

Donna Selman
Eastern Michigan University

*I*N 1999, THE WORLD BANK ranked Albania as "The Most Corrupt State in Europe." Two years later, after the establishment of an anti-corruption commission, Albania ranked as the seventh most corrupt nation. Bribery, as Cao and Stack point out, is a major component of this concept of corruption. Media communications within and outside of Albania report corruption from the highest levels of the state administration to impacts on individual citizens, including the necessity of additional payments (bribes) to obtain phone lines, automobile registrations, adequate medical care, employment and fair treatment in the justice system.

Cao and Stack acknowledge the ambiguous nature of the word "corruption" as it is used in Albania. To the problems acknowledged by the authors presented by this specific case study, the culturally specific meaning and history of 'bribery' need to be addressed. Whether or not one agrees with the authors' contention that Albania is not a Muslim society, given the religious history there remains the possible influence of the Muslim traditions in shaping beliefs and opinion. After 45 years of Communist rule it is not surprising that people would be reluctant to identify religious affiliation or perceive themselves as being influenced by religious tradition. Nonetheless, the history is there. Thus, when seeking determinants of attitudes regarding bribery, one must consider the practice and meaning of "bakshish". Understood as charitable giving, giving to show gratitude, respect or veneration and often involving an appreciation for the recipient for allowing one the opportunity to earn merit through giving, there may or may not be a perception/belief of wrong doing attached with either giving or receiving a bribe. This could quite possibly help to explain the significantly high levels of tolerance of bribery in Albania.

Commentary

One point worth considering, which is somewhat related to the above point, is "need." In transitional societies corruption and bribery persist partly because of structural insufficiencies. Specifically, when the tax structure is insufficient to pay civil servants adequate salaries, bribery—both giving and receiving—is perceived as not necessarily altruistic, as the case of "bakshish," but as a necessity to the functions of everyday life. As with any behavior, when large numbers of people participate in the behavior and/or can neutralize negative stigma attached to it or justify the need for it, the tolerance of it goes up, often to the point that the behavior loses the status of being a "problem" (Pfuhl and Henry 1993). Considering that the minimum monthly wage of a state administrative employee in 2001 was 7,000 lek ($47.14) while the highest paid state job in the country, that of the president of the republic, was 156,000 lek ($1,051) (Peza 2001), one can identify the basis for both the justification for bribery and the ability to neutralize the negative stigma.

As Cao and Stack point out, the development of the structures of a civil society including the press (a new phenomena), and the educational system will play an important role in the future. More specifically how it chooses to frame bribery and thus contribute to what the public comes to believe as unacceptable and therefore intolerable will be crucial in determining Albanian attitudes toward bribery. Equally important is how these attitudes will—or will not—shape the legal reactions to bribery and corruption, including the critical aspect of deciding which behaviors will be included in the legal definitions.

Cao and Stack have contributed a piece of the puzzle that is Albania. As is the case with most exploratory research it has also raised questions and pointed to some important considerations. Methodological issues with translation of survey data, how to compare what on the surface look like comparable countries but indeed have distinct political, religious and cultural differences are only a few of the challenges researchers will face when studying Albania. On the other hand, this and future work can provide Albanian citizens and policy makers with the opportunity to avoid costly mistakes made by the West. Social problems vary across space and time. Reactions to them, whether formal or informal, are at least partially impacted by the process of how they are presented to the public and vice versa. Understanding of this reciprocal relationship between public opinion/attitudes and the development of laws is crucial if a transitional society hopes to move toward democracy while reducing the harm done to citizens in the process. Cao and Stack stress, "In its recent move toward Westernization, the overt legal structure in Albania has changed, while the underlying legal substructure may remain largely unchanged." Similar claims exist in western countries; justice systems that claim to be blind and impartial have been revealed to be racist and biased. Laws that proclaim to protect all citizens benefit the wealthy. The nature of the reciprocal relationship mentioned above and the importance of the process in the shaping of laws, defining behaviors and societal reactions is revealed. In the west, definitions of what constitutes bribery vary from state to state, but generally it includes: giving a benefit (e.g., money) in order to influence the judgment or conduct of a person in a position of trust (e.g., an official or witness). Accepting a bribe also constitutes a crime. However, the granting of favors to a public official or giving a gift is not a bribe unless it is given with some intent to influence the recipient's official behavior. Intent to influence is strictly defined and very difficult to prove. Thus, campaign donations by corporations, political action committees and lobbyists with interests in policy decisions are common practice even though many citizens consider it bribery (Selman and Leighton 2007). These practices are routinely cast as the norm, as a necessity, as just the "way business gets done in a bureaucracy" and thus tolerable despite the damage done to citizens in the long run. Let's hope that tolerance of bribery in Albania as it is defined right now does not lead them down the same path.

References

Henry, Stuart, and Edwin Pfuhl. 1993. *The Deviance Process*. Aldine Transaction
Peza, Alfred. 2001. "Corruption in Albania: Up from the Bottom," *World Press Review* http://www.worldpress.org/1001cover5.htm

Selman, Donna, and Paul Leighton. 2007. *Punishment for Sale: How Big Business Bought the American Correctional System*. Roman& Littlefield.

Donna Selman *is Assistant Professor of Sociology and Criminology at Eastern Michigan University. She is co-author (with Paul Leighton) of* Punishment for Sale: How Big Business Bought the American Correctional System, *forthcoming in 2007 by Roman & Littlefield.*

Printed in the United States
96458LV00002B/251-310/A

9 780977 666294